Shattered Vessels

SUNY Series in Modern Jewish Literature and Culture
Sarah Blacher Cohen, editor

Shattered Vessels

Memory, Identity, and Creation in the Work of David Shahar

Michal Peled Ginsburg and Moshe Ron

State University of New York Press

The Northwestern University Research Grants Committee has provided partial support for the publication of this book. We gratefully acknowledge this assistance.

Published by
State University of New York Press, Albany

Printed in the United States of America

For information, address State University of New York Press,
90 State Street, Suite 700, Albany, NY 12207

Production by Michael Haggett
Marketing by Fran Keneston

Library of Congress Cataloging in Publication Data

Ginsburg, Michal Peled, 1947–
Shattered vessles : memory, identity, and creation in the work of David Shahar / Michal Peled Ginsburg and Moshe Ron
p. cm. — (SUNY series in modern Jewish literature and culture)
Includes bibliographical references and index.
ISBN 0-7914-5919-5 (alk. paper) — ISBN 0-7914-5920-9 (pbk. alk. paper)
1. Shahar, David, 1926—Criticism and interpretation. I. Ron, Moshe. II. Title. III. Series.

PJ5054.S33Z67 2004
892.4'36—dc22

2003069328

10 9 8 7 6 5 4 3 2 1

Contents

Acknowledgments

The authors are grateful to Shulamit Shahar, Meir Shahar, and Madeleine Neige for their cooperation and encouragement. We also wish to thank Murray Baumgarten, Yair Mazor, Alan Mintz, and Henry Sussman for their help and support. We are beholden to Tamar Sofer and Mark Shaeffer for the maps included in this book. We thank Avner Treinin, Hayim Beer, Hanan Hever, and Michal Oren-Nordheim, who discussed with us portions of the manuscript, and Jenny Navot for her friendship and hospitality.

An earlier version of chapter 1 appeared in *Prooftexts* 19 (1999): 151–77. We thank the editor for the permission to reprint.

Introduction

At the time of his death, April 2, 1997, David Shahar had not become a household name. He died in France, and his body was transported back home to Jerusalem, where a brief ceremony was held before the funeral procession to the Mount of Olives. A few dozen people gathered in the little plaza outside Beit Hasofer in downtown Jerusalem around a slightly raised stone platform on which the body was laid. Midday traffic was heavy, as usual, in the adjacent streets of this busy commercial district. Some speeches were given. While Avner Treinin, professor of physical chemistry at Hebrew University and a poet, spoke of Shahar's passionate interest in the phenomenon of vision and his intense ambivalence about the mind-body duality, hundreds of high school students began streaming out of the nearby Beit Ha'am auditorium, where they probably had attended an educational program. Some lingered a moment on the crowded sidewalk to stare, by no means disrespectful, obviously nonplussed. Who was this guy? A writer, ah, yes. A Jerusalem writer.

Is this odd event a proper emblem of the saying *Ein navi be'iro*, so often applied to David Shahar? Though he himself was not averse to cultivating the mystique of the prophet unrecognized in his hometown, the notion that he has been totally or willfully ignored is not quite accurate. Not only did he receive important prizes and honors (Agnon Prize, 1973; Prime Minister's Grant 1969, 1978, 1991; Bialik Prize, 1984; Bar-Ilan University Newman Award, 1986–87), but many critics recognized him as one of Israel's foremost novelists, an author whose oeuvre is unique and unparalleled in scope and force.[1] Yet reviewers of Shahar's work also have noted that his reception, both by the general public and by professional critics, has fallen short of what was his due.[2] Given the magnitude and quality of his literary project, his relative marginalization within Israeli culture is in itself of considerable interest.

The reasons for this marginalization are both poetic and ideological (and, in our mind, these two aspects cannot be separated). Poetically speaking, critics were not wrong to read Shahar as a realist who chronicled life in Jerusalem during the British Mandate period. But perhaps because the mimetic aspect of his writing does not easily accommodate national-allegorical or symbolic readings (as do, for example, works by A. B. Yehoshua or Amos Oz), it often was perceived simplistically and reduced by critics to a literal realism of a rather naïve kind: personal reminiscences or a *roman à clef*, an assortment of anecdotes characterized, at best, by vividness and local color. Since the "reality" in question was deemed to have little bearing on the problems and issues at the center of current debates in Israeli culture, his writing could be dismissed as sheer personal nostalgia. This is perhaps why the leading critical voices in Israeli literature have had little or nothing to say about Shahar's work.

As we shall argue in what follows, Shahar's realism involves much more than local color and personal nostalgia. His depiction of Jerusalem during the British Mandate period (which we analyze in chapter 3) projects a sociocultural world that does not embody any historically defined ideological position in the context of the debate around and within Zionism. This is not to say that Shahar engaged in any overt critique of Zionism as such; his personal politics were staunchly nationalistic, and this occasionally rises to the surface of his fiction. Still, the milieu he chose to depict in his major work, the novel sequence *The Palace of Shattered Vessels*, can best be described as an in-between world: his Jerusalem is one that no longer conforms to the values of the Orthodox "Old Yishuv," nor does it fit into any of the other recognized ideological tendencies of the day, least of all labor Zionism. Some of the attitudes manifested in his fiction exhibit an affinity with Canaanite ideas—especially the attitude toward the territory and its traditional material culture—but Shahar can hardly be said to adopt the full Canaanite platform. His mimetic enterprise may be characterized as the personal recreation of an alternative sociocultural world whose demise he elegizes.

Paradoxically, however, Shahar has been described quite often also as someone who rejects "despicable, time-worn" material reality and yearns for "transcendent essences that lie beyond it."[3] Again, there is no doubt that many of Shahar's characters are dreamers and visionaries of one kind or another, and that the narrator himself often is dissatisfied with the world of the here and now. But discontent and dreaming in Shahar do not entail a renunciation of reality or a retreat into a world of pure mind or imagination. If Shahar's realism is not "pure," this is not because he aspires to a realm of the spirit that would transcend, reverse, or supplement material reality but, rather, because he recognizes and contends with the force of desire. With all his insistence on the referentiality of literature, documented in many interviews, his literary texts also stage the dramas of individuals (foremost among them the narrator) motivated by wishes and desires that exceed the boundaries of the real. What is particular about Shahar's poetics is that his longing to free himself from the constraints of empirical reality is paradoxically linked to an unwavering investment in the material and the sensuous. No matter how lacking reality is found to be, no matter how abundant, even excessive, the demands of imagination and desire, in Shahar's world there can be no satisfaction that is not firmly anchored in the empirical. His writing is marked by paradoxical representations—by what we call in chapter 1, a "flirting with the uncanny"—the result of the incommensurability and tension between the laws that govern empirical reality and those that determine desire and the imagination.

The commitment to the reality of the senses is nowhere more obvious than in the highly erotic nature of some of Shahar's writing, with which critics who wish to cast him as longing for a purely spiritual world had a hard time coping. Such critics, therefore, tended either to ignore this aspect of his writing or to be scandalized by it, branding it as shameful and a sellout to the base tastes of the uncultivated public.[4] But, as we shall argue in chapter 2, in Shahar's world, the erotic and the sexual, with all of their attending ambivalences, are inseparable from artistic creation. The artist-surrogates appearing in the short stories and novels (especially *His Majesty's Agent*) privilege the art of painting as a personal act of creation, not only emulating divine creation itself but doing so in its own medium of light, color, and matter. What is peculiar to these Shaharian protagonists is that the space of visuality is both made available and denied to them by the agency of a woman, initially the mother and subsequently other female figures exempt from the incest taboo. The turning away from the male protagonist of the loving gaze of a woman is experienced as an offense to his very maleness and/or as a fatal blow to his ability to paint. Such narrative moments are the closest analogue to the metaphor of the "breaking of the vessels" derived from the account of creation in Lurianic Kabbala—a catastrophe of enormous magnitude. Thus Shahar's great cosmological, metaphysical, and aesthetic themes both concern the world of the senses and are inscribed within highly eroticized interpersonal patterns.

Shahar's strong commitment to the body may also be seen as a corollary of the investment in "place" or "territory." The relation between place and identity (which we discuss in chapter 4) is raised in Shahar's *Palace* novels both implicitly and explicitly, both in phenomenological and even metaphysical terms (e.g., through the problematic of the relation of body to soul), and in a way that relates clearly to the national question and conflict over the land between Jews and Arabs. It is in the latter context that Shahar's specific brand of Zionism, strongly tinged with the Canaanite privileging of the territory as a source of national and cultural identity, comes most explicitly to the fore.

Shahar's critics (and he himself) liked to point out his ideological or political "apartness," his refusal to belong to literary or political cliques.[5] This characterization was used primarily to explain his relative isolation from the mainstream of literary and cultural life in Israel, but what is surely more interesting is that this "apartness" translates into or derives from a conception of identity dramatized in his fiction. Shahar's individualism is not simply a sociological fact or a psychological character trait of the man but a basic mode of conceiving the relation between personal identity and a group—be it national, ethnic, or racial. As we argue in chapter 4, his marked investment in unorthodox individuals (people who escape definition in terms of group affiliation) is part and parcel of his view of individual identity as fluid, heterogeneous to the point of being self-contradictory, free to change; rigid, well-demarcated definitions are, in contrast, the hallmarks of "group identity," and they are repeatedly depicted as fostering violence. The valorization of flexibility and fluidity is certainly linked to the poetics of the uncanny where, through the narrator's practice of entering the experiential domain—one would almost say "the body"—of other characters, the boundaries between self and other become shifting and porous. This has some consequences on the thematic level: it accounts, for example, for the importance in Shahar's work of the figure of the "Oriental" (or "Levantine") represented both by the Sephardi Jew and by the Arab. Though the view of the "Oriental" as being "fluid" or having no stable identity may strike us as banal (given that it is a common stereotype), the fact that this mode of being is generally valorized in Shahar's fiction goes a long way toward reducing the alterity of the Oriental. In particular, it establishes a continuity between the representations of the Arab and Sephardi Jew, in contrast to the prevailing tendency of much Zionist discourse to make the strongest possible case for their difference. In contrast to the fluid Oriental is the violent "other"—the other who lost his or her individuality by being absorbed into an homogenizing group (represented by both the Ashkenazi orthodox Jew and the Arab).

This already suggests that the highly personal narrative of the *Palace* novels is not at all indifferent to the social and political issues that are at the center of Israeli culture. But it also suggests that Shahar's way of approaching these issues is very different from that of mainstream authors not only of his own biological generation (e.g., Shamir or Megged) but also of "*dor hamedina*" (Yehoshua and Oz). His narrative does not deal with "collectives" (except to denounce them as violent mobs), and the individuals he describes are both idiosyncratic and somewhat indeterminate—hence, they cannot allegorically represent a collective. The nonallegorical nature of most of Shahar's writings means that the reality he depicts, rich and varied as it may be, is not posited as a totality, and his realism is not the synecdochical one of "part for the whole." This can be seen most clearly in his representation of Jerusalem: as we argue in chapter 3, unlike most writers on Jerusalem who see the city as a totality because they attribute to it an "essence" (which, in turn, explains why it can function as a powerful symbol), Shahar chooses to focus in the *Palace* sequence on a part of Jerusalem that lacks a homogenous identity and whose "otherness" bars it from standing as part for the whole.

The reluctant acceptance of Shahar as a major author by Israeli critics has been compared, *ad nauseam*, with the warm reception he received in France, where he won, in 1981, the prestigious Prix Médicis Etranger and where he was hailed as "the Israeli Proust." The comparison of Shahar to Proust, which has become a cliché of Shahar criticism, has mostly been based on a superficial understanding of both Proust and Shahar. In chapter 5 we revisit this analogy in order to show the important differences in the way these two authors approached issues crucial to both: time, memory, art, and autobiography. Rather than being an "Israeli Proust," Shahar is an author whose take on the issues central to both Romanticism and modernist fiction is both specific and complex.

Throughout our critical engagement with Shahar's work, we have tried to remain attuned to his narrative art. The temporal disjointedness of his associative style will not have escaped even a casual reader of his fiction. What repeated and more focused reading reveals is the depth and pervasiveness of some of these patterns. Analogies, connections, and verbal echoes appear—often unexpectedly—across vast stretches of text and many years of writing acitivity. The astonishing richness and coherence of these clusters of meaning make it possible to tease out of Shahar's work a complex position on matters both poetic and ideological—a position that, for the most part, his writings do not expound in direct expository fashion.

A Note on Texts and Translations

In the following pages, all references to Shahar's works will be given parenthetically in the text, with the Hebrew original followed by the English translation (when available). Translations were silently modified when a more precise literal translation was needed; when no English version was available, translations are our own. Emphasis in quotes is ours, unless otherwise indicated.

The following editions of Shahar's works are referred to in this text:

The Pope's Mustache. Tel Aviv: 'Am 'Oved, 1982; *The Death of the Little God*. Tel Aviv: 'Am 'Oved, 1982. These two collections gather together all of Shahar's short stories previously published in *Of Dreams* (Tel Aviv: 'Am 'Oved, 1955), *Caesar* (Tel Aviv: Agudat Hasofrim/Dvir, 1960), and *The Fortune Teller* (Tel Aviv: Agudat Hasofrim/Massada, 1966). Some of Shahar's short stories appeared in English translation in *News From Jerusalem* (Boston: Houghton Mifflin, 1974).

His Majesty's Agent (Tel Aviv: Hadar, 1979). English translation by Dalia Bilu (New York and London: Harcourt, Brace, Jovanovitch, 1980).

The Palace of Shattered Vessels: I. *Summer in the Street of the Prophets* (Merhavia and Tel Aviv: Sifriat Po'alim, 1969); II. *A Voyage to Ur of the Chaldees* (Merhavia and Tel Aviv: Sifriat Po'alim, 1971); III. *Day of the Countess* (Tel Aviv: Sifriat Po'alim, 1976); IV. *Nin-Gal* (Tel Aviv: 'Am 'Oved, 1983); V. *Day of the Ghosts* (Tel Aviv: 'Am 'Oved, 1986); VI. *A Tammuz-Night's Dream* (Tel Aviv: 'Am 'Oved, 1988); *The Nights of Lutetia* (Tel Aviv: Ma'ariv, 1991); VII. *Of Candles and Winds* (Jerusalem: Yedi'ot Aharonot, 1994). A boxed, revised edition, including *Of Candles and Winds* (as the seventh "gate") but excluding *The Nights of Lutetia* (listed on the frontispiece as an eighth novel, classified as *hasha'ar hasatum*, the blocked gate), appeared shortly before Shahar's death (Jerusalem: Sifriat Hasha'ot, 1996). We have referred in this book to some of the changes that Shahar made in revising; we have, however, kept quotations and page references as they appear in the original publication, since the revised edition, of which only 120 copies were printed, is not widely available. The first two volumes of the *Palace* were translated into English by Dalia Bilu and appeared in one volume (New York: Weidenfeld and Nicholson, 1988).

To the Mount of Olives (Jerusalem: Mossad Bialik, 1998) (a posthumously published fragment).

In this book we do not refer to Shahar's early novel, *The Moon of Honey and Gold* (published originally in 1959), or to his children's book, *The Adventures of Riki Maoz* (published originally in 1960).

Chapter 1

Flirting with the Uncanny

Somewhere near the middle of the first volume of David Shahar's novel sequence *The Palace of Shattered Vessels*, the narrator describes a scene he witnessed many years before. He was a ten-year-old boy sitting on the verandah reading a book (Bialik's adaptation of *Don Quixote*) when judge Dan Gutkin, a Jewish magistrate under the British Mandate administration, came to pay a visit to the landlady, Mrs. Gentilla Luria, the widow of Yehuda Prosper Bey:

> The Officer of the British Empire climbed the steps to the home of his old friend the Officer of the Ottoman Empire, who had departed this world only a few weeks before, reaching the verandah just as the Jerusalem widow of the departed was shutting herself in her room and her sister, Pnina, was drawing up the three-legged iron table standing in the middle of the flagged floor to the red plush armchair which had been kept up till then for the exclusive use of Yehuda Prosper Bey. As soon as he had seated himself in the armchair with his face toward the setting sun, Pnina hurried off to bring him some biscuits and a cold drink. (*Summer*, 101; 84)

This description, quite typical of Shahar's style, is replete with precise spatiotemporal notations and correlations. First, the immediate scene itself: Judge Gutkin reached the verandah "just as" Mrs. Luria "was shutting herself in her room"; "As soon as he had seated himself," her sister, Pnina, "hurried off" for refreshments. Then, the recent past of the individuals involved: the decease, several weeks earlier, of Yehuda Prosper Bey, which, among other consequences, brought to an end his "exclusive use" of that particular armchair. The long-standing relationships among the characters, too, have an implicit temporal dimension: the judge had once been the Bey's protégé, and Pnina had once been her sister's rival for his affections. The reference to the two men as officers of two different empires enriches the passage with the notion of historical change, the British having displaced the Ottoman Empire in Palestine some eighteen years before the time of the scene (of course, both the publication of the book and the narrator's recollection take place after a further change, with the State of Israel replacing the British Mandate). There is perhaps a touch of irony in that the officer of an empire on which the sun never sets should take a seat "facing the setting sun." This particular detail evokes even more readily a symbolic sense of the waning of life toward decrepitude and death. Returning to the logic of the scene itself, the failure of Mrs. Luria to welcome her visitor in person is due to her reluctance to show the ravages that time and neglect brought on her physical appearance.

Taking this analysis one step farther, we might note that spatiotemporality here is profoundly linked to notions of identity and potential rivalry. In a reality understood by empirical and rational principles, time is irreversible, and two entities cannot occupy the same place at the same time. Thus the Ottoman Empire had to give way to the British one, and unless Yehuda Prosper Bey had disappeared, Judge Dan Gutkin might not have been seated in his armchair.

This latter image, however, produces in the narrator at first a different, powerful reaction:

> Meanwhile I was flooded with a sense of uncomprehending wonder, delightful and frightening at the same time, as if I had suddenly stepped into a magic palace, at the sight of the judge with his mane of white hair combed severely back from his forehead on both sides of the middle parting above the square-jawed assertiveness of his lean face, lowering his strong limbs into the armchair of the old Bey, who used to sit up excitedly and call out "Of course, of course" as he drew a large red handkerchief over his smoothly shaven, shining head to wipe away the beads of sweat sparkling like fireworks in the setting sun. The picture of the old Bey, as I had last seen him before his death, sitting on this red armchair with the checked scarf his Jerusalem wife had wrapped around his neck, his hoarse old voice shouting in impotent rage "Our master Moses, our master Moses," superimposed itself on the picture of the judge sitting on the same old verandah in the same armchair without either picture blotting the other out, blurring or erasing its lines to the slightest degree, and my heart feared and expanded in an abundance of joyful wonder in the palace in which I had suddenly found myself. (101–102; 85)

The scene, then, is perceived as a telescoping of two moments in time, and the elation it produces in the narrator is attributable to an apparent victory over the destructive irreversibility of time and/or the mutual exclusion of personal identities. The characterization of his sense of wonder as "uncomprehending" suggests a perspective other than that of a ten-year-old boy. That it could be articulated retrospectively, at a distance of many years, is itself another implied triumph over mutability and oblivion. At the same time, this delayed coming-to-significance bears all of the hallmarks of that *Nachträglichkeit* Freud associated with the retroactive emergence of trauma.[1]

Several such moments, in which a person long lost seems to come back to life or is suddenly glimpsed in another, or a situation recurs with apparently the full force of its original occurrence, are to be found in *The Palace of Shattered Vessels*.[2] A reader of European literature will recognize here an experience (or a narrative trope) akin to, if not at all points identical to, Proustian privileged moments of remembrance or Wordsworthian "spots of time." Shahar's term here for such a moment is the word "palace," a choice that may seem odd to the uninitiated but whose importance is underlined by its figuring in the general title of the novel sequence.

First it must be noted that the Hebrew word rendered here as "palace" is not *armon*, usually used to designate a royal abode, but *heikhal*, which can also mean "shrine," that is, a holy place, and often is used in connection with the Holy Temple itself. More specifically, the key to the use of this term by Shahar is to be found in the literature of the Kabbala. Indeed, any reader alerted to this connection must recognize immediately that all the elements of the general title (as well as the subtitle, *Lurian*, dropped from later volumes but reintroduced in the revised edition) point in the same direction.[3] In early Kabbalistic literature, "Palaces" (*Heikhalot*) were texts describing the mystical ascension to the celestial palaces and the meeting with the "King of Kings"; the latter is depicted as seated on a celestial throne in the seventh of these palaces and is described in great anthropomorphic detail. Since the ascension of the mystic follows in reverse the process of creation, it leads him back from the world of plurality and particularization to the original divine unity.[4] We cannot, at this stage, point to any closer parallels between the Heikhalot literature of the second to fifth century A.D. and Shahar's work. For our purpose here, suffice it to say that in this passage Shahar uses the word "palace" specifically to designate the locus of a quasimystical encounter. The centering of the scene on a father/judge figure on a thronelike seat also contributes to this parallel. What makes the experience mystical is the appearance of freedom from the limitations of empirical existence, in particular, from the irreversibility and destructiveness of time rather than any other divine attributes of power or holiness. And yet the mystical encounter occurs most emphatically on the ground of empirical reality. In Shahar's fiction, on certain extraordinary but not all-too-rare occasions, the divine, thus understood, is glimpsed precisely in the mundane.

The "abundance" (*shefa'*) characteristic of such experiences is precisely the overdetermination or excess disallowed by a rational-empirical conception of reality governed by the law of excluded middle. And here, as elsewhere in *The Palace of Shattered Vessels*, this cannot last longer than a brief instant, as the text continues: "But the palace vanished as suddenly as it had appeared, and with it the picture of the old Bey, and I said to myself, 'No, it's quite impossible that this red chair should have room enough for both of them, the old man and the judge as well—and besides, the old man's dead and gone'" (102; 85–86). Why should the exhilaration of the palace disappear so abruptly? The text presents it as a sober return to common sense, but surely that is just what the narrator's consciousness had to take leave of in order to have its quasimystical experience in the first place. A stronger explanation is suggested by the ambivalence characterizing this experience from the start: it has always been both "delightful" and "fearful," caused the heart to both "fear" and "expand."

Affective ambivalence such as this often accompanies accounts of mystical experience. If transcending the destructive power of time appears desirable, then the abolition of the difference between life and death (and, even more so, between the living and the dead) can be felt as a threat to life. Likewise, the union with the absolute being of the divinity is the ultimate goal of mystical yearning, but at the same time it spells the dissolution of the subject's personal identity. Certainly in Shahar, as our subsequent discussions will show, personal identity as the locus of desire is a *sine qua non*, the basis for any possible development. The awe inspired by the palace experience is also plain fear.

Such affective ambivalence characterizes as well the experience Freud discusses in his essay "The Uncanny" ("Das Unheimliche," 1919). Freud there talks about situations where the subject is suddenly faced with an aspect of external reality that bears a powerful and close kinship with something buried deep in his unconscious (a repressed complex or a stage of development presumably long since overcome). When this aspect of reality assumes anthropomorphic features, the subject is faced with what has been called a "double." Freud highlights the intense affective ambivalence elicited by such figures, giving it a temporal inflection. Originally, he writes, the double was "an insurance against the destruction of the ego," "an energetic denial of the power of death," but such belief in the indestructibility of the self is relinquished when the evidence of empirical reality begins to assert itself. The double then reverses its aspect, inspiring terror instead of joy: "From having been an assurance of immortality, it becomes the uncanny harbinger of death."[5]

Placing his poetic, personal version of the topos of the *Heikhal* so early in his text, Shahar invites us to consider it as emblematic of the work as a whole. We can then read the scene as indicative of a tension in his poetics between two elements: on the one hand, an "adult," prosaic commitment to a rational-empirical conception of reality; on the other hand, an ambivalent fascination with the suspension of rules governing such a reality.

Of course, the former, grown-up conception does not necessarily amount to a naive belief in a strictly "objective" reality, but it does presuppose a discrete self with a sensorium, a consciousness, and a memory relating to a world that is actually "out there," a world of linear temporality and well-defined identities. Positing such a world is the foundation of realist poetics and, indeed, it is in his success as a mimetic writer that critics of Shahar often locate his unique power. Thus, for instance, the most assiduous of Shahar scholars, Sarah Katz:

> For Shahar is, after all, one of the most gifted novelists in our literature, and he represents his creative world and the Jerusalem milieu in a manner so plastic and colorful, so authentic and convincing, that the fictional story appears to be literally true [*emet la-amita*]. Shahar's characters are so fresh and credible, so energetic and lively, that the reader feels as though she has met them in reality, somewhere in the streets of Jerusalem or one of its neighborhoods, in a café, a garden, or one of their private basement love-nests.[6]

The other element, opposed to a rational-empirical conception of reality and to a straightforward mimetic poetics, is more complex and somewhat more difficult to describe. We believe it can be accounted for in three ways. First, it often appears as a mystical yearning to transcend or transgress the limitations of plain reality (but then, Shahar can no longer be committed to any traditional, let alone institutional, religious discipline). Second, and no less frequently, it may be construed as a privileging of what Freud called "primary process," where time is reversible and distinctions between self and other tend to blur. Finally, it manifests itself in narrative patterns that, through repetition, doubling, and the blurring of borderlines, challenge the punctuality of events, the linearity of time, and the discrete existence of individuals. It is the interplay between these two commitments and the paradoxical representations that it generates that this chapter sets out to explore.

Narrative Organization

The remarkable opening paragraph of *Summer in the Street of the Prophets* (and of the whole *Palace* sequence) posits as a general framework the voice of a narrator recounting experiences recalled from the past, by way of autobiographical, retrospective narration:

> Light and cistern water, the mouth of the cave and the rock at its side: these four have been connected in my memory with the figure of Gabriel Jonathan Luria ever since the time he came to stay in our house when I was a child. From Paris he came straight to our house, and since he entered the yard just before the King of Abyssinia entered the Ethiopian Consulate across the road—which is to say, just as I was drawing water from the cistern—his figure was fixed in my memory as rising from its mouth together with the pail of water splashing radiant, dancing light in all directions, which I was drawing up with a peculiar kind of pleasure from its bottom: rising and opening like the Japanese paper flower in its glass of water which he himself was later to buy me from Hananiah's toy shop. (9; 7)

As a global motivating device, this framework allows for associative leaps and bounds, an episodic and nonlinear organization of plot materials, while at the same time not relinquishing the claim that the contents of these memories might be pieced together into some coherent reality. Wherever this reality does not meet the requirements of external verisimilitude, one expects it at least to be attributable to the consciousness of the narrator. The focus on consciousness may go so far as to make the very plot assume the appearance of being the story of this consciousness. Indeed, the very title of the work leads one to expect it to constitute a piecing together of memories and experiences into some sort of architectural whole.

At the center of the narrator's reminiscences stands Gabriel Jonathan Luria (who gave the sequence its subtitle "Lurian"), with whom the novel opens and who dominates the seventh and last "gate."[7] He is the son of old Yehuda Prosper Bey, former Consul of Spain in Jaffa, and his much younger wife, Gentilla, in whose house the narrator lives as a boy. The narrator meets Gabriel upon his return to Jerusalem after a long stay in France and tells of what he saw of him that summer, up to the moment at which Gabriel kills an Arab rioter, is arrested, and then is released. But the narrator also tells of Gabriel's life prior to his departure for France, especially his love for Orit (often called Orita) Gutkin, the beautiful and proud daughter of Judge Dan Gutkin, with whom he had a stormy love affair, as well as his concurrent liaison with Bella, the wife of Fat Pesach (co-owner of the Café Cancan). Following his ten-day fling with Orit at the King David Hotel, Gabriel leaves for France, ostensibly to study medicine; some time later, Orit (possibly pregnant by him) marries the much older Dr. Landau, a famous ophthalmologist. We are told also of Gabriel's life in France: upon finding out that he dropped out of medical school, his father cuts him off financially, and during the last year of his stay, he becomes a simple farmhand in Brittany.

The narrator was also acquainted in his childhood with some of Gabriel's friends, and he relates episodes from their lives prior to and following Gabriel's departure: Israel (Srulik) Shoshan, the little librarian of the Bnei Brit library, whose long-standing dream to travel to Ur of the Chaldees, birthplace of the patriarch Abraham, is repeatedly frustrated by family mishaps and obligations, and who disappears one day from Jerusalem, only to return many years later as a Protestant doctor of theology and missionary; and Berl Raban, alias Eshbaal Ashtarot, an admirer of the biblical Joshua son of Nun, conqueror of Canaan, who works as Dr. Landau's assistant before deciding to devote himself entirely to the writing of poetry. In telling the story of these characters' desires and disappointments, the narrator digresses into the lives of their relatives and friends: Srulik's father, the carpenter nicknamed Temple-Builder; his sister Rina and her husband, the dance teacher Oded; his aunt, the coppersmith Elka, and her sister Ethel; Berl's brother, Haim Longlife, always excited by some new idea for a money-making invention; Berl's wife, the pretentious art critic and intellectual Lea Himmelsach; Shoshi Raban, the wife of the ultra-orthodox greengrocer Reb Itzhok, who discovers one day Berl's poetry and falls in love with him; Judge Gutkin and his other daughter, Yael (often called Yaeli); his Anglophile Arab chauffeur, Daoud, later killed by Gabriel, possibly with the same dagger that had killed Daoud's father a quarter of a century earlier; Wertheimer, a half-Jewish professor of Germanic mythology, who escaped from Germany when Hitler came to power, lives as a peddler in Jerusalem, becomes a British intelligence officer during World War II, and ends up a professor in Oxford; his friend, the violinist Brunhilde, who dies of cancer; Boulos Effendi, the rich Arab antique dealer; William Gordon, chief of a British police station in Jerusalem, whose passion for photography brings about his death during the riots in the summer of 1936; and Louidor the Silent, whose unrequited love for Yaeli Gutkin as well as his disappointment at finding Eretz Israel full of Arabs leads to his conversion to Islam and subsequently to his murder. Later volumes expand the story to include the next generation: Berl's daughter Nin-Gal, whom the narrator loved in his childhood and who dies mysteriously at an early age; his son Tammuz Ashtarot, the narrator's schoolmate and best friend, who may or may not be the same person as a drama critic named Thomas Astor he encounters many years later in Paris; Arik Wissotzky, another school friend of the narrator and of Tammuz, also encountered later on in Paris; and Orit's granddaughter, Yaeli Landau, who may be mysteriously connected to Tammuz/Thomas.

Chronology

Shahar's rhetoric often highlights the various "spatial" relations of analogy between characters and events, but insofar as his narrative invites a conventional mimetic reading, it calls for a chronological piecing together of these life fragments, an attempt to construct the sequence of events that makes up the main trajectory of the plot.

This attempt at chronological construction must hinge on the scene opening the text, a scene that posits the promise of a chronological referent with particular force. For this scene anchors the narrator's personal experience in *historical* reality: the day on which the narrator, then a ten-year-old boy, was so impressed by the return from Paris of Gabriel Luria, so we are told, was the very same day on which Emperor Haile Selassie of Ethiopia made his entry to Jerusalem (9; 7). This latter event can be easily looked up in historical records: fleeing from the Italian invasion of his country, the emperor came to Jerusalem on May 8, 1936.[8]

By the middle of volume 3 (*Day of the Countess*), we realize that the crucial point toward which the various narrative strands lead is a particular day later that summer, a day branded as the "enchanted day" (52). This is the day on which Gabriel came with Orit to the Café Gat and played Brunhilde's violin in the street outside, the day Wertheimer sold that violin to Boulos Effendi, and the day the narrator discovered the volume of poems by Eshbaal Ashtarot under the peacock ashtray made by Elka. This day, too, presumably is anchored in public historical record: it is said by the narrator to be exactly eight days prior to the outbreak of violence in Jerusalem as part of the Arab Uprising (referred to in Zionist historiography as the 1936 Riots).

Such cross-references are not absent from the later volumes of the sequence. Thus in volume 7 (*Of Candles and Winds*), as Gabriel is in his basement, deep in the study of Spinoza, Bella breaks in with the shocking news: "They murdered Brenner" (105). In fact, Chaim Yossef Brenner was murdered on May 2, 1921. This invites us to date several fictional ongoings: Lord Radcliffe's visit to Jerusalem; Gabriel's affair with Bella; and his fateful fling with Orit at the King David Hotel. In *The Nights of Lutetia*, upon being invited to celebrate that lady's fortieth birthday, the narrator comments that she is as old as the State of Israel (28). His stay in Paris and his second meeting with Tammuz/Thomas must therefore take place in 1988.

Such references to external chronology invite us to consider the personal fictional narrative as an integral part of general history. If so, we might expect this private story to consist of discrete events that occupy specific points along the axis of time. However, if we proceed on such assumptions in the attempt to locate other fictional events, we run into considerable difficulty. In some cases, the relative temporal position of important events becomes problematic when we try to correlate them with such external references.

Thus two of the major characters of the whole saga, Gabriel and Srulik, disappear from Jerusalem in separate events, only to run into each other again years later in France, before one of them, Gabriel, makes his return to Jerusalem (Srulik will return, too, but only some twenty years later). Srulik's disappearance is not dated in the text. The story of his experiences in Jerusalem continues for several years after Gabriel's departure for France, since his desire to travel to Ur of the Chaldees is reawakened for the last time when Orita has long been married and is mother to a three-year-old daughter (*Voyage*, 125; 354; she was unmarried and childless when Gabriel left). Elsewhere, Gabriel's return after a nine-year stay (*Voyage*, 190; 428) is said to be "long after" Srulik's disappearance (*Voyage*, 38; 252); this would put Srulik's disappearance somewhere near the middle of Gabriel's absence from Jerusalem. Srulik's disappearance can also be related to several other events. "A week or two before he disappeared," he discussed with the narrator himself the visit to the studio of his Aunt Elka by Yehuda Prosper Bey in the company of Sir Ronald Storrs, identified in the text as "formerly governor of Jerusalem and *now* governor of Cyprus" (*Day of the Countess*, 11). During this memorable visit, Storrs mentions a conversation he has had with Lawrence (of Arabia) only "last week," in which the latter maintained that the only people worthy of one's admiration were artists and creators. Some time during the same period, and certainly while Aunt Elka was still alive, the narrator was asked by Srulik to fetch from her house Sir Leonard Woolley's book *Abraham*. So far, so good: there is no violation of *internal* temporal coherence.

Since Storrs, Lawrence, and Woolley were actual historical figures, the appeal to historical chronology seems to be warranted. But when we try to map the sequence onto external chronological indications, things begin to show signs of crumbling. In his autobiography, Storrs (who was governor of Cyprus from 1926 to 1932) mentions that particular conversation with Lawrence, dating it September 1926.[9] Since Woolley's *Abraham* was not published until 1936,[10] Srulik's disappearance would have to be dated soon after September 1926 and not before 1936, a full ten-year discrepancy. Either one of these dates would also contradict, of course, the aforementioned correlation with Gabriel's absence. Rather than disappearing at some point around the middle of Gabriel's absence from Jerusalem, Srulik's disappearance would have to be dated either just prior to Gabriel's departure (c. 1927) or around the time of his return (1936). Furthermore, if the narrator was about ten years old upon Gabriel's return in 1936, he must have been a babe in arms when he heard from Srulik about Storrs's recent visit to Elka's studio (externally dated 1926) and was asked to fetch Woolley's book (not published until ten years later).

There are other such cruxes in the eight volumes of the *Palace*, where references to historical chronology lead to contradictions in the construction of the fable.[11] It is quite possible that some of these inconsistencies are due to authorial oversight, or the gradual elaboration of the plot in the author's mind over a period of some twenty-five years. Indeed, in revising his text for the definitive edition, Shahar addressed himself to some issues of this kind (cf. note 13 below). Our pointing out these details is not offered in a spirit of pedantic fault finding. The fact remains, however, that it is the author who insistently studs his text with such external chronological notations. Taken together, these notations add up to a sense that it is important to him to anchor his narrative in documented historical reality. At the same time, the existence of such discrepancies indicates that the author's fictional creation and/or the characters' subjective experiences do not easily fit into a consistent, linear mold. To use the central conceit of the work as a whole, if empirical reality is the vessel then the poetics of verisimilitude cannot quite contain the overabundance of imaginative energy.

But inconsistencies also may be noted when we try to piece together *internal* temporal indications rather than just relate them to external chronology. Gabriel's return from Paris coincides not only with Haile Selassie's entry to Jerusalem but also with the narrator's act of drawing water from the cistern. In remembering that particular occasion, the narrator emphasizes the particular care he took not to spill any of the water. This is related directly to the anxious watching by Pnina, Gabriel's old aunt, of the decreasing water level in the cistern located beneath the house. Her present cause for concern is contrasted with last year's: "The year before we worried about floods. . . . But this year was dry and rainless" (*Summer*, 10–11; 8–9). Dry and rainy years can alternate in Jerusalem, then, and Gabriel's return happened to take place on a dry year.[12] In the next paragraph, however, we find him standing at the window, "smoking one of his Latif cigarettes and looking out at the rain pouring down in a steady beating rhythm as if it would never stop" (11; 9). The worry here is that the cistern may not be large enough to contain the abundance of water, so that the house erected over it might be in danger of crumbling. It is conceivable, of course, that having returned on a particular day in a dry year, Gabriel should have stayed in Jerusalem long enough to witness a rainy one. At the very least, however, it should be noted that there is no textual indication whatsoever that the time of the occurrence has shifted. If anything, the association of excessive rain with the previous year creates the odd impression that Gabriel was somehow there to say some particular words that have some particular effect on the narrator the year prior to his actual return.[13]

The oddity is that while, on the one hand, the narrator expends considerable effort in anchoring each event and each experience in a specific time and place, on the other hand, the characters appear to lead a ghostly life that at times seems to float rather freely over this meticulous spatiotemporal grid. A partial motivation for this kind of freefloating scene is its attachment to temporal realities that are in principle iterative or repetitive (the four-season cycle reiterated each year, with the possible alternation of rainy with dry winters; iterative situations such as sitting on the verandah or standing guard with a comrade during military service; event types repeated in the course of the plot, such as wars and journeys abroad). However, if verisimilitude is the desired effect, the problem still remains: the year of Gabriel's return could be either a dry or rainy one, but not both.

There is, however, a sense in which it hardly matters whether the cistern is depleted or overfull. Either one of these eventualities is fraught with unease, and both are allayed by the actual or remembered presence of Gabriel Luria:

> "Yes, yes," he said, showing no signs of making ready for the necessary plugging operations, "the vessels will never be able to contain the abundance," and I was for some reason reassured, sinking into a strange kind of calm acceptance that this, in fact, was the way things were. Just as my anxiety lest the cistern be emptied left me now at the sight of his face appearing suddenly as if rising from the pail and the sound of his saying, "Yes, yes. The vessels are emptying." (11; 10)

Passages such as this indicate that what matters here most is positing—and overcoming—the opposition excess/dearth rather than this or that eventuality. This applies not only on the psychological level, in the narrator's relation to Gabriel, but also on a more general, symbolic level. The text establishes a metaphorical equation of water and light: the inability of the cisterns to contain the excess of water has its equivalent in Gabriel's eventual eye condition, "when his eyes were no longer able to bear the abundance of the light" (*Summer* 12; 10). In Lurianic Kabbala, the "shattered vessels" are the lower of the ten spheres, which could not contain the abundance of light in the process of creation. But the absence of any such light would have meant that no creation occurred at all. Gabriel, who is described as a source of "comforting emanation, instilling security and joy in which he abounds," and who is enigmatically said to have been "the author of 'The Palace of Shattered Vessels'" (*Summer*, 19; sentence omitted from the English and French translation but not from the definitive edition), is also the first and foremost "shattered vessel" in Shahar's *Palace*.

Often, inner temporal contradictions result from the telescoping of several (possibly mutually exclusive) occurrences or events into a more or less limited time/space. Thus under the designation "Summer in the Street of the Prophets," at least three summers are conflated, confused, or superimposed: the summer of Gabriel's return from France, the summer of his departure, and the summer of Srulik's last dream of Ur. However, inner temporal contradictions also occur when a relatively short and well-demarcated period of time (between two punctual, decisive events) is overcrowded with occurrences (and especially repetitive ones) beyond the limits of verisimilitude. This happens in the initial description of the narrator's introduction to the Luria household. The narrator and his family, we are told, have moved into an apartment in Mrs. Luria's house only a few weeks before Gabriel's return. This relatively short period of time is further divided by another punctual event—the death of the old Bey, Gabriel's father, which took place several weeks before Gabriel's return (*Summer*, 36; 29), hence, soon after the narrator had moved in. Yet the narrative describing the short period between the narrator's coming to live in the house and the return of Gabriel, or the even shorter period between the death of the father and the return of the son, gives the unmistakable impression that a long time has elapsed, a time during which the narrator has become an intimate member of the household: "Ever since her husband's death, but especially since the old judge had wound up the affair of her inheritance to her complete satisfaction, Mrs. Luria had become so worried about her finances that she had stopped sending her son any money at all, and contented herself with sending him parcels tied up with whole balls of string which I would carry to the post office for her" (*Summer*, 166; 151). Parcels did not go by airmail in those days.

Similarly, the relatively short period between Gabriel's return from France (a day of great importance, at least for the narrator) and the beginning of the riots in Jerusalem on the fatal day in which "the world was divided in two" (*Voyage* 194; 433) is filled with an overabundance of incident. According to the narrative sequence told at the end of *Voyage* and the beginning of *Day of the Countess,* about two weeks separated these two turning points. Orit first saw Gabriel a week after his return (*Voyage*, 189; 428, "ten days or a fortnight," according to *Voyage,* 167; 401). The day following their first meeting was the "enchanted day" (*Countess*, 52), and that, we are told, was eight days before the eruption of violence that brought about the death of Gordon and Daoud (*Countess*, 41).

Day of the Ghosts, too, covers the same time period, in fact ending on a verbatim repetition of the description of the riots as given at the end of *Day of the Countess.* But new characters and new events have been introduced into this short interval. We are told (in *Ghosts)* of Gabriel's half-serious attempt to help Lea Himmelsach, Berl's wife, whose previous attempts to "mount the barricades" in order to bring progress to the Arab populace have been frustrated by her ignorance of the Arabic language. Gabriel suggests that she launch her mission by addressing those Arabs who were educated by German missionaries. Lea accepts; a first meeting is organized in Gabriel's house; a second meeting takes place a week later in the Bnei Brit library, following which Daoud drives Lea back home and is "seduced" by her into a sexual encounter (a seduction that is presented as contributing to his turning against the Jews and thus explains his participation, soon after, in the Arab riots). The impression fostered by this section is of a Gabriel long since back in Jerusalem, an active member of a social set; it is hard to imagine all of these developments occurring in a period of two to three weeks.

The difficulty increases if we assume that this brief span also saw the "benefit" concert Gabriel held in his house on Brunhilde's birthday. There is no direct indication in the novel when this event happened (it is mentioned several times, e.g., *Countess*, 126; *Nin-Gal,* 138), but this could not be before Gabriel left for France (presumably around 1927), since Wertheimer and Brunhilde only came to Palestine with Hitler's takeover. Moreover, Gabriel explicitly compares and contrasts his effort and motives in organizing these two affairs (*Ghosts*, 110), thus suggesting their proximity in time. A week after Gabriel's return, however, Brunhilde is already dead: on the "enchanted day" Wertheimer sells her violin to Boulos Effendi to raise money for her tombstone. Brunhilde's concert and the events surrounding it can hardly fit into this chronological straitjacket. In order to accommodate the narrative impression of iteration and duration, we have to "forget," or at least shift, one of the punctual events demarcating this period—Gabriel's return, the "enchanted day," the riots.

But the events demarcating those miraculous two weeks during which so much is supposed to have transpired are not indifferent occurrences that might simply be shifted around to make as much room as would be reasonably necessary for everything to happen. They are repeatedly characterized as exceptional moments. We have already alluded to the day of Gabriel's return to Jerusalem and its internal as well as external chronological correlations. As the narrator resumes his narrative in chapter 2 of *Summer in the Street of the Prophets*, he insists on the momentousness of the event: "I saw Gabriel Jonathan Luria for the first time on a great and strange day in my life" (*Summer*, 23; 19). He then goes on to repeat the correlation with his own act of drawing water and with Haile Selassie's entry into the Ethiopian Consulate. The same phrase is repeated at the end of chapter 7, as the narrator once more recalls "the first time I saw Gabriel Jonathan Luria on a great and strange day in my life, the day on which my eyes beheld, on the other side of the street, the King of Kings Haile Selassie, Elect of God, Conquering Lion of the Tribe of Judah, the Emperor of Ethiopia, in the middle of summer in the year 5696 from the Creation of the world, 1936 according to the Christian calendar" (*Summer*, 150; 136). A substantial portion of this sentence is repeated verbatim in the beginning of chapter 4 of *A Voyage to Ur of the Chaldees* (157; 388).[14] Each time the text insists on its being the *first* time the narrator actually saw Gabriel Luria, a meeting that affected him for the rest of his life.

The miraculously eventful fortnight comes to an end on the day the riots broke out in Jerusalem. It may not be irrelevant to note that, historically, the 1936 Arab Rebellion was triggered earlier that year and away from Jerusalem, and that no riot similar to the one Shahar describes here is documented in easily accessible records.[15] The momentousness of the particular day he describes is, then, a compositional feature of his own fictional creation, and it would be hard to outdo his highlighting of the significance and irreversibility of that day, "the day of the outbreak of the riots [*meora'ot*, literally, "events"] that split the world and time in two, a day that became a turning point in Gabriel's life no less than it was Berl's day" (*Countess*, 135). This sentence echoes a previous one in which the narrator demarcates the period in question, with Gabriel's image rising before him "as I first beheld it on the day of his homecoming, and as it remained until the events that split the world and time in two" (*Voyage*, 194; 433).

One expectation powerfully raised by this kind of emphasis is that subsequent portions of the narrative should tell us about Gabriel's later experiences, and that these should be significantly different from those that transpired till then. Thus the day of the riots was also said to be Berl's day (*Countess*, 135, quoted above), and the change in this character's life is indeed remarkable: having resigned from his position in Dr. Landau's clinic, he moves out of his home and into Mrs. Luria's cellar to devote himself entirely to the writing of poetry; later volumes suggest that he has subsequently gained wide recognition as a poet. But of Gabriel's life after his killing Daoud, his arrest, and his release, we are told next to nothing. From volume 4 on, he is largely relegated to the background, and when he does reemerge as the protagonist in *Of Candles and Winds*, it is only as the subject of events prior to his homecoming and the day that "split the world and time in two." All that we ever learn of his life after 1936 concerns the deterioration of his eyesight and some meetings with the narrator, during which he tells him of earlier periods in his life. A curious detail is that Gabriel seems to be absent from his mother's funeral (which must have taken place after 1936), since Blum, the pharmacist, on that occasion, voices to the narrator his displeasure with himself for not having asked the deceased lady for her son's address while she was still alive.[16] In brief, after that *annus mirabilis* of 1936, Gabriel hardly seems to exist in the world and time of the *Palace*. In contrast, we might note that the character of Srulik does reappear on a much later date in the fable. Some twenty years after his disappearance from Jerusalem, now the Protestant clergyman Dr. Shoshan, he comes to David Shahar's door to urge him to translate into Hebrew a *Life of Calvin* (as Shahar, both in the fiction and in real life, had translated some book on Zen), and in the various meetings that ensue, he tells the narrator of his life after his conversion.

Gabriel's presence in the life of the narrator (which is, to a large extent, the "subject" of the story) does not, then, fit easily into a temporal narrative with a beginning, a middle (a turning point), and an end; yet the narrative also insists precisely on these moments in their punctuality, uniqueness, and irreversibility. Though in a general way we can attribute this to the incommensurability between the requirements of the imagination or desire and those of empirical reality, it is not easy to sort out which elements of the text belong to one category or the other. Both the temporal grid—with its precise notations—and the events (detailed, varied, iterative) that should, but do not quite, fit within it can be claimed with equal justice to obey either one of these logics.

Identities

During those stretches of fable time from which Gabriel is absent, it is the figure of the narrator that to some extent assumes his role. The narrator is not just the witnessing and remembering character for those times but also the traveler (specifically to France) and the lover—as Luria had been before him. One should note, however, that even if the narrator is seen as in some sense stepping into Gabriel's shoes, the emphatic "splitting of the world and time in two" is not substantiated by any narrative material about him either. This substitution can be explained in various ways. The narrator has become *like* Gabriel, since Gabriel was his admired example, his role model; imitating Gabriel and Gabriel's desires, the narrator takes his place. Conversely, one can argue that Gabriel is not so much a model in the real world as the narrator's ideal self, a fictional projection of his wishes and desires. In the first case, the narrator is shaped or created by Gabriel; in the latter, it is Gabriel who is created, or imagined into fictional being, by the narrator. However we explicate the substitution, Gabriel and the narrator, with all of their similarities, remain distinct (whether as model and imitation, or as self and ideal).

There are, however, numerous places where the narrator and Gabriel are conflated in ways that cannot be easily explained by either one of these logics. Thus on occasion, experiences attributed to one of them are elsewhere predicated of the other. For example, the text narrates twice Mrs. Luria's griping over what happened during her weekly visit to the eye clinic: in the very midst of administering her eyedrops, Dr. Landau became involved in a dispute over a biblical verse with his assistant, Berl. But while on one of these occasions the addressee of this harangue is her son, Gabriel (*Voyage*, 168–69; 402), on the other, clearly referring to the very same event as having happened "two days ago," it is the narrator (*Countess*, 13). Similarly, in the early volumes, the narrator recalls time and again his visits to the Bnei Brit library and the late afternoon meals, largely consisting of canned foods sent from America, that Srulik's aunts arranged there and that these ladies liked to call "by the elegant title of 'five o'clock tea'" (*Voyage*, 17; 233). Much later in the text, as Gabriel returns to the library some time in 1936 for Lea Himmelsach's attempt to enlighten the Arabs in dialectical materialism, he, too, reflects nostalgically on those meals, with both the canned foods and the "elegant title of 'five o'clock tea'" figuring in the text (*Ghosts*, 134).

These instances of conflation suggest a relation between the narrator and Gabriel at once more superficial and more intimate: it is as though in the routine events of everyday life the two are one and the same. Indeed, the narrator claims that in some sense they are one and the same person. The first sentence of the novel evokes the figure of Gabriel as the narrator saw him when "he came to stay in our house when I was a child. From Paris he came straight to our house" and entered the yard when the boy-narrator was drawing water from the cistern (*Summer*, 9; 7). The narrator, however, is quick to "correct" himself, pointing out that "our house" is actually Gabriel's house: "On that very day Mr. Luria had returned from Paris to his late father's house—for our house was, in fact, his father's house, and the well we drank from was his childhood well" (*Summer*, 23; 19). The opening sentence also calls the well (or cistern, *bor*) one of the "four fathers of memory" (9; 7; missing in translation). The narrator's (metaphorical) well of memory is, then, Gabriel's (actual) well, so that when he draws from it, it is, in fact, not just his own childhood but also Gabriel's that "he" remembers. When we add to this the frequent equation in the novel between house and body, the narrator's claim that "our" house is, in fact, Gabriel's house leads us to the conclusion that, in some sense, the two are actually one, body and soul.[17]

The narrator also seems to be conflated with the character of Srulik. Reflecting on Berl's suggestion that the Arab dervish, or *willi,* they both saw by Jaffa Gate was actually Louidor the Silent, the narrator comments that this character "disappeared from my mind and Jerusalem and the life of Yaeli many years ago" (*Countess*, 94). However, since this disappearance took place "many years ago" the boy narrator, who is ten years old at the time he sees the *willi* in the Jaffa Gate, could not have had any personal recollection of the actual Louidor and his unrequited love for Yaeli Gutkin. Rather, it was Srulik who overheard from behind a partition Louidor's confession to the laundress Rosa of his unfortunate encounter with Yaeli Gutkin (*Countess*, 113 ff.), so that the mind in question is, in that sense, his.[18]

A similar conflation occurs when we juxtapose two scenes involving the Café Gat. In the later of these, a preamble to the "enchanted day," the narrator goes to the Café Gat on Mrs. Luria's orders to fetch Gabriel away from Orit's company for lunch at home (*Countess*, 32). On arrival there, he notes (in the first person) the absence of Gabriel and Orit and the presence of "three people out there under the marquee" (*Countess*, 34): William James Gordon, chief of the Mahaneh Yehuda police station, with his camera; and Boulos Effendi, about to conclude the sale of Brunhilde's violin with Wertheimer (34). In the earlier Café Gat scene, Srulik passes by on his way to an important appointment. In the ensuing account (narrated in free indirect discourse from Srulik's point of view), Orit's and Gabriel's absence is noted; Boulos Effendi is in a corner smoking his houka, and by the bar Gordon is showing

Joseph Shwili, the owner, his photos of Jericho and Wadi Kelt (*Voyage*, 90–91; 314–15). After some further associative digressions, which take the narrative far afield both chronologically and geographically, to a point decades later in a shop in Amsterdam, where Srulik is overcome with emotion at the sight of a fashion watch that reminds him of Haim Longlife's old ambition to patent such watches, the text returns Srulik to the Café Gat moment: "He suddenly realized that the tears he was shedding were not only in memory of Haim Longlife, but also in memory of the boy he had once been, nearly fifty years before; the boy to whom I now return, as he peered into the doorway of the Café Gat on his way to the Café Cancan" (*Voyage*, 104; 331). As the narrative point of view changes abruptly from that of Srulik to that of the narrator, a curious confusion occurs between the two: at the time of "his" Café Gat scene, Srulik was not a boy but a man in his mid-twenties, and so the boy "he" remembers with tears cannot be the boy to whom the narrator "now return[s], as he peered into the doorway of the Café Gat." If anyone was still a boy witnessing three men in the Café Gat, it must have been the narrator, and on a different occasion.

The similarity between these two café experiences is both less and more meaningful than an ordinary plot analogy. Less meaningful, because for two individuals to see people at a café on different occasions is quite plausible and does not in itself generate any significant plot development or suggest a thematic analogy. However, it is precisely the cumulative repetition in both scenes of details that are in themselves poor in significance that suggests an odd conflation of the character of Srulik with that of the narrator. This repetition tends to evoke in the reader's mind an odd question: "Whose memory is this, after all, and of whose experience?"

Uncanny Photo

From this double scene, the chains of repetition extend in still other directions by means of memory and representation. When Gordon invites Srulik to enter the café and look at pictures of Jericho, the young man first declines in spite of "a delicate feeling invading him at the sound of 'Jericho'"; then, leaning forward, he sees "three people sitting next to the mirror that took up the whole of the inner wall," and this makes him change his mind (*Voyage* 91; 315). The text never names the three people. If they are the same three observed before—Gordon, Shwili, and Boulos—as the English translator assumes (and which is quite unlikely, given their different positions in the café and the fact that Gordon is addressing Srulik), then it remains unclear what caused Srulik to change his mind. The allusion to "a delicate feeling invading him at the sound of 'Jericho'" points us, however, in a different direction. This allusion introduces into the present scene the memory of another, earlier scene of *Srulik himself* sitting in the Café Gat with Orit and her sister Yaeli (after a plan to go together to Jericho had to be canceled); finding himself next to the beautiful Orit was "a dream too good to be true, his dearest wish . . . suddenly realized" (92; 316–17). What Srulik then "sees" in the Café Gat that persuades him to stay is an image of a moment in his past life when his dearest wish was fulfilled—and both the image of the past and the fulfillment of his wish appear to him in the real world and in the present (though the presence of a mirror in the vicinity may suggest, allegorically, the imaginary or subjective nature of this appearance).

Just as Srulik's Café Gat scene is doubled by an earlier scene in his memory, so the boy-narrator's Café Gat scene will be doubled by both a personal memory and a photograph. To appreciate the conceptual network governing this narrative sequence, we must backtrack to the point where the account of the child-narrator's Café Gat experience begins. We recall that he was sent there by Mrs. Luria to fetch Gabriel away from Orita to lunch at home (32), and that his narration of this sequence is intertwined with his recollection of the first time he read Eshbaal Ashtarot's poems, which in turn is related to the goings-on at the eye clinic on the day Berl quit his job there to devote himself to poetry. The narrator recalls some reflections he had then (he must have been quite a precocious ten-year-old boy) on the metaphysics of body and soul in its specific relation to the organ of sight. The paradox he reflects upon is that our "spiritual pleasure . . . of light with all its colors and shades" depends on a "ball of flesh"—the eye (*Countess*, 33). His recent experience at the eye clinic (the sight of the Arab boy's dislodged eye) has led him to realize how fragile this piece of flesh is. Hence, his following thought (or wish):

> This reflection did arise in me as a sort of flickering sense that it may be possible to have sensations and feelings and visions and melodies which are not of this world, without the mediation of the body, but the possibility of this indeterminate, disembodied being, hovering in empty space between nothing and nothing, frightened me so much, that I repressed it immediately, opening wide both my eyes in a wonderful sense of relief at their being both in excellent health. (*Countess*, 33–34)

Alluring as the idea of visions and sensations that do not depend on physical reality may be, the narrator recoils from it in panic. Both the eye and what it wants to see may lead a precarious existence in physical reality but must nevertheless be anchored in it; the possibility of an experience that is beyond or outside of this reality (such as the "palace" experience) is briefly considered and rejected.

These general reflections on vision and physical reality remind the narrator of Dr. Landau's philological inquiry into a possible biblical distinction between physical and moral blindness and send him on his journey to the university library in search of this article. As he makes his way across Jerusalem, he feels at odds with the world around him: all that was valuable and worth preserving is gone—Orita is dead. The response to this loss is a retreat to the world of "memories and thoughts and imaginings and reflections and dreams" (55), where he can still find her. But as his musings continue, they betray a growing dissatisfaction with mere spiritual entities, whether internalized or not:

> Surely even if [Orita] subsists as a disembodied soul, the eyes of the flesh cannot see her since she is outside the world of matter, and if she did become clothed in another, new body, we can all be quite sure of her being so changed, that not only could I not recognize her, but she herself could not recognize herself nor remember anything at all of her previous metamorphosis. (*Countess,* 55)

Without a stable adherence of personal identity to perceptible shape, nothing can have value in Shahar's world.

At the same time, by a nefarious irony, so familiar from Romantic and post-Romantic literature, those perceptible shapes that the author in his personal identity here and now finds himself surrounded by all seem to him ugly, alien, corrupt, degraded, and even directly hostile. The sight of the building housing the eye clinic, where he once had some moving experiences, fails to move him now. People at the bus stop push and shove. Still more depressingly, the article cannot be found after a three-hour search in the library. Smoking a cigarette and staring at some long-haired students on the Hebrew University campus lawn, the author is driven back into his private literary world:

> Suddenly it dawned on me that this dejection stemmed neither from the elbows that had pushed me getting on the bus nor from the failure of my search for Dr. Landau's article which may never have been published, but from the very interruption of my writing the story of that day and my going out into the reality of this day. . . . Just as there is little chance that walking down the street today I would meet Gordon or Daoud Ibn Mahmoud, who were both killed at the beginning of the 1936 riots . . . so there is little chance that I would find today in the National Library a trace [memory trace, *zekher*] to Dr. Landau's linguistic theories. This world here and now not only would not aid me in constructing that other world but, on the contrary,

> would prevent me from concentrating on it, and I have no choice but to escape it as soon as possible. (*Countess,* 58)

It may be tempting to take this passage as a programmatic declaration of Shahar's poetics,[19] which would then appear as a particularly maudlin version of the escape into subjectivity and rejection of the outside world. "This world here and now" seems not just indifferent to the heart's desire but actively hostile to it in some sort of universal conspiracy. All the author can do is withdraw into the world of his memory, where he can retrieve the images that are dear to him. The passage seems to suggest that the whole literary project of the *Palace* is the outcome of this activity in the medium of writing.

But again, the point is that the turn inward is presented as a rather reluctant last resort. The author cannot really be content with memory traces of absent entities; his desire is for nothing less than a reappearance of his past in the here and now of the present. The object made present again need not be desirable in itself (like the figure of Orita); it may be devoid of any special emotional investment (like Gordon or Daoud) as long as it brings back to life the author's own past. Aware, in the adult rational part of his mind, that even this is too much to ask, he denies this wish (much as the "palace" experience we analyzed in the beginning of this chapter gave way to a sense of the impossibility of the dead Bey and the living judge occupying the same chair at the same time). This, then, is the dilemma that shapes Shahar's poetics: on the one hand, an uncompromising desire to preserve his past and, on the other hand, a refusal to accomplish this only in the purely mental realm of subjectivity, the literary equivalent of which would be indulging in fantasies of wish fulfillment and pure fictionality.

It is against this background that we can appreciate the full import of the surprise for which "this world here and now" sets him up. Among the bric-a-brac offered for sale on the campus plaza by a young Englishman, he spots a photograph of the monastery of Saint George in Wadi Kelt. As he turns the photograph over to look for a mark of its origin, he comes face-to-face with another picture, hitherto screened by it:

> All at once I was flooded by an abundance of wistful longing that squeezed my heart and I felt that my eyes were filling with tears. Boulos Effendi was watching me [*nishkaf elai*] from the photograph, sitting under the marquee, one hand holding a houka and the other on the violin, in an unexpected materialization here and now—and even if it is only a realization by means of a picture it still has the concrete materiality of a picture and its form in the external world—of the tale of memory that was interrupted by this very external world

> when I set out to consciously and deliberately search in it a trace of the reality of my story. (*Countess*, 59)

The dead come back to life, as in the "palace" passage; but an important difference is that this "unexpected materialization here and now" is achieved through the material and formal agency of a surviving photograph "in the external world" rather than by the purely personal, internal, and momentary act of imagination (or of memory, as in the case of Srulik).

Following the logic of the scene, the next discovery is perhaps as expected as it is astonishing: after the first surge of surprise, the narrator notices "the thin figure of a poor boy standing behind Boulos at the picture's corner—I don't know why everything in the photograph looked so poor and piteous—his knees sticking out of his thin legs as he leans with care over a bird quivering in his hands. Another glance revealed to me that it is not a bird but a booklet and that the poor boy is I myself" (*Countess*, 59). So the here and now does unexpectedly bring back to life, as it were, a scene from the narrator's past. The mere existence of the picture is perfectly banal in a modern world where the mechanical reproduction of images we call "photography" is so widely available. What animates its emergence with an aura of the uncanny is the extreme unlikelihood that it should appear, precisely to, of all people, the narrator specifically at a moment when he has just about abandoned his search for tangible evidence of his past under the pressure of a hostile present.

This hostility has not yet spent its force, as the ensuing discussions of the photograph will indicate. First, understandably, the narrator is overcome with emotion. Against his better judgment, he unburdens himself to the indifferent young picture seller, telling him not only about Gordon and Boulos but also revealing that "the child in the corner . . . is none other than me as I was at age ten" (60). Regretting his outburst and the intimacy it implies, he asks to buy the two pictures (61) only to be rebutted, first by the young man, who refuses to sell, saying that they are already sold, and who insists that they were taken in Cuba, not in Jerusalem, and then by the present owner (as it turns out, none other than Srulik's grown son), who asserts, rather testily, that they are the work of Man Ray, or "another photographer of the same school" (67). When in response to the narrator's request to photocopy the pictures young Shoshan just "rolled them without responding and put them in the trunk of his car" (69), the narrator is left "shaken with helpless rage" (ibid.).

It is easy to see the narrator's predicament. The combined weight of Dr. Shoshan and the other young man's denials of his self-recognition in the photo raises the stakes considerably: "The simplest way to drive a man mad, quite literally, is to explain to him that what he sees isn't what he thinks he sees, that the picture of Boulos Effendi is not the picture of Boulos Effendi, that the picture of St. George monastery is not the picture of St. George monastery, and that his own picture is not his own picture. To convince him with every possible evidence that he is living in hallucination, in a world of his own misleading imaginations" (70). In such a world, anything can be made out to be the picture of anything else, and the heart's desire would reign supreme. The point is, of course, that though the narrator has every reason to be particularly susceptible to this temptation, he insists, once again, on anchoring his inner world in the outside one.

Thus he is able to persist, waiting on the campus lawn for the "original" owner of the pictures to show up. This young man is a "nice fellow, with blue eyes and a red, curly goatee, carrying a guitar" (71), and he says he obtained the pictures from yet another young man who had received them in Oxford from a "political refugee," none other than Professor Wertheimer, who settled there after the war (75). The circle is thus closed, with the external world, however grudgingly, corroborating the narrator's personal knowledge of his own past self.

And so the quest for Dr. Landau's article actually leads to the narrator's own photograph, a more focused, more powerful evocation of his own past world. The existence of such a record, which might have been preserved in some family album or the like, is little more than trivial. What is remarkable is the complex set of circumstances Shahar (as author) constructs to surround its appearance. Set against the richness of his evocation of the past, its documentary value seems slight. Strictly speaking, it does nothing more than confirm a piece of personal knowledge by objective evidence. But its emergence against all odds as a phenomenon in a reality indifferent or hostile to the narrator's innermost desire is nothing less than uncanny: both wish fulfillment and plain fact. In the context organized for its emergence, this plain fact becomes a sort of Archimedean point outside of the narrator's private, subjective world, lifting and anchoring it in material objectivity. Ultimately, this is obviously little more than a sleight of hand, and having managed his uncanny effect, Shahar wisely does not dwell on it. As the narrator, he is quite happy to settle for indefinitely waiting for the return of the young man who obtained the pictures from Wertheimer. And so his interruption of the process of reminiscing and writing for an excursion into the actual world comes to an end, allowing him to plunge once more into the narrative of that "enchanted day" in 1936.

It is as though Shahar's creative effort is geared toward organizing such moments of uncanny experience—moments in which outside and inside, present and past, the objective and subjective are miraculously joined together (but, as we have emphasized all along, in "the world here and now"). However, when these moments are reached and their significance is realized by the narrator, he either retreats in fear from the quasimystical vision (as in the "palace" episode) or allows his experience to dissolve back into the mundane (as with the photograph). Whether he is too weak a vessel to retain the uncanny apparition or is strong and generous enough to let go of it, even a brief glimpse seems sufficient to reinvigorate his imagination in its self-avowedly impossible quest. This is why there is never anything *final* about any of these episodes. Shahar constantly flirts with the impossible possibility of the uncanny, but he never allows it to take over his fictional world. Leaving the "palace," where the heart's desire miraculously materializes in the midst of the everyday, he returns to the ongoing construction of the *Palace*, where the everyday world is represented bearing the mark of the desires that exceed it.

Chapter 2

The Eyes of a Woman in (and out of) Love
Creation, Painting, and Betrayal in Shahar's Fiction

> From *Adam Kadmon*'s ears, mouth and nose lights issue forth, constructing systems of inner worlds invisible to any living thing. But the major role of creation pertains to the lights shining out of the eyes of *Adam Kadmon*. And so the vessels, themselves constituted from a mixture of lower-quality lights, now destined to receive the light of the *sefirot* emanating from the eyes of *Adam Kadmon* so as to serve as receptacles and instruments of creation, could not withstand the power of the abundance of the lights emanating into them and broke. This is the *Breaking of the Vessels*—the crucial crisis in the divine being and in the whole of creation.
>
> —Shalom

In this chapter we set out to explore the peculiar and recurrent association in Shahar's fiction between painting, betrayal, and the ambiguity of the female gaze. We begin by tracing this pattern through several short stories and the novel *His Majesty's Agent*. We then return to *The Palace of Shattered Vessels*, where the art of painting does not figure prominently but where, as we propose to show, the female gaze is made to play an extremely dramatic, even a founding, role, closely related to the overarching cosmogenic Kabbalistic imagery of the title.

In retrospect, the short stories Shahar began publishing in the early 1950s appear as a series of études toward his crowning major work, *The Palace of Shattered Vessels*, launched near the end of the following decade. Given the romantic problematic at the heart of his poetics, which we explored in the previous chapter, as well as his widespread reputation as "the Israeli Proust" (cf. chapter 5), it might have been expected to find in his great novel sequence something like an artistic autobiography—the story of an aesthetic education. But while a reminiscing first person leading an active subjective life does play a constant role throughout the sequence, there is hardly anything in it adding up to a portrait of the artist as a young man. To find something answering to this description, we must turn to Shahar's short fiction.

"Of Shadows and the Image"

"Of Shadows and the Image," the story that opened Shahar's first book, *Of Dreams*, relates the history of its protagonist, Ephraim, from early childhood to the threshold of manhood. The text opens by describing his situation at the end of the story's chronological sequence: "When Ephraim was seventeen years old he left home and went to live at Hospitality, where he stayed for several weeks" (*The Death of the Little God*, 151). This departure is the event framing the text and retrospectively endowing the sequence with meaning and purpose. In making his move, the boy turns his back upon the religious-orthodox as well as the practical-bourgoeis law of the father to adopt the free, artistic way of life embodied by the female painter, Varda. Both aspects of this move are marked by profound ambivalence and a powerful sense of guilt related to the mother and to the paintress who becomes her substitute in the latter stages of the story.

The narrative is introduced by a first-person narrator who drops out of sight after the first paragraph, giving way to an impersonal voice that has complete access to the protagoninst's mental processes and often modulates into free indirect discourse, without ever becoming anything like the voice of a community. This is worth noting, precisely because the protagonist's sense of a unique personal destiny is constructed in a way reminiscent of the recurring motifs in myths of the birth of heroes in diverse cultures (as identified by Otto Rank[1]). After the description of Ephraim's parents (in chapter 1) the text goes on (in chapter 2) to touch upon Ephraim's prenatal experiences ("while still in his mother's gut, Ephraim knew no rest"), his difficult birth ("during birth his umbilical chord got tangled and while emerging from his mother's womb he nearly choked to death"), and his precarious health as an infant ("a feeling of suffocation and a fear of suffocation haunted him like nightmares throughout his childhood," 154). His early aesthetic sensibility, his theogenic heresy as a young schoolboy, and his being branded a "redhead" (the colloquial Hebrew word *djinjee* has mostly pejorative connotations; while not explicit, the allusion to King David, and thus to some great messianic calling, seems inevitable; David is also, of course, the author's given name) all point to a sense of a unique destiny. The text will end on an imaginative projection assigning to no less than God the role of a distant but very much interested observer of the protagonist's fate: "Ephraim looked up to heaven: it seemed to him God was still sitting there, watching him through a telescope. Watching, smiling and waiting to see how things should turn out" (184). Despite this pattern, Ephraim (or later avatars of the Shaharian protagonist) will not become the hero of any community or culture, and there will be no creation other than that of his own personality.

Ephraim's aesthetic sensibility is awakened at an early age. The founding experience takes place "after a severe crisis of his illness" and after "his mother propped him up with pillows so he could sit up and look through the window." What he sees through that window is the sun setting over Jerusalem:

> It was dusk and the setting disc of the sun radiated orange light among fiery clouds suspended over the Jerusalem mountains. The awestruck child did not remove his eyes from the spectacle until the sun was gone and the roofs of the neighborhood were revealed in all their naked ugliness. This was the first clear memory to be etched in his mind along with intense secret longing for the light shining from beyond the distant horizon. The yearning for beauty was always combined with the hatred of ugliness. He was pervaded by an acute sense of color that often induced in him a feeling of great happiness. (154)

This primarily visual experience opens up for the protagonist a space that is illuminated and intensely colored, giving him a sense of liberation and relieving his physical feeling of constriction. As soon as the sun disappears over the horizon, however, this elation turns into intense longing. The founding aesthetic experience, then, is almost simultaneously both the visual impression of a present spectacle and a yearning for something that is absent. That the narrator, who might have simply described the exprerience as such, chooses to position himself at a later point in time so as to characterize it as Ephraim's "earliest clear memory" strengthens the impression of absence and loss. The setting of the sun causes, at the heart of natural reality itself and within the protagonist's experience of temporality, a double rift: a rift between the beautiful and the ugly as well as between presence and absence. Thus the hero is left faced with an inferior reality (ugly and man-made) and is in a state of longing for that which is no longer visible (possibly also of longing for that "original" experience of longing). As in many examples of European Romantic poetry, this is clearly a figure of transcendental yearning, although its object remains an essentially terrestrial, natural spectacle.

The founding aesthetic experience is not without some complications of the family romance (which is precisely how Freud characterized the myth of the hero elicited by Rank): it is the protagonist's mother who puts him in the position to have this special spatial experience, and the mother is put, from the very first chapter, in telling oppositon to the father. The father is a "bookkeeper," whose "chief virtue was the love of order and the imposition thereof" (151); "his beard would never exceed its measure and was ever neatly clipped and squared as befits an orderly man" (ibid.). The mother is not only prettier and younger than her husband but also "taller [than him] from the nose up" (152), and the father seems unable to impose his law upon her: his "penetrating and coercive gaze would melt and disappear from his eyes whenever he looked at her" (ibid.). In placing the mother at the opposite pole, the narrator finds it necessary to enter some apologetic reservations:

> It was said about her that she was frivolous, certainly that she was an oddity among all her female friends and neighbors, although compared to secular women her conduct was highly religious and her requirements were small, modest and quite obvious ones . . . The more he strove to save and economize and lead a thrifty life, the more she would spend his wages left and right—such, at any rate, was his opinion as well as that of her female neighbors. (152)

Shahar's narrative voice insists here that the mother's opposition to paternal order need not be interpreted as pure lawlessness or, worse, lewdness (*pritzut*), but the very concern betrays a certain ambivalence (whose dark side will be thematized in later works by overtly outrageous representations of women). What appears to the orthodox milieu as frivolity and wastefulness is, in the narrator's implied view, nothing but the love of beauty: "She would . . . dress her children in very handsome clothes, and she herself sported dresses that would embarrass all those around her, most of all her husband. . . . She was not, lord forbid, lewdly dressed, but the colors of her dresses were too bright, her stockings were thin, transparent and made of silk, and rather than tying her hair in a kerchief she appeared in public wearing small, lovely hats" (152–53). This love of beauty is presented as neither sexually provocative nor strictly selfish, but despite the narrator's qualifications, the beauty in question remains inescapably physical and thus nevertheless of erotic significance. There may, after all, be an essential opposition between this love of beauty and the strict observation of order and propriety, or one could say that there is a continuum leading from generosity to wastefulness, and from there to excess and transgression, and finally to lewdness and promiscuity—and that the love of beauty is related to this continuum as a matter of principle.

The scenes that constitute the following narrative present the tangled implications of the conjunction of the polarity of beauty versus law and order with the Oedipal triangle. The first of these scenes follows immediately upon the founding physical-aesthetic experience. It may be regarded as exemplifying one such moment of happiness deriving from Ephraim's newfound acute sense of color:

> When he was six he took a walk with his mother on Jaffa Street. It was a spring day and the entire street was bathing in light, the rays of the sun bouncing off every window pane. She was wearing a white dress with large blue flowers printed on it and a wide-brimmed straw hat, and suddenly he raised his eyes and was flooded with great love for her. He was glad to be alive and healthy, glad that the one walking next to him was his own mother, glad that the street was brimming [*shofe'a*] with light. Along the way they stopped by a picture shop. Having rapidly surveyed the shop window, his mother turned to go on, but Ephraim detained her and kept gazing. In the middle of the window there was a large picture of three horses in a meadow. Two of them were rubbing each other's neck in an outburst of love and energy, while the third was chewing grass. The two cuddling horses were reddish-brown in color, and the third one was blue. The colors were vivid not due to the figures but on their own account, and they were so palpable and alive that they seemed to be leaping off the canvas and pouring into one's thirsty mouth like some refreshing drink. Ephraim refused to budge from the shop window, kept drinking that picture in. (154–55)

This artifact and what it represents (which exists only in the illusionary mimetic space of the picture) fascinates the child with an intensity far exceeding the mother's fleeting interest. Should we be guilty of antiquated dogmatic Freudianism if we construe the content of the picture—a pair of loving horses with an odd third eating grass—as an obvious representation of an Oedipal triangle? What little Ephraim beholds in the picture of the horses behind the windowpane is surprising yet familiar, an engrossing reflection of his own inner psychic landscape, and the picture's functioning as such a reflection depends both on the pattern of the figures and, as we shall find out subsequently, on the distribution of colors among them. Thus the emphasis on the vividness of the colors at the expense of the figures themselves is both a denial meant to distract and a clue to a subjective truth. This "truth" is the mother-child specular relation that results in—or is caused by—the exclusion of the father, of the Law that prohibits such excessive proximity/identification. That this "truth" is more a fantasy fueled by desire than an "objective" fact is suggested by the description of the horses as "rubbing each other's neck in an outburst of *love and energy*"; clearly, the sentiments imputed to the horses are not, strictly speaking, elements of the pictorial representation but the transposition into the world of the picture of the child's love for his mother, a love the narrator represented him as becoming aware of just before chancing on the picture.

The affinity between Ephraim and his mother, which puts them in opposition to figures of law and authority, can be seen in two subsequent scenes. First, during a Bible lesson on Genesis, Ephraim upsets his teacher by asking "and who created God?" only to be reprimanded for not raising his hand before speaking. At home he feels that "his father's reply would be uttered with the same angry countenance" (157). His mother, on the other hand, "picked him up in her arms and hugged him closely to her chest and kissed him with much warmth. 'Mein kind,' she told him, 'there's none like you in the whole world.'" Ephraim is "flooded by a feeling that he and his mother alone are privy to a deep, dark secret" (ibid.). God, too, must have been created by someone: a mother?

Then, immediately following this episode, Ephraim is teased by another boy about his freckles, branded a "redhead," and beaten up by the other boys. He falls ill and upon recovery glimpses in the mirror "a big, unruly shock of hair, whose color was reddish-brown" (157–58). Once more, mother to the rescue:

> "You have nice hair, Ephraim'l, your hair is the same color as mine, and no one ever called me 'redhead'." She undid the kerchief she used to hold her hair while at home, and plentiful [*shofe'a*] chestnut silky hair cascaded over her nape. Just then his father came in and saw her passing her hair over her cheek, stroking it with her fingers. He stopped short, his face turning white, as though he had seen her naked, but rushed to another room without saying anything, his heart still fluttering. (158)

This scene bears an obvious structural resemblance to the scene in the picture: three figures, two in a relation of proximity and similarity (expressed in both cases by their identical hair color), the third different and apart. The relation between the two scenes is a textbook example of what Freud called *Nachträglichkeit*: the latter scene allows us to interpret the boy's fascination with the picture as recognition/projection of his identification with and desire for the mother, while the physical contact between the two cuddling horses allows us to read into it a stronger erotic significance. The father, who is supposed to occupy the position of power (within the order/freedom opposition made explicit by the text), fails to intervence, which suggests that he has neither real control over this situation nor the ability (or wish) to exact retribution for the offense that he is supposed to be suffering (since it is he who is assigned the role of the accidental voyeur coming upon the scene of the mother's alliance with the son and shamefacedly skulking away). Interestingly, in a rare departure from Ephraim's point of view, the last sentence of this excerpt adopts the father's emotive point of view. This perhaps indicates the inception of an identification with the paternal position, but specifically with the father as a victim of embarassment and humiliation by the mother.

Following this crisis, Ephraim refuses to go back to school, even when he is well again. Against the advice of his father (worried particularly by his failure in arithmetic) but with the support of his mother, he keeps up his truancy for another week. One spring day, while wandering near the Sanhedrin Tombs, "he saw a man and a woman sitting and painting. The man was sketching in charcoal while she was coloring with a brush" (159). When asked by the man "which picture is more beautiful," the seven-year-old boy proceeds to reconstitute—probably availing himself of the implied opposition between black line and vivid colors—the old familial triangle: "'Your wife's picture,' said Ephraim. In his heart, he thought the man's picture not only not beautiful but downright ugly. He saw in it nothing but blotches of charcoal" (ibid.).

This variation with difference on the familial triangle renders explicit the provoking sexuality of the woman—which, in the description of the mother, was both implied and denied—a move made possible by the fact that this new female figure is exempt from the incest taboo: "She was wearing an orange shirt that clinged to her body and blue slacks. . . . When she extended her arm her tight shirt lifted to reveal a segment of white hip and a piece of pink woman's underwear. The painter stuck out a little finger and tickled her bare hip, and she uttered a shrill cry, hitting his hand hard" (ibid.). It seems as though, from the male point of view (and this may be the ground for the identification between son and father), the freedom of the woman from patriarchal law is tantamount to her promiscuity. The focus in Shahar, however, will not be on the moral aspect of this "danger" but, rather, on the affective one: the shattering unreliability of the woman/mother as a vital source of unwavering acceptance, approval, and love.

At this stage, however, the woman artist, like the mother before her, represents the possiblity of freedom and is thus an enabling figure, even a possible role model.[2] When she tells Ephraim that she "must wash dishes in a restaurant every evening for a living and so [she] can later sit down and paint," he "enthusiastically" declares his own willingness to do the same: "he saw himself washing dishes at night and being free all day to sail away into the distance to his heart's content" (160). Ephraim's fantasy, then, is not to dedicate himself to the diligent pursuit of the art of painting, or even to the achievement of glory as a famous artist, but only to "sail away into the distance to his heart's content," that is, to break out of the constricting home and family environment, possibly also to overcome the empirical limitations of time and space.

Here the text leaps over a ten-year period to throw the protagonist once more in with the paintress Varda. He is now at the threshold of sexual maturity and far more critical of her artistic endeavors: he believes the Jerusalem views she paints deserve the intensity of oil rather than the mere pale watercolors she is using. When she invites him over to her apartment, he is disappointed to find there an older man who turns out to be not her father but her husband. This confusion leads to a dream:

> When he got up in the morning he recalled nothing of all his dreams except the end of a strange dialogue that took place between him and his father. His father was standing on the Old City wall clad in his talith and tephilim while he, Ephraim, was sitting down below, painting him. Suddenly his father leapt off the wall, tore up the painting, and shouted with all his might: "You prodigal, rebellious son, fornicator, fornicator, fornicator, you have fornicated a married woman, fornicated a married woman." Suddenly Varda appeared and picked up the torn shreds of paper and his father came up to her and beat her, and as he was beating her she was no longer Varda but his mother, and she took the beating humbly without saying anything.
>
> "Don't hit mother!" exclaimed Ephraim. "She's a fornicatress and an adulteress!" cried his father. "Fornicatress, fornicatress, fornicatress!" (170)

One can hardly imagine a clearer expression of oedipal guilt. The son punishes himself in his dream by having his father tear up his painting, that is, by castrating his creative power. However, what is more remarkable is the verbal and physical abuse of the mother. Although the son protests this paternal aggression, the fact that it is after all *his* dream betrays a certain identification with the father, with violent resentment at the mother's alleged waywardness. It is this inner conflict that seals the fate of his painting.

The next day, returning home late at night, Ephraim finds out that his mother is dead, having been run over by a drunken British military driver. Once more, a dream:

> The first night after his mother's death he dreamed he'd gone out to the field to paint with Varda. She wore the same orange shirt and blue slacks she had worn when he had first seen her at the time he was a child of seven. He painted a wonderful picture in oil and she gave him

> an admiring look, then abruptly took off her shirt and said "come, lie with me," and he bent over her, reaching to remove her slacks, but just then he woke up and the first thought that occurred to him was that his mother was dead. (173)

Whether the mother's death is *Ephraim's* punishment for his incestuous desires (and for his lust for Varda, seen as a substitute for this forbidden desire) or *the mother's* punishment for disobeying the law of the father,[3] it also frees him in his dream to desire other women and thus to accede to the symbolic place of the father: the biblical phrase (Genesis 39:7) turns Varda into Potiphar's wife and the dreamer into Joseph, that is, into his own father, since he is "Ephraim." However, in contrast to the biblical forebear this is a Joseph who is more than willing to be seduced, and this resolution is crowned by his imagined success as a painter and its correlative: the gaze of a woman who admires his feat—the fantasized basis for his male appeal and sexual prowess.

In "real life" (that of the story, which is of course itself a fantasy), things take a different course: on his next visit to Varda's apartment, his desire almost overcomes him. She, however, only offers tender consolation over his mother and a semi-innocent goodbye kiss. Ephraim is sorely humiliated, thinks of himself as a "worm of a man," and takes off in quite a state. Presently he gets into a fight with a British policeman and is thrown into jail, where he has time for further reflection (in sarcastic second-degree free indirect discourse):

> This little playboy dug up a woman fifteen years older than himself and "fell in love with her at first sight." He imagined he fell in love with her when he was merely seven years old. Already then, so he imagined, he felt jealous of that skinny painter with the moustache who stuck out his little finger to tickle her hip. *Of her whole figure he saw nothing but her eyes, which appeared to him that day with a power that smote him into submission, crushed him to the ground. Her eyes were large and brown and luminous. When he looked at her he saw her eyes only, and when he saw them his own eyes were blinded and he could no longer do anything; his thoughts became confused and he felt nothing but longing—longing to the point of death.* (179)

The focus of these reflections is clearly the gaze of the female painter. It is precisely a gaze that does not requite what he bitterly calls his "love at first sight" by sexual acceptance, conferring upon him instead mere friendly affection. This withholding of sexual love seems to endow those eyes with an overwhelming power to the point of depriving him of his own eyesight: their radiation of light, being somehow simultaneously both denied and excessive, turns noxious.

This amounts to a humiliating negation of that much-valued sense of freedom: "Yes, he was free to love a married woman, but was this perhaps no freedom but horrible enslavement, the enslavement of his soul?" (179). The moral or religious edge of this formulation seems little more than rhetorical (and in later configurations of this pattern will drop out entirely). Despite the figure of God hovering over the ending, the story is not concerned with any Faustian *or* Don-Juanesque problematic involving the fires of hell or the fate of the soul in the hereafter. The core issue is one of power relations between other and self here and now, in this world. As experienced by Ephraim, Varda's gaze condemns him to permanent occupation of the position of desiring (the topos Shahar will later designate by the expression *'einayim ro-ot vekhalot*—eyes seeing and perishing [sc. with desire]).

The overall movement of this seminal early fiction may then be summed up as follows: from a protective woman who opens up and makes available to the hero's gaze the freedom and beauty of the space of visuality, light, and color to a provocative woman of artistic pretenses whose inviting/forbidding look can deprive him of his freedom, his eyesight, his sexual and creative prowess.

"Of Dreams"

The title story of Shahar's first collection exhibits a minor variant of this configuration.[4] Here we find the typical Shaharian first-person narrator, whose retrospective narrative focuses on his close affinity with an older male figure. The protagonist is Uncle Zemach, who, following some studies at the Betzalel art academy, decided to give up painting, sailed to England and returned to Jerusalem several years later a doctor of law and husband of the caring (and rich) Stella, only to betray her with other women, notably with a paintress he had known in his early bohemian days. After his wife's death, he finds out that she has kept every one of his occasional sketches, those he tossed off from time to time and never thought much of, so that now he is condemned to live out the rest of his days full of compunction at never having kept his promise to paint loyal Stella's portrait.

The man of talent's betrayal of his wife is a betrayal of his own artistic vocation, the worst kind of self-betrayal. It is expiated to some degree by transmitting the bitter fruits of his grim experience to his young nephew, the narrator. A cautionary tale. But if, in a somewhat more cynical vein, we put a little extra pressure on the moral, we might get the following: do not give up painting, but most of all, do not get involved with female painters. Appreciate the woman who does not pretend to paint, the one who would dedicate herself to endorsing and admiring *your* talent.

Women with creative (or intellectual) ambitions will continue to be chastised throughout Shahar's mature fiction, either for poor achievement or for inflated claims. To his credit, however, let it be said that the simplistic circular arrangement, whereby an adulating female gaze is pressed into service, does not much figure in his later work.[5] His preferred ideal model is one of reciprocity, the timely meeting of two desiring gazes—still, as we shall see later, a precarious situation indeed.

"First Lesson"

Written just a few years before the first novel of the *Palace* sequence, this short story—in fact, more of an autobiographical sketch or a meditative memoir—offers another take on the same concerns. This may not be obvious to the casual reader, as the surface thematics often seems a far cry from "Of Shadows and the Image." Since this is a rather rambling text and extremely rich in associative possibilities, we will not attempt to tie all loose ends into a full coherent account of it.

"First Lesson" is dedicated to "My Shula," with Shahar's wife Shulamit also mentioned (in parentheses) in the text itself, so that the first-person narrator is deliberately not distinguished from the biographical author. The text sets out on the grand declamatory tone of a creation myth: "In the beginning was the miracle, and the miracle was and is, and will be to be marveled at always" (*The Pope's Mustache*, 242; *News From Jerusalem*, 209). This announces the recollection of an originary experience dating back to a time when he was "a small child of about three years old," one that the author will later link with the avatars of his artistic vocation. This experience, then, parallels the one described in "Of Shadows and the Image," but this version of Shahar's personal myth is constituted in terms that are the opposite of the previous one.

Having stayed up late one night while his father sat poring over his textbook in accountancy, he approached his father who "rose from his place, took [him] in his arms, and went outside with [him] into the night."

> The first meeting with the night sky filled me with an obscure terror. I saw the sky and suddenly it was black with tiny points of light in it. "Those are the stars," said my father, and added, "the host of Heaven." Somewhere a door creaked open and a stream of light poured out of the crack which opened in the blank dark wall, reaching the foot of the cypress tree which stood in our yard and wrapping its trunk in a mantle of day. Soft chill tongues of wind whispered between the branches, bringing with them from afar, from beyond the

> tombs of the Sanhedrin, a smell of damp earth and small humming, cricking, buzzing voices, the voices of night animals suddenly signaling and suddenly stopping, and the existence of the surrounding mountains—the mountains of Nebi Samwil and Sheikh Jarach and Mount Scopus—was present and breath-stopping and heavy with the weight of an ancient-breathed quality, terrible in its dimensions, which were beyond the dimensions of man, and its eternities which were beyond the eternity of man, and in its indifference to the little men stirring on its back. The same quality of mountain and sky dimly perceived on my daytime ramblings along the mountain paths between the thistles and rocks . . . oppressed me now more strongly in the night world revealed to me. The mountains and the sky at night became more tangible in their distance, more oppressive in their tangible presence in the darkness.
>
> I clung tightly to my father's neck, to the strong pleasant smell of his tobacco. "Come, daddy, let's go back," I said to him, "let's go in." He looked at me and said, "Good, let's go inside." I saw in his eyes that he understood that the fear of the elements in the night [*mora ha-eitanim balaila*] had overcome its powers of attraction, and with his first surprise had come the understanding that I was not yet old enough to live both in the world of the day and the world of the night. (242–43; 210–11)

This encounter, then, takes place under the aegis of the other parent, the father, who now appears in a kind and sympathetic light in a direct autobiographical context (even his activities as bookkeeper are fondly recalled), with the mother nowhere to be seen (and barely mentioned in the rest of the text). Rather than looking out at a visual world full of light and vivid colors, here the child is surrounded by the palpable, audible atmosphere of the night with sporadic starlight barely puncturing through its "blank dark wall." The emphasis here is not on visible beauty but on invisible, incomprehensible power (*eitanim)*, and whereas in the earlier story the child almost immediately starts longing for the vanishing light, here light is scarce to begin with, and his reaction of wonder rapidly modulates from awe to terror. Subsequently this fear will turn to longing for this mystical moment.

A variant of the first encounter with the night sky takes place later on at the grandmother's house, where the narrator's family must live because of his father's financial setbacks. There, the lit stove provides the boy with an inverted image of the awe-inspiring star-spangled night, turned, as it were, inside out (or outside in). As he sits happily painting away (of which more later), grandmother seems to doze off, and Aunt Pnina, the daughter she practically made into a servant, promptly turns off the light to save the expense—in total disregard of the young protagonist's wishes.

> I stayed rooted to my chair full of helpless rage at my Aunt Pnina. Through the mist of tears which dimmed my eyes I was suddenly aware of the flickering dance of points of azure light rising from the stove which was drying Grandmother's giant bloomers. . . . In the darkness the stove lengthened to a towering lighthouse with a blueness of soft light flowing through the blue glass of the square window set in its center near its base, and a row of blocks of yellow light shining through the little air vents underneath the cap on its head. The wreath of light burning steadily on its round wick was reflected through the glass of the window like a sunflower of azure light rising out of the darkness and hovering suspended in a square frame. The square frame became the gateway to a castle [or palace, *armon*] far away in the depths of the dark. In the castle was a great light, and its radiance burst out through all the doors and windows and orifices and apertures of its towers and wings and stories and cloisters and halls. The castle walls kept guard on the world of light stemming from within in the calm of the great silence, and I remembered that I had once been inside and wanted to go back, although I didn't have the right clothes to wear and knew that even if I found them I wouldn't be able to put them on because they no longer fitted me . . . I glided through the air as if I were a bird. I flew a blue point of light with high-flying sparks of fire in a dance of red and green and gold and blue and lemon-yellow and orange splinters of light, and in the blue light I shed all along the walls of the great hall, a row of idols sat stiff and solemn in their masks, but they all melted away with the dying of my blue light when Aunt Pnina came back and turned on the light in the room. (260–61; 232–34)

Any reader of *The Palace of Shattered Vessels* will have no trouble recognizing here several strands of imagery that announce the central metaphorics of the later novel sequence, even before Shahar adopted the Lurianic figure for its title. The passage is particularly valuable in providing a clear picture of Shahar's imaginative cosmology, which is also his metaphysics and his aesthetics.

The principle of it all is light, the source of all beauty, value, and power. However, to the child, the artist, the individual subject, or, ultimately, to any mere part of creation, its modalities are never simple and unproblematic. Too much of it blinds,[6] too little negates and terrorizes; it may be freely available or frustratingly withheld. This delicate balance is rendered all the more precarious by the temporal condition of all created things; thus the balance itself is subject to change. The long passage just quoted deals mostly with the possibilities of its nearly total obfuscation by material barriers such as the night sky or the iron walls of a kerosene stove. In the former case, the light seems to be banished to a literally *meta*-physical domain, beyond that boundary of the natural world that the firmament (*raki'a*) is imagined to be. In the latter case, the light may be thought of as contained—either cruelly imprisoned or safely treasured—within some vessel or shell.

For Shahar, however, it is fundamentally the same light. All of these formulations, in fact, represent local spatial and temporal perspectives, since it is the same light that exists both within and without,[7] potentially emanating from the individual human self as from the divine cosmic principle called "God." And sometimes the subject locates itself as the obstacle or shell, that material body or surface which finds itself in the path of light and therefore becomes, to varying degrees, sentient and able to register it. Shahar shows his awareness of the far-reaching ambiguity of this quasimystical conception of consciousness when in an earlier passage of "First Lesson" (inserted in a rapid associative zigzag that defies brief summary) he writes:

> I only said I would have ascribed this writing to God because of the fog, so to speak, in which I find myself, this blurring of the boundaries between what comes from outside and exists from within, the feeling that I myself am the firmament dividing the waters from the waters, a sort of skin [*klipa*, shell] separating two worlds, the inside world and the outside world. If the fence of this garden . . . were to write its sensations they would surely resemble my own. (247–48; 216)

The two "visions" we have discussed—the first sighting of the night sky and its inverse, the watching of the light of the stove—are opposed also, as we have already suggested, in that the first is under the aegis of the father, whereas the other is haunted by the figure of the grandmother (and of Aunt Pnina). The strict regime and even stricter pious talk at this lady's house are contrasted with the freedom from any compulsion or formal requirements in the boy's parents' house. In this text, the well-meaning, kindly father is not party to any kind of repression. He is, at worst, a father who proves unable to protect his son, since it is his unfortunate bankruptcy that puts the child into the household and under the thumb of his unsympathizing, tyrannical grandmother. It is the grandmother who takes it upon herself to represent the Law, and this is not unrelated to her attitude toward painting:

> Between God and my Grandmother . . . as I gathered from her words and actions, there did appear to be some connection, and the more she stressed this connection, berated and reproached my mother and my father in His name, the more rebellious I became and the more strongly I sensed . . . a kind of outrage: the kind of outrage Agur ben Jakeh must have felt on seeing a slave turned king, or an artist would feel if he were compelled to paint according to the dictates of a ruler who not only knew nothing about art but were colorblind to boot. . . .
>
> Grandmother was not, like the rulers in my parable, colorblind, but she had lost her eyesight owing to the trachoma endemic in the country during the days of the Turks many years before I was born, and it was in no other than the sphere of painting that she first chose to impart to me the commands of God in Yiddish, since Hebrew she did not know. (251; 220–21)

The grandmother is not only blind; she is also, as the boy soon discovers, ignorant of the quality of color as such, and with it of any aspect of the shape and makeup of anything concrete. When his interest in color awakens (and in a show of sympathy about her much-regretted lost coal stove), the boy tries "to get her to say something clear about the color of the stove and its shape. Was it black or yellow, square or round, high or narrow, or low and wide, and a chimney—did it have a chimney or not?" (257; 229). But all the grandmother can muster is obtuse repetition of these questions without providing any additional information about this, supposedly the most cherished possession she has ever had. So cherished, in fact, that it seems to take precedence over her own son, Avremele, whose untimely death never comes up in her conversation, and about whose loss she is not just at a loss to offer concrete detail but utterly disinterested in doing so: "In decided contrast to the catechism of the stove, however, Grandma showed no interest at all in response to my questions about Avremele, but answered briefly, dryly, and lucidly, 'I don't remember. He died many years ago, shortly after the stove was lost'" (258; 230). The bitter irony implicit in the narrator's characterization of this mother (his mother's mother) registers fully when we backtrack a couple of pages to his free-indirect-discourse reporting of her account of missing the stove while moving to a new apartment: "And after all the goods and chattels had been moved, and also the children, that is to say, my mother and my Aunt Pnina and Avremele, who died a few weeks later in Doctor Wallach's hospital of typhoid fever, when all the children and the goods had been moved and Grandma returned with Bulbul [the carrier] to supervise the removal of the stove, and opened the cupboard with the key she kept in her purse, lo and behold, the cupboard was empty and the bird had flown [*vehayeled einenu*, 'and the child is gone'[9]]" (256; 228). The grandmother, then, is represented as both lacking in motherly affection and being indifferent to the physical qualities of concrete objects. Her condition of blindness is symbolic of her total lack of love for (or even sheer hostility to) creation as such.

This being the case, the conflict between her and the boy who loves to paint is inevitable. The final showdown, a life-and-death struggle fought *mano a mano,* takes place when she tries to get the boy to give up painting. First she instructs him that "it's forbidden to draw on the Sabbath," and then she tries to bribe him: "You may not draw on the Sabbath. And now be a good boy and stop drawing and I'll give you a sweet." Then she supplements her tactic by trying to terrorize him: "And now be a good boy and stop drawing at once or else God will punish you." Finally, she extends the prohibition to make it general: "And in general, you should know that a Jew is forbidden to draw and make pictures even on ordinary weekdays, let alone on our holy Sabbath. And here is a sweet for you" (264–65; 238–39). He deliberately squeaks his crayon on the cardboard, she tries to push the sweet into his hand, he throws it away in anger, accidentally knocking over her teacup. And now, it comes to fisticuffs:

> "Hah!" she cried at the sound of the glass falling. "Please see what this child is capable of! Things he throws in the house! And what's the wonder, isn't he bone of the bone and flesh of the flesh of his father the *soldat*? Why, it's mortal danger just to be in the same room as him! And now, my little savage, give me the page!" And she seized it with unexpected strength. I grabbed it out of her hands and began tearing the picture to pieces with all my might, tearing and scattering pieces on the ground, tearing and throwing the crayons in all directions, tearing and crushing and grinding to powder with my feet. Tearing and crying. At first she shouted "criminal, destroyer of Israel, robber!" But her shouts soon turned to cries for help, to the thin piercing hysterical screams of an old Jewess with a sharp sword at her throat: "*Gewald! Gewald!* Jews, to the rescue!" Had she sensed the curse I was cursing her within my heart, "I wish you were dead, I wish you were dead?" (265–66; 240)

The first thing to note is that the boy defends his right to paint as though fighting for dear life; the intensity of his reaction is a measure of the value placed by Shahar on the activity of painting. When the enemy lays hands on his handiwork, he responds by destroying it all himself,[10] a desperate act of protest and defiance that is nothing less than self-martyrdom. His then wishing her dead is simply tit for tat.

The demonization of the grandmother, however, should not blind us to the fact that in trying to enforce a taboo on painting she is merely towing the orthodox rabbinical line on Exodus 20:4 ("Thou shalt not make unto thee any graven image, or any likeness of any thing that is in heaven above, or that is in the earth beneath").[11] It is a quirk peculiar to Shahar that, in this story at least, this should be ascribed to the mendacious Law of the (mother's) mother rather than to that of the father. To the extent that the father is an all-powerful creator, he not only permits painting but may even enjoin it: "the God that created the heavens and the earth and said, Let there be Light and there was light, did not forbid me to draw on the Sabbath" (267; 241). Painting, then, is a celebration of the world of light and color, a world-creating, fatherly act, performed in emulation of the father rather than in rebellion or competition against him. In defending his right to draw, the narrator can consider his father a natural ally. But, again, in characteristic Shaharian fashion, the father is unfortunately suspected of being unable to provide his son with the protection he so sorely needs, when he needs it. As the boy runs for his life, expecting grandmother's shtreiml-wearing fanatic allies to come after him, his chief concern is that "when I was dead Father would be sorry. He would be so very sorry. And I couldn't bear his sorrow and couldn't endure his bereavement" (266; 240). If the father cannot defend the child against the blind, unloving gaze of the (grand)mother, then how can the child paint?

After the considerable literary effort to present the grandmother as the deadly enemy of his desire to paint, in the final paragraph of the story the narrator takes a different tack: he now admits that if later in life he in fact gave up painting, it is not grandmother who is to blame. First it was the practical necessities of daily life, and now he has no explanation at all, really. Given all of our foregoing comments on this story, we are led to think of this anticlimactic ending as a defensive gesture: a refusal, in the final analysis, to grant that controlling female figure such an absolute determining power.

But the end of the story also comes back to a point made at its very beginning: the child grew up and became a man, and though he does not paint, he does write. Indeed, "First Lesson" is the text in which Shahar comes closest to articulating his attitude to language and writing. The view he articulates is essentially a metaphysical one, as evidenced by the following episode:

> When my teacher read aloud during the Bible lesson the words, "In the beginning God created the heavens and the earth and the earth was without form and void, and darkness was upon the face of the deep," the quality of the elements made tangible in the darkness suddenly welled up in me unendurably. "And God said, Let there be light," and in the wall of darkness a crack was revealed and the imprisoned light burst through it to wrap the rocks and clods of earth in a mantle of day. I had sensed things as they were, from inside myself, and the written and spoken words garbed them in phrases like currency which could be passed from hand to hand. (248; 217)

Language is an outer shell, clothing or containing (preserving or concealing) things as they are. None of "In the beginning was the Word" for him. The order of precedence seems to be: thing, then image, then word. Things emerge as they are affected by light and become images. The visual medium of painting emulates directly God's creation itself and is thus an expression of the human subject's god-like creative capacity.[12] Language only comes in later, at a second remove, as a conventional medium of exchange and communication.

Writing, it would seem, is never *quite* the thing to do. It is repeatedly presented by the narrator of "First Lesson" as second best in comparison, first to divine revelation, then to the pursuit of erotic desire, and finally to the art of painting. Indeed, writing seems opposed to the "freedom" which, as we have seen, is intimately linked both to erotic desire and to aesthetic experience and painting: writing, the narrator tells us somewhat enigmatically, is a "tax" [*mas*] he has to pay:

> If I were living my life according to my true inclinations and the impulses of my heart, I would not be sitting and writing now but casting a line into the waters of the Marne by the side of that slender Frenchwoman. . . . This elegant fisherwoman is in all probability one of the mistresses of one of these rich men, which would of course not prevent me, if I were living my own life, from wooing her so that she would lie with me on the riverbanks after the sun had set . . . I do not paint but yearn and marvel instead—and pay, it seems, the price in writing, one installment after the other." (244–45, 268; 212–13, 242)

To love, to paint, is to be free; to write is to pay for alternating between marvel and yearning. This is the closest Shahar gets anywhere in his published work to commenting on his choice to express himself through the art of writing (in fact, to devote to it the major part of his life). Nevertheless, we can try to articulate an argument for the usefulness, or even necessity, of writing in terms of the experience he does describe.

As we have seen, the "miracle" of the night sky or the mystical/uncanny "palace" experience (discussed in the previous chapter) can last but a brief moment before being relinquished. They share this brevity with the early aesthetic experience of beauty and freedom (in "Of Shadows and the Image") which, as the sun sets, gives way to intense longing. It would be misleading to assume that the longing is occasioned simply by the withdrawal of light: when the narrator of "First Lesson" has relinquished the night-sky experience, that too becomes the cause of longing (albeit with some delay, 244; 211). And the deprivation of light can have its unexpected benefits: if Aunt Pnina's turning off the light thwarts the boy's painting, it also sets the stage for his imaginative vision of the palace with its row of idols, and it is that magnificent vision[13] that then "melts away" precisely by her turning the light back on. What seems constant in all of these founding experiences of the self as artist is the rapid *alternation* between wonder and longing, too much and too little, presence and absence. This alternation can hardly be captured by the static, spatial art of painting, despite its apparent ontological advantage. It seems to require an art whose medium has a temporal dimension, such as language, and it finds its most adequate expression in writing, whose very structure exhibits the alternation (or indeterminacy) of presence and absence.[14]

This phenomenological argument for the necessity of writing must be supplemented by a psychological explanation that has a special validity for Shahar. It is a peculiarity of his work that painting should be represented as an artistic pursuit much desired by his male protagonist and repeatedly crossed by the vagaries of a fickle female gaze. For whatever reasons—perhaps precisely due to its supposed ontological inferiority, or to its being firmly and squarely on the "right side" of the Law—writing seems to be exempt from this threat and from the erotic charge that makes it so damaging.

His Majesty's Agent

In its original Hebrew publication, the title page of this novel featured the subtitle (or in-cover blurb) "A Story of Love and Betrayal Which Begins with the Second World War and Ends with the Yom Kippur War." This was dropped from the English publication[15] which, however, carried on the next page the following disclaimer:

> While all the details of the wars, battles and operations—including the underground activities—described in *His Majesty's Agent* are authentic and based on firsthand reports and experiences, His Majesty's agent himself is a creature of fiction. Everything connected with him is imaginary—his personal, underground, and assumed names, his personality, emotions, thoughts and deeds, attitudes and activities. Any resemblance between him and any living person is purely coincidental.[16]

This may seem the usual precaution required by a publishing company's legal department, but whether the job is done in this case may be questioned in more than one way. First, logically speaking, it is hard to see how His Majesty's agent himself can be said to be "a creature of fiction" and his underground activities "imaginary" if all of the details, "including the underground activities," are "authentic." Second, the above statement is disingenuous, or at least counterfactual, since the resemblance between the protagonist and a particular living person is far from purely coincidental. "Heinrich Reinhold" and the code name "Yannai" (241; 251) were, in fact, the names of an Irgun member who was thought to have betrayed his comrades during or after the bombing of the King David Hotel in 1946, was secretly condemned and sentenced to death, escaped Palestine, was pursued in Belgium, and got away; his subsequent whereabouts or possible assumed identity remain unknown.[17] No less remarkable is the fact that "Jacob Amrami—whom everyone calls by his underground name—Yoël" (5; iv), the book's publisher and dedicatee, as well as a character in it (he is the man who moves into the fictional Reinhold's room after the latter's disappearance[18]), was actually the senior underground member who determined the real Reinhold's guilt and approved the death sentence against him, a fact he tells the narrator in the novel with full details of the evidence he had to determine Reinhold's guilt (234; 243–44).[19] Third, the statement that His Majesty's agent is a pure creature of fiction may be considered valid (without ceasing to be misleading), in the sense that no such person appears in the novel: by any reasonable reading of the plot, it is clear that the protagonist did *not* betray his fellow underground members, so that he was not in (fictional) fact His Majesty's agent, nor is there any other character who can lay serious claim to this title.

The far-reaching moral ambiguities of Shahar's literary use of Heinrich Reinhold[20] suggest a profound affinity on his part for this character that goes straight to the heart of the thematic complex we are exploring in this chapter: the question of guilt and betrayal and its association with the familial triangle, on the one hand, and painting, on the other hand. In this novel we have once more a first-person narrator who bears the author's real name and is deliberately made indistinguishable from his real-life persona. As in many of Shahar's works, including the *Palace,* this narrator tells of an older man he knew as a child, not restricting himself to the role of an eyewitness but often indulging in extensive descriptions of his hero's thoughts and feelings in clear transgression of the "normal" conditions governing access to other minds. This older character, Heinrich Reinhold, is in several ways conflated with Gabriel Luria, the character who plays such a central role in the *Palace* sequence as well as in the short story "The Pope's Mustache." Just as *Summer in the Street of the Prophets* opens with the emergence out of the cistern of the boy-narrator's cherished recollection of the first time he saw Gabriel, so on the fourth page of *His Majesty's Agent* we are told that "the sight of Yoël suddenly looming up out of the desert sand, like the reincarnation of a past buried in the depths of time, flooded me all at once with a wonderful sensation, the memory of *one of the happiest days of my childhood—the day I first saw Heinrich Reinhold*" (6; 12). Like Gabriel, Reinhold is a handsome man in his prime, sexually active and attractive to women, who is living in the narrator's family's courtyard; he too has an illicit love affair in Jerusalem, is offended by his lover's conduct, goes into exile overseas, and learns belatedly that she has borne his child. Unlike Gabriel, however, Reinhold is a would-be painter. And in addition to being suspected of treason, he is both the perpetrator and the victim of several acts of betrayal having to do with women. These are vital links for the coherence of the interpretation we are attempting in this chapter.[21]

One mark of the exceptional significance of the visual in *His Majesty's Agent* is the insistent proliferation of mirrors. Mirrors are also a notorious source of the uncanny, and they repeatedly put into question the logic of identity that is essential to maintaining the straightforward, mimetic character of the novel.[22] Such is the mirror Reinhold buys from Jamilla, the old Arab cleaning woman, complete with the tale of the evil eye haunting it. The evil eye in question is a mother's envious resentment of her pretty little daughter, which is blamed for the child's horrible death by fire. As this and other anecdotes related to the child's father, Ismail Bey, are told over several pages of text, Reinhold listens good-humoredly, bandying ironic comments with old Jamilla. But his mood changes abruptly when Jamilla speaks of the wise and honorable Bey as having "abandoned his little daughter, Rowada, who was dearer to him than the light of his eyes, to the cruelty of the Evil Eye which looked out at his wife, Sitt Fatma, from this very mirror when she was dressing the little girl and making her ready for her meeting with the German empress." It is the word "abandoned" that seems to rattle Reinhold, who immediately turns pale, feels dizzy, and must lie down, muttering to himself in German, "God almighty! God almighty! How can the father save the child from its mother's claws?" (24; 21).[23]

"Its mother's claws"—sharp words indeed! This apparently disproportionate reaction puts us in a psychic territory that we have already encountered near the ending of "First Lesson" (and that will crop up again in Gabriel's dream near the conclusion of *Of Candles and Winds*). And the story of Reinhold's problematic relationship of solidarity with a weak father and horror of a loved but treacherous mother will turn out to be also a story about the desire to paint. This story, about "a little boy who liked to draw," Reinhold tells the boy-narrator when he sees him drawing. The boy-narrator understands at once "that he was going to tell [him] a story about himself . . . even though he used the third person throughout the story and called the boy in it Joseph" (27; 23)—which later turns out to be Reinhold's actual middle name. The story—to be labeled eventually "the day of the crayons"[24]—takes place in Berlin, against the background of the deteriorating relationship between Joseph's parents, due to the financial reverses suffered by the father. The boy tries to shore up this crumbling family, and just one aspect of his predicament is his abstention from asking for the costly watercolors and large paper for which he so ardently longs. As he sits there daydreaming about his mother coming out of her room all dressed up to take him out on a walk and his father returning home with colors for him, aware all this time of the disagreeable reality of their actual lives, suddenly the dream seems to be coming true:

> The child raised his eyes and saw his mother, who had just emerged from her room like a materialization of that sweet vision she herself had dispelled by opening the door: in a wide-brimmed hat and long gloves and high heels, with a conspiratorial smile that lashed at his heart and made it beat wildly, she approached him and said with impetuous gaiety, "Come, sweetheart, let's go for a little walk. What? Are those all the crayons you have left? We'll go into a shop on the way and buy you a box of twelve new crayons! No, not twelve—we'll buy you the biggest box of crayons in the shop, and then we'll go into the Romanisches Café and call your father, and then we'll go somewhere special together—to the zoo, or anywhere else you like!" (29; 26)

But this is, of course, just a ploy: taking advantage of the boy's passion for painting, the mother uses him to draw the father out so that he can be served a court order sentencing him to a term of imprisonment for failing to provide for his wife. In acting that way, Reinhold's mother reiterates the grandmother's attempts in "First Lesson" to bribe the boy into obeying her wish (which, in that case, was that he should cease to draw); and however deceitful her behavior is, however outrageous the boy finds it, she still manages somehow to have the law on her side (rabbinical law in one case, the law of the land in the other).

As we should have come to expect by now, the episode of "the day of the crayons" is doubled by another scene that takes place later in Reinhold's life and which he recalls many pages after (but chronologically before) he told the boy-narrator of the former. The trigger for the recollection is a pain in his side:

> The pain had not started on the day of the crayons itself, or even soon afterward, but years later, when he graduated from the gymnasium and decided to study painting. He had always loved painting and paintings, more than anything else. He filled in the application and waited confidently for the official letter inviting him to submit his drawings and paintings and take the entrance exams; quite sure he would win the scholarship, he went on painting as he waited for the letter. He preferred oil paints, because with them he felt the color as an actual body. One day, he sat down for some reason before the hall mirror and started painting his own face. He mixed the paints and had begun applying one brush after another to the canvas, without making any preliminary sketch, when he was interrupted by the doorbell. Sure that it was the postman with his registered letter, he jumped

> up to answer the door, still holding the palette in his hand. With the other he took the letter from the postman, who stepped into the hall to peep at the picture that was coming into being on the easel. Reinhold disliked having anyone peer over his shoulder, and he never showed his unfinished pictures even to those closest to him, but always took care to turn them to the wall. Perhaps if he hadn't opened the door with such eager anticipation the postman would not have come in as if he had been invited to look at the painting on the easel. In the mirror Reinhold saw the bronze badge glittering on the postman's cap as he leaned to look at the first layer of paint of the self-portrait. Reinhold's anger flared up. "You're not allowed to look!" he shouted, and the postman, since he was in a hurry to finish his round and had no intention of staying, escaped quickly from the man who only a moment before had welcomed him with a cordial smile. With his palette in one hand and the letter in the other, Reinhold rushed in an uncontrollable fury to kick the door shut behind the fleeing postman. It was only afterwards that he was able to reconstruct what had happened to him then: when he drove the postman out, his eyes were on the mirror, so his kick was also aimed in that direction, and instead of hitting the door it hit the leg of a table. Catching his breath at the sharp pain as his ribs collided with the corner of the table, he collapsed and fell flat on his face, right into the palette on his thumb. The paints stuck to his face and he breathed them in. For a moment he thought he would be suffocated by the mixture of oil and turpentine. He felt a little better after he vomited, but the first image that flashed through his mind when he had managed to get to his feet and go to the faucet to wash his face was that of a puppy having its nose forced into its own excrement, to train it not to perform its natural functions inside the house. But even the best-trained dog goes on performing its functions outside the house, whereas Reinhold was obliged to give up painting altogether, both inside and outside, because of this nausea: he could no longer endure the smell of oil paints. At first he tried to continue painting anyway, but the nausea and vomiting brought on attacks of asthma that sometimes lasted for days, and on his last such attempt—on the very eve of his entrance examinations—it seemed to him that he was going to die of suffocation. The asthma did not let up until he realized that he would have to choose another career, and, abandoning painting, he turned to languages. (99–101; 98–100)

The narrative of this scene (a small masterpiece of storytelling worthy of E. T. A. Hoffmann) is cast almost in the mold of a little tragedy. Reinhold's hubris is his ambition to be a painter and more particularly his egotistic indulging in self-portraiture. His tragic flaw, a common one, is a headstrong intensity of temperament. The tragic error stemming from it is compounded by his first welcoming the postman too cordially, which opens the door to his unwelcome trespass, and then overreacting to it by trying to kick the door after him. And as is often the case in tragedy, the punishment is both disproportionate and self-inflicted.

Since it affects his ability to paint, this punishment also points back to the self-destruction of the protagonists' drawings out of Oedipal guilt (in the first dream of "Of Shadows") and in self-righteous martyrdom (in "First Lesson"). Both of these motives—identification with the father and protest against the mother's domination—animate "the day of the postman" and invite us to read it as an echo and a rejoinder to "the day of the crayons." Reinhold's anger at the postman "flares up" when he sees in the mirror "the bronze badge glittering on the postman's cap." Surely this official badge recalls the "shining brass badge" on the "peaked cap" worn by the court messenger on the day of the crayons and thus reveals the intolerable truth that this bearer of good news is nothing but the messenger of his enabling, lying, domineering mother. And if Reinhold is in the position to receive such great news, a budding young painter about to be granted official recognition, this is because he went along with his mother's act of treachery against his father and presumably used the crayons that rewarded his doing so. Reinhold is locked in a powerful double bind, which finds vent in the sudden flare-up of fury and violence. But since the whole drama is really an internal one—a point Shahar encodes and realistically motivates by the role played by the mirror—the kick directed at the departing postman ends up hurting no one but himself. In both identifying himself with and protesting against both the weakness of his father and the control of his mother, the double-bound hero inevitably has incapacitated himself. The specific nature of the affliction—an asthmatic condition, inducing attacks of suffocation—puts Reinhold in the state young Ephraim was in before his mother opened up to him the vista of light and color. This analogy comes close to equating painting with life itself, since Ephraim's breathing problems began during birth, the very process of his being put into the world by his mother. In giving up painting and settling for a career in languages Reinhold echoes the judgment of the narrator in "First Lesson" that writing is only a second best.

If painting is life, then not to be able to paint means to suffocate and die; and for the protagonist who feels confident in his potential as a creator and who has a strong sense of his unique destiny, what is at stake in this death is not just his own life but the very existence of the whole world. This is made explicit in an episode dating from Reinhold's days in the Underground, an episode narrated three times in the novel, first by Yoël and from his point of view (237–38; 246–48), then twice by Reinhold himself (312–13, 330–31;

324–26, 346) when, in the guise of the arms-dealing tycoon, Joseph Orwell, he meets the narrator in his mansion in Beverly Hills after the Yom Kippur war.

Shortly before the bombing of the King David hotel, Yoël and Reinhold are among a group of some fifteen Underground members waiting in an apartment in Haifa for a signal to move against a British destroyer docked in the harbor. In the apartment Reinhold's attention is caught by a reproduction—a page torn out of some art magazine—of a painting by Chaim Soutine, a powerful painter whom he discovered a year earlier when in Paris.[25]

> The reproduction was bad and the colors lacked the living ferment of the original. Nevertheless, it seemed to peel away, layer by layer, the outer shell of his life as with the point of a knife: a tremendous tide-like desire began sweeping through every part of his body to set up a blank white canvas on an easel and to start covering it with paint. A desire as fresh and vivid as in the days of his childhood, as on the Day of the Crayons, as during the days he was preparing to enter the Academy of Art. He rose and went into the second room, where he found an easel—the room belonged to a woman painter then living in Jerusalem who had made it available to the Irgun. "I'm dropping everything and going back to painting at once," said Reinhold to himself, not because he had weighed the possibilities open to him and resolved to choose a particular way of life, but because he knew that this was what must happen, as one would know that water would flood out because the dam had been breached. The knowledge that he was about to begin painting was accompanied by a feeling of freedom and strength—the thrill one would feel on entering an enchanted palace [*armon*]—and everything was bathed in a new light. . . .
>
> He was about to begin painting again not because it was more important—the demolition of the destroyer was far more important, especially to all the refugees from the concentration camps—but out of an inner compulsion, because he couldn't help it, because he was coming home at last, after all these years, to breathe the air of his own world.
>
> With the first step he took towards the easel, his chest tightened and everything grew dark. He made for the balcony door to get some fresh air, and overturned a can of turpentine holding a few paint brushes. He gripped the balcony railings to stop himself from falling; as he breathed in the cool, salty sea air, he felt cold sweat streaming down his face. The moment of joy was cut short [*niktam*, was clipped or shorn], the light in all the windows of the palace went out, and the whole world lost its taste. A tidal wave of rage overflooded him—an

> ocean of bitter anger. No, blowing up one destroyer was not good enough. It was nothing. The whole world must be blown up! If he could have prayed, if he had believed in any kind of god, he would have implored him, "Please, dear God, turn me into a bomb to blow up this whole world you created!"[26] (312–13; 324–25)

If I cannot paint, then let the whole world perish! This extreme sentiment—stated specifically in terms of desire, light, palace, constriction, clipping, and overflooding (all already associated with the influence of a woman)—prepares us for a possible interpretation of the cosmic metaphor of the broken vessels in the title of Shahar's novel sequence.

Reinhold, however, does not blow up the world,[27] not even the destroyer—the operation eventually is aborted when the ship unexpectedly takes to sea. Nor, however, does he paint. What he does do is repeat the experience of betrayal in his love relations with Tamara Koren, the wife of his friend, Daniel, who, like Varda in "Of Shadows," is a paintress. On one of his visits to her home, Tamara leads him downstairs to her spacious, well-lit workshop to show him her ceramic sculptures and various paintings, which he judges to be "not simply dull and shallow [but] bad from every point of view" (93; 91). This display of her hollow artistic pretense is a galling reminder of his own abandoned ambitions (which, presumably, he believes would have yielded far better works of art). Both oddly and typically, this becomes the ground for his (morally sleazy but psychologically telling) identification with the lawful but weak and unloved husband and father, his friend, Daniel Koren, who, like him, had to give up his artistic aspirations (Daniel has told him that he gave up his love for the theater because of his marriage) and who is thoroughly cuckolded by none other than himself. What "arouses his wrath" in that house which Tamara herself was responsible for designing (and causes the pain in his side, reminding him of the day of the postman's visit) is the tiny space she allowed for her husband's study, an "alcove, squeezed [*nimhatz*, crushed] like something superfluous between the living room and the nursery" (95; 93–94). From the protagonist's perspective, it is a life-and-death struggle against a female presence that both enables and blocks a man's access to a space of air and light.

That Tamara is yet another member of the mother paradigm is confirmed by a broad hint dropped by the author's choice of detail.[28] When she first comes to visit Reinhold at Augusta Victoria, we are told that "the tune from the days of his childhood, still echoing in his ears, gave him the sudden sensation, as in a twice-dreamed dream, that this very same woman with the wide-brimmed hat and mysterious smile had appeared to him once before exactly so, suddenly, like the coming true of a daydream, a miracle accelerating his heartbeat" (53–54; 54). So she is an uncanny reincarnation of Reinhold's mother in her day-of-the-crayons manifestation, harking back to Ephraim's mother before the picture shop on Jaffa Street. This is further corroborated by the otherwise insignificant repetition of a small detail from that earlier work. Let us recall that in "Of Shadows" Ephraim's initiatory vision was made possible by his mother's propping him up with pillows in his bedridden condition. During the visit that begins Reinhold's firsthand acquaintance with Tamara, the first thing she does is arrange his pillow (an action mentioned twice) "as if he were a helpless baby" (54; 54). On her second visit, the specific opportunity for his being able to slip his hand up her dress and into her panties, thereby initiating their unbridled sexual liaison, is provided by her leaning over his body to arrange his pillow once more (and in the brief paragraph concluding that scene, fixing or arranging a pillow is mentioned no less than three more times; 67; 69). This is insistence.

In the love relationship between Reinhold and Tamara, surely the most outspokenly erotic in the annals of Hebrew literature, a major role is played by the sense of sight. Vision was, from the outset, the hinge that linked the erotic and the aesthetic, and it seems as though in *His Majesty's Agent* the surplus psychic energy welled up by the inability to paint is invested in the erotic, in a process we can call "de-sublimation," producing a novel and a text where the erotic is hyperbolic and excessive.

In one of their encounters, Reinhold insists on making love in a room equipped with a mirror, "a big one," and he explains why: "I want to see everything. I want to see the royal scepter penetrate your soul!" (85; 85). If seeing is dominating that which comes under view, then a mirror enhances this domination by showing angles otherwise blocked from view; but at the same time it necessarily involves the splitting of consciousness.[29] Such splitting means being simultaneously positioned at different points in space and/or time, and therefore may entail occupying simultaneously the dominating and dominated positions in the force field of desire. Precisely at the felicitous moment of the most assured possession, with Tamara ecstatically mounted on his triumphant member, Reinhold will identify with the literal viewpoint and violent affect of the excluded subaltern (but not with the woman, who is imagined as unseeing, hence, no subject at all):

> Using that style of hers he always found troublesome except when making love to her, during which time it added a flavor of amusement to the pleasures of feeling and seeing, he hummingly drawled to her: "Feel Tamara'le, feel well how the divine abundance fills your heart." A verse from the Epigrams of Martial, from the days he studied Latin, echoed in his ears: "masturbabantur Phrygii post ostia serui/Hectoreo quotiens sederat uxor equo." And they could not see! They only knew and heard the moaning of the bed and the groaning

> of the rider! What would have happened to those wretches had the door suddenly opened and they could also behold! They would be blinded with desire [*'eineihem hayu ro-ot vekhalot*], and they would go mad, raving mad! They would kill the husband, Hector, to take his place between her legs! They would probably kill each other too, fighting for the woman! They could not see how in the heat of riding her hair flies wildly, falling over her eyes and covering her face entirely! (89–90; omitted in translation)

Just when Reinhold asserts his divine omnipotence, his power over the loving/treacherous woman, he also identifies with the point of view of the one condemned to permanently occupy the position of desire, of *'einayim ro-ot vekhalot*—the position of the weak father or the defeated rival/double.[30] Alternating endlessly between these two positions, Reinhold attempts to break free of his "enslavement" but finds himself again and again caught in the web of treachery. Thus at a certain moment of longing for Tamara (which quite resembles what one would describe as "love"), he starts drawing again and even rushes into town in search of paint. But the imminent discovery that Tamara is betraying him too (with the British Colonel Drake) as well as meddling against his will with his military assignment renews his symptoms of old. He will not be rid of this femme fatale, and he will never be able to paint.

Of Candles and Winds

While Shahar never declared *The Palace of Shattered Vessels* complete, his death, shortly after the publication of *Of Candles and Winds* and of the boxed edition in which it was included as the seventh and last "gate," in fact determined this novel as concluding the sequence. It is only befitting, as the cliché goes, that this final installment should return to Gabriel Luria and just at that stage of his (fictional) existence preceding his return to Jerusalem and appearance to the boy-narrator that inaugurated the first novel of the sequence, *Summer in the Street of the Prophets*. It also may be worth noting that Shahar dedicated *Candles* as follows: "And this is in your memory, Mother."

At the center of this novel is the relationship between Gabriel and the lovely Orita, Judge Gutkin's younger daughter, who throughout the representation of Jerusalem in its Shaharian halcyon days is the very incarnation of unself-conscious libido, the secret or obvious object of desire for just about every male character in the book, often referred to as "Jerusalem's Queen of Hearts" (see, e.g., 60). Her sheer sexual attractiveness puts her on a par, in Shahar's fictional work, with the Tamara of *His Majesty's Agent*. But whereas in Tamara's character Shahar's admiring, philandering eye for women is more than outweighed by an often nasty misogyny, the character of Orita has been kept in all of the earlier volumes of the *Palace* quite on a pedestal. Unlike Tamara, there is no suggestion of Orita being promiscuous (or, after her marriage to Dr. Landau, guilty of outright adultery). Her very name—Orita—suggests her affinity with light [*or*], the divine principle of creation. And even though in *Candles* she will be depicted in the enjoyment of the sexual act, she will remain on the whole dignified, imperious, autonomous—to a fault, from Gabriel's point of view.

The book is constructed of two major scenes with all of its other components being preparations, commentaries, elaborations, repetitions, parallelisms, and connections leading from one to the other: from the scene of Orita's cutting look (proleptically anticipated in summary form [45], narrated as a scene [56-67] and analeptically recalled [97]) to the scene of her symbolic killing and ritual commitment to memory in a retroactive modification of that first scene in Gabriel's imagination (98 ff.). The first of these major scenes takes place in 1924[31] in a bedroom of the King David Hotel. Following the early departure of the visiting Lord Radcliff, Orita is granted the use of a luxurious suite for a week and invites Gabriel to join her. This is the fulfillment of his most cherished dream which, as we shall see, will turn into his worst nightmare. Since what Gabriel experiences as a catastrophe of hyperbolic dimensions involves a slight that under different circumstances might seem almost trivial, it is important to note the way in which Shahar orchestrates the scene to give it a rich, symbolic aura and to endow the moment of reversal with a transcendent sense. On his way to the King David, Gabriel indulges in some metaphysical meditations, insisting on the presence of the spiritual within the physical and rejecting any otherworldly domain where the sensuous qualities of things are idealized away.[32] He then falls into a meditation on the relative virtues of various visions of Paradise, asserting the supremacy of the Islamic paradise where lovely houris, who "keep their *eyes downcast*[33] to earth out of great modesty" (37), are always available for the sexual gratification of the just. Later on, a little disappointed that the royal suite paid for by a prince of the realm does not contain a gramophone, Gabriel wonders why it is that music gives him "something above and beyond physical pleasure . . . something which provides a sort of glimpse into eternity, so to speak, gives meaning to inflated vague figures of speech such as 'ecstasy', 'abstraction from the body', 'forever and ever', 'highest heaven', 'divine,' and the like" (44). This makes it all the more poignant that the lyrics of a song on a distant radio— "your eyes are the eyes of a woman in love"—should waft in from the corridor, echoing the special quality of the moment. With Orita's "frank look, alive with provocative gaiety, even insolence" (38) responding to his own, this is, indeed, heaven.

But there is the promise of even more, a little extra gratification. "When the look of a woman in love in Orita's eyes opened wide to him the gates of

Paradise, unbolting the sluice-gates of his lust pool, his energies were diverted to stemming the tide breaking out of his depths" (56). He interprets his own deference to her libidinal interests as partaking of the spirit of medieval chivalry (62) as well as of Zen-Buddhist detachment (58, 64). He has thus worked himself up to the position of being able to "fully relish his rush of happiness at the sight of Orita's face giving herself over to the complete enjoyment of her own climactic release" (58). And he seems to feel—concurrently or in retrospect—that his having exerted himself to contain himself has earned him some extra credit. This is when everything is reversed.

> It rose in him, that sense of utter joy, together with pride and gratification at the whole scene: here is this royal bedchamber decorated in Louis XV style, delightfully paid for by a real prince and blood relation to His Majesty King of Great Britain and her overseas dominions, and here is the Jerusalem Queen of Hearts lying open-thighed, ready and willing to pleasure him in any imaginable manner, and now that he has retained himself and maintained his upright position till she should get her full satisfaction in her own way, and if this were not enough, he was prepared to risk his life to defend her from any monster or windmill in the whole world, now, when his lust reawakened in all its vigor, surely now she should only be too happy to give him every subtlety and nuance to his heart's content. And she, who even while she was submerged in the depths of her inner rumblings seemed to keep floating on his own wave as well as hers, that common wave of lovers, at that very moment opened her eyes as though responding to the movement of his heart.
>
> "Your eyes are the eyes of a woman in love," came wafting in yet again the refrain with her eyes opening on his rising manhood, and his heart rejoiced at the pleasure awaiting him. So did the notion that had come to him last night . . . that should he ask himself, when his time is up: "Gabriel, Gabriel, what were the most charming moments of your life that you wish to remember before the candle is snuffed out," why there is no doubt at all that this image should be one of the foremost—the image of a beautiful, desired woman, kneeling to kiss; a loving woman eager to bestow more and more. And he grasped at her hair with the palm of his hand, all expectant and wound up ahead of imminent pleasure.
>
> And then it happened: before her lips came close enough to flutter, she retracted her head backwards with unexpected force, shot a sharp look at him as her lips crumpled in a thinner-than-thin smile reflecting the distant disdain of a cold-hearted ruler. It all happened at once: using the disingenuous tone of a petulant girl pretending

> acquiescence, she inquired: "so where exactly would you like it—here, or there, or maybe over there?" tentatively marking the spot he had in mind with her fingertip. In the raging fury that flooded him over he needed every ounce of his mental power to restrain his hand palming her nape from pressing and crushing that long dainty neck and keep his free hand from landing one slap after another on either side of those high-colored, dimpled cheeks. He might have, in this murderous rage, strangled her to death had his powerful hands held that delicate neck a moment longer. (61–63)

If Orita's loving, willing gaze of a short while before "opened up for him the gates of paradise," now "this same gaze has turned[34] and cut him out as something contemptible, worthless, casting it down into hell for his eyes to be blinded with frustration [*ro-ot vekhalot*]" (65). What in earlier enactments of this reversal in Shahar's fiction was merely mental, or involved personal, political, and spatial difference (a slave, a door), here is a very rapid, purely temporal transition. It is this fiasco, and possibly also the suggestion that Orita may be carrying his child, that makes Gabriel Luria betake himself out of Jerusalem and into exile in faraway Paris.

The other significant events take place many years later, on a farm in Brittany, where Gabriel stays first as an honored paying guest, and then, when his father finds out he is not attending medical school and cuts his allowance, as a lowly farmhand. In an important transitional episode, Gabriel, who has humbly performed any hard labor, refuses to take part in the gelding of pigs; the special knife used by an old laborer reminds him of Orita's malicious grin. He then reflects once more on the King David fiasco in a passage using almost the exact same words (98), except that this time Gabriel does not hold back but gives his fury full vent: he imagines himself slapping Orita hard and forcing her to enjoy the act. The mental realization of this fantasy suddenly takes his breath away "with the sharp edge of the painful knowledge that Orita is no more. Orita is dead" (101). *Orita meta*—a lapidary, rhyming phrase. Having killed her symbolically, Gabriel prepares to mourn her: he buys seven special candles and finds an abandoned, half-ruined church where he sets out to light them one by one in memory of the "dead" Orita. With the mourning nearing its completion, the novel comes to an end, implying that the hero is now ready to return home from his self-enforced exile.

In his subsequent life in Jerusalem (told in the previous volumes of the novel) we see Gabriel not avoiding but keeping a certain distance from the beautiful Orita. Unlike Reinhold, who cannot liberate himself from the loving-manipulating Tamara, Gabriel seems autonomous and free. It may be that the symbolic reenactment of the traumatic moment of betrayal has served as a cure. Yet his finding some solace in writing (which never seems to amount to anything much), and the worsening condition of his eyes, which "could not bear the abundance of the light" (*Summer*, 11), suggest that his encounter with Orita's beneficial/noxious gaze has left him a broken vessel indeed. That this should be the nearest analogue to the Kabbalistic figure may be seen as anticlimactic in more than one sense. It need not be: it is another indication that for Shahar the cosmic and the individual, the divine and the human are one. Most peculiar of all is his persistent projection of the light that can make and break as emanating from the eyes of a woman.

Chapter 3

Shahar's Jerusalem

Critics and reviewers of Shahar's work have long recognized him as a "Jerusalem author."[1] Jerusalem is not only the city where Shahar was born and where he lived most of his life, it also is the setting for most of his works; *The Palace of Shattered Vessels* bore, for a while, the subtitle "Jerusalem Scrolls." But how exactly does Jerusalem function in the *Palace* novels? How does the representation of the city relate to the particular kind of novel Shahar writes and to other elements of the novel sequence, such as themes and plot? Is the Jerusalem that Shahar represents in the *Palace* the same one represented in his other works, most notably his short stories? How does the represented city relate to the "real," historical Jerusalem of the 1920s and 1930s? These questions, which have remained to a large extent unexamined by critics, will be the focus of the following discussion.[2]

Whereas a map projects the territory of a city as a schematized totality, a novel about a city may ignore whole parts of the "real" city and zero in on others. Fictional discourse is even free to create "additional" buildings, streets, and neighborhoods. This process of selection, of inclusion and exclusion, of possible extrapolation and interpolation, which happens in each and every text, differs from text to text (even when they are about the "same" city) and determines what "the city" would be in each particular case. In what follows, we show that in the *Palace* novels Shahar focuses on a very small part of Jerusalem, to the exclusion of the rest of the city. In this, the *Palace* novels differ significantly from Shahar's other works. Since the choice of spaces to be represented is intimately linked to the kind of plot the novelist wishes to create, a comparison between the representation of the city in the *Palace* novels and its representation in other works by Shahar will allow us to distinguish between different kinds of plot.

Like most novels set in real, historical cities, the *Palace* novels move between "real" places (streets and neighborhoods, public institutions) and fictional places (most often private residences).[3] By resorting to such an apparatus, a novelist does not only bolster his or her claim for veracity (enhancing what Barthes called "the effect of the real"[4]). Since specific areas and institutions have particular sociocultural value attached to them, their mention in the novel helps evoke the sociocultural world where the characters live and act and defines their positions within this world. Historical information about Jerusalem of the British Mandate period and about the specific part of Jerusalem that Shahar has chosen to represent in the *Palace* novels can help us understand the implications of his choices and clarify the social vision of his work.

We are aware, of course, that there is no absolute, objective standard against which Shahar's fictional practice may be measured. Any discourse about an object as highly charged and controversial as the city of Jerusalem is necessarily colored by its authors' affiliation, bias, and place in history. Thus the historical and geographical accounts to which we resort are all ideological constructions of their subject matter. For the most part, these accounts are part and parcel of what might be called the "Zionist narrative" of Jerusalem. Even in the absence of an Archemedean point outside of this particular orbit, we believe that an examination of Shahar's choices within it is of considerable critical interest.

Small World/Liminal Space

The title of the first volume of the *Palace* sequence indicates quite clearly the place and time in which the novel is set: *Summer in the Street of the Prophets.* However, whereas "summer" proves to be a rather slippery temporal indicator (as we have seen in chapter 1, several summers are collapsed in the novel into one), Street of the Prophets, "between the Italian Hospital and Abyssinian Road" (*Voyage*, 9; 223[5]), is and remains the center of the world represented in the novel sequence. This is a very small world, and a crowded one. Indeed, in the few-blocks' area covered by part of Street of the Prophets and some side streets that branch off from it (Abyssinian Road [today Ethiopia Street], Bnei Brit, Harav Kook, Chancellor [today Strauss] and Belilios streets), most of the characters whose stories the novel tells live, work, and interact with each other. This is where the narrator's house, which is also Gabriel Luria's, stands; some other main characters—Judge Dan Gutkin and his family, Dr. Landau and his wife Orita, Srulik Shoshan (as well as his father, the Temple Builder, and the rest of his family), and William Gordon, the chief of the Mahaneh Yehuda police station—live there too. This is also where the most important public places where various characters meet and interact—the Café Gat, the Bnei Brit Library, and Dr. Landau's eye clinic—are located, as well as some less important public places, such as Café Paramount and the Edison cinema, the grocery store of the Red Ear and his son Reb Yitzhok, the tailor's shop of Antignos (frequented by Srulik, Gabriel, and Dr. Zondack, among others), the Bikur Holim Hospital and the Haddasah clinic (where certain events involving Lea Himmelsach, Daoud, and Talmi occur), the police station of St. Paul Street, and the dancing school (run by Haim Longlife and Oded, Srulik's brother-in-law). The Teachers' College (where Gabriel and Srulik studied), the Gymnasia (the high school where Rina, Srulik's sister, studied, as well as later on, the narrator, his friend Erik Wissotzky, and Berl's son, Tammuz), and the Evelina de Rothchild School (where both Gentilla Luria and Shoshi Raban received their education) are all to be found in this area. On the "enchanted day," Gabriel plays Brunhilde's violin in the middle of Street of the Prophets, while Wertheimer, Orita, Boulos Effendi, William Gordon, and the narrator watch and applaud; and a week later, during the riots, Daoud is killed there.

The extreme smallness of this world and the proximity of characters that this smallness generates can be seen from locating the main fictional and real sites in this area on a map (see map 1, p. 60).

The map is not, however, an exact replica of the novel. Though the narrator sometimes gives us very precise spatial indications, especially when following the movements of characters (see e.g., *Voyage,* 55, 189; 272, 427–28), his main concern is not to give us geographical information but to show what the characters (including himself) see and encounter in their movement through this space or from specific points they occupy in it. Therefore, the exact location of some of the fictive sites can only be conjectured from the partial information given in the text (sometimes with the help of external, historical information). More importantly still, the narrator's habit of locating points in space in relation to other points creates an even greater impression of proximity than the map layout one generates from these descriptions does. Thus we are told that Srulik lives "in an alley branching from Street of the Prophets" (*Voyage,* 104; 331), and that the Bnei Brit Library is located "in an alley off the Street of the Prophets" (*Summer,* 42; 34); the location of the Café Gat is indicated by its proximity to Street of the Prophets (*Countess,* 43), as is the location of Red Ear's grocery store (*Countess,* 86) and Antignos's shop is located in relation to Red Ear's grocery store (*Countess,* 130). A reader who is not very familiar with Jerusalem tends to assume that the Ethiopian consulate would be on Ethiopia Street (called in the novel by the old name for Ethiopia, "Abyssinian Road"), so that when the narrator's house, on Street of the Prophets, is described in relation to the Ethiopian consulate, as it often is, the impression

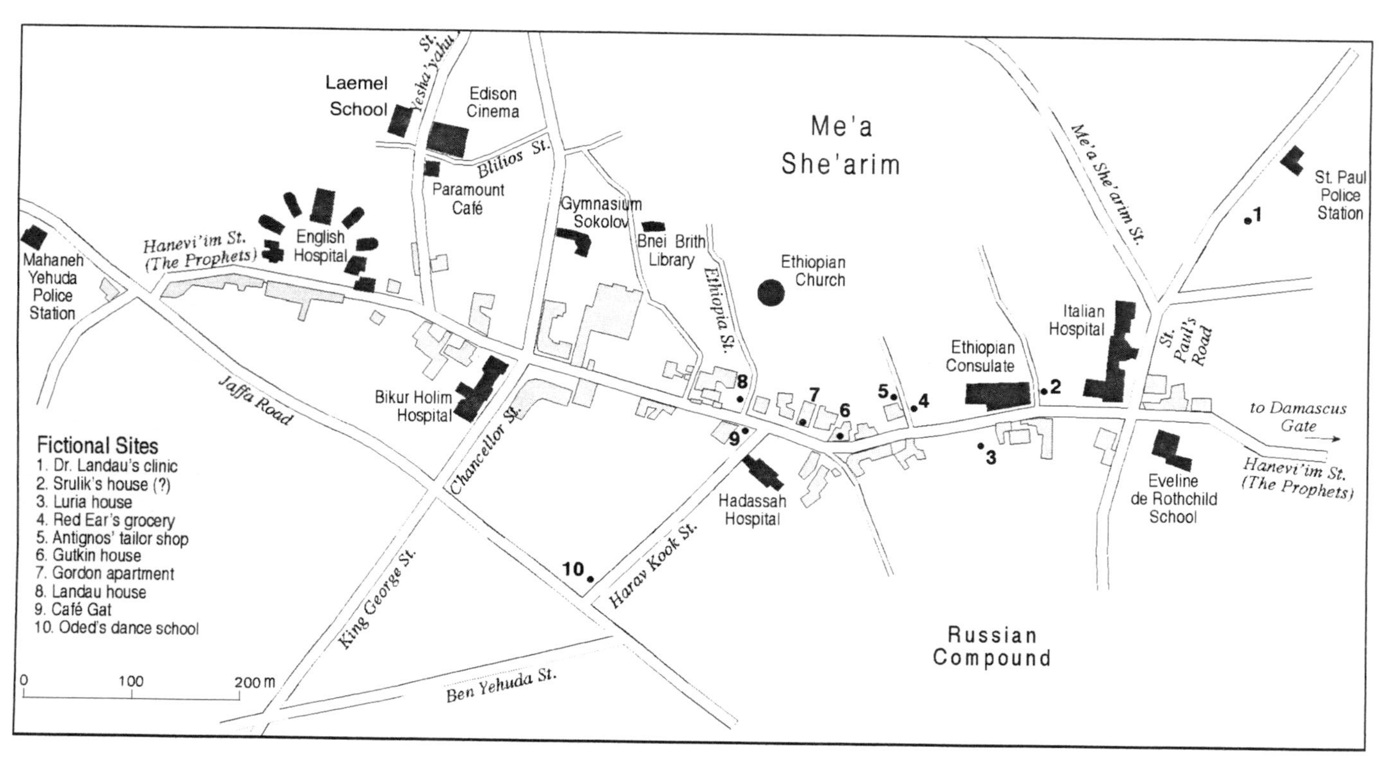

MAP 1. Street of the Prophets in *The Palace of Shattered Vessels*

Note to Map 1: Fictional Sites

1. Dr. Landau's eye clinic "was then situated in St. Paul's Road next to the police station" (*Summer*, 85; 71).
2. Srulik lives with his parents "in an alley branching off Street of the Prophets" (*Voyage*, 104; 331). Walking every day from his home to the Teachers' College, Srulik goes "up the steep incline of Street of the Prophets and pass[es], near its highest point, the Judge's house" (*Voyage*, 55; 272).
3. The narrator's house "was, in fact his [Gabriel's] father's house." The "Ethiopian Consulate [is] opposite the house" (*Summer*, 23; 19).
4. Reb Yitzhok tells his father, the Red Ear, that one of the rioters "was found dead just in front of the grocery store [*mamash bafetah*] (*Countess*, 146); this dead rioter is Daoud, who "was killed on Street of the Prophets at the corner of the Ethiopian Consulate" (*Countess*, 144). However, the grocery store is not on Street of the Prophets itself but in "an alley," "close to Street of the Prophets" (*Countess*, 86).
5. The shop of Antignos the tailor faces the grocery store of the Red Ear (*Countess*, 130).
6. On his way to the doctor's house, Srulik goes "up the steep incline of Street of the Prophets and "pass[es], near its highest point, the judge's house (*Voyage*, 55; 272).
7. Gordon's apartment is on Street of the Prophets; the windows of his apartment look over the alley where the Red Ear's grocery store is situated. On the day of the riots, the English police car, arriving from the English Hospital, stops by Gordon's apartment; some of the policemen continue along the street toward Gabriel, who is still sitting by the body of the dead Daoud (*Countess*, 137).
8. Dr. Landau lives in a big house with a stone fence on Ethiopia Street [Abyssinian Road], at the corner of Street of the Prophets (*Voyage*, 11, 12; 225, 226).
9. Café Gat is on Street of the Prophets, at the corner of Harav Kook Street (*Countess*, 43). Shahar's Café Gat is clearly modeled after the real Café Pat.
10. Oded's dancing school is in an apartment on Harav Kook Street, at the corner of Jaffa Road (*Voyage*, 133; 363).

created is of its proximity to Abyssinian Road. And when the Edison cinema, which in reality is almost as far from Abyssinian Road in one direction as the narrator's house would be in the other direction, is described as "near our house" (*Summer,* 12; 11; trans. modified), a further telescoping occurs, and what is in reality a small area appears even smaller. Some of the narrator's "errors" increase this effect. Thus the narrator tells us that the Bnei Brit Library is located on Abyssinian Road (*Voyage,* 15; 229), and that he goes there by way of Abyssinian Road (*Summer*, 77; 64), whereas it is, actually, on Bnei Brit Street (a short block away from Abyssinian Road). The geographical proximity is thus increased by the reference (in this case inaccurate) to Abyssinian Road. What the narrator feels strrongly and wishes to communicate to the reader, is the closeness and denseness of this world where everything branches off from and comes back to a well-demarcated center.

The area around Street of the Prophets on which the novel centers has an "extension" in the nearby Russian Compound. This is where Judge Dan Gutkin works, where his daughter, Yaeli Gutkin, rents a room, and where the Café Cancan, frequented by Yaeli Gutkin, Louidor, and Berl, as well as by Shoshi and Bella, is located. This extension is extended farther southward in later volumes of the novel where, with new characters such as Nin-Gal, Tammuz, Lea Himmelsach, Bella, and Yaeli Landau, episodes now take place at the King David Hotel, Mishkenot Sha-ananim, Abu Tor, 'Emek Refa-im, and the Rose Garden. Some of these new characters take part in episodes occurring at a later time period: the narrator's meeting with Yaeli Landau, Orita's granddaughter, first in Paris and then in Jerusalem, happens, obviously, many years after the summer of 1936. Likewise, his relations with Nin-Gal and Tammuz date to a somewhat later period, around the mid-1940s, when he was already in high school. But other new characters, such as Lea Himmelsach, Shoshi, and Bella, belong to the narrator's childhood, or even to an earlier period, prior to Gabriel's departure for France. What all of these characters (with the possible exception of Lea Himmelsach) have in common, however, is that they "come into focus" and become part of the story, because at a certain point they enter the geographical purview of the novel. Thus both Shoshi and Bella, through their relation with Berl and Gabriel, respectively, show up in Mrs. Luria's basement on Street of the Prophets, and the narrator meets Nin-Gal (whom he had briefly sighted at a Lag Ba'omer bonfire) in the Bnei Brit Library, where she works. Finally, it is important to note that the southward extension shares with the area around Street of the Prophets one of its most important features: that of being a border zone. We should recall here that Shahar's *Palace* novels are set in Jerusalem of the British Mandate period, that is, before the city was divided by a cease-fire line that skirted the entire area from Mea She'arim in the north to Abu Tor in the south on the city's eastern side. The characterization of the area around Street of the Prophets as well as around Mamilla Street and Abu

Tor as "border zone" is not the result of confusion (on our part or on Shahar's) between the pre-1948 and post-1948 period. We discuss the notion of "border zone" below; what is important to note at this point is that as the story develops in time, it does not move geographically in the direction taken by the Israeli city's historical expansion—toward the west; rather than moving away from the border, it moves to other stretches of the border.

One could have thought that the restriction of the novel's space to a small part of the city reflects the restricted movement and limited experience of the child-narrator, but this is not the case since, in fact, the boy-narrator enjoys greater spatial mobility than most of the characters. Though his life is firmly anchored in Street of the Prophets, he also often goes outside of this area (as in the episode where he attends the coronation of the new Chief Rabbi narrated in *Countess,* or when, in *Nin-Gal,* he goes for a Lag Ba'omer bonfire near Malha). Taking walks with Gabriel (or in his footsteps), he reaches the periphery of the city: Nebi Samwil, the Tombs of the Sanhedrin, Mount Scopus, Kidron Valley. His spatial mobility is further enhanced by a panoramic vision: the narrative is punctuated by moments in which the narrator looks around him and sees far and wide (see, e.g., *Summer,* 13, 24, 63–64; 11, 20-21, 50; *Countess,* 91–92; *Nin-Gal,* 203; *Ghosts,* 20–21; *Tammuz,* 44–45, 47). The novels' restriction of space, therefore, cannot be aimed at representing the limited experience of a child.

The novel presents the area on which it centers as a liminal or an interstitial space: neither the historical Old City nor the rapidly expanding new city, it is, both physically and metaphorically, in between.[6] Despite its proximity to what became the heart of downtown West Jerusalem (the "triangle" created by Jaffa Road, King George Street, and Ben Yehuda Street), Street of the Prophets is depicted in the novel as a border zone between the modern, Jewish, secular hinterland and the potentially violent world of the Arabs of Mussrara and Damascus Gate and the Orthodox Jews of Mea She'arim.[7] We see this most clearly in two episodes of *Day of the Countess*: the first takes place when Reb Yitzhok, the inhabitant and representative of Mea She'arim, attacks a young couple, visiting the area "between Mea She'arim and the Italian Hospital," and they are advised by sympathetic bystanders to run for safety "to Street of the Prophets" (*Countess,* 85, 87). The second is the scene of the riots, which happens a week later, when Arab rioters come storming from "St. Paul Street [now Shivtei Israel]" (131), and Gabriel kills one of them (Daoud) "on Street of the Prophets, at the corner of the Ethiopian consulate" (144), while another runs off "towards Damascus Gate" (137). Since we are not told anything further about the riots, the impression created by the novel is that Gabriel's action in fact stopped the riot at the border zone.

The Old City—associated both with the Arabs and with the Orthodox Jews—can be seen from the distance: "On summer afternoons I would stretch out full length on the round windowsill—the walls were so thick—and look out toward Tur Malka at the top of the Mount of Olives and the section of the Old City walls facing the crowded square in front of the Damascus Gate" (*Summer*, 24–25; 20–21). The Old City remains distant throughout the novel: the narrator, in all his roaming around, never gets closer to the Old City than the Jaffa Gate and prefers to view it from afar (and this in spite of the fact that the Old City is accessible both to the boy and the adult narrator, since the events of the novel take place mostly before 1948 and its narration after 1967).

Temporally, the Old City is distant, too: it belongs to the childhood of the adult characters, or even of their parents. Gentilla Luria, Gabriel's mother, born on Midan Street (Misgav Ladakh Street) at the heart of the Jewish Quarter of the Old City, left it with her family already in her childhood, and Dan Gutkin lived in the "Deutscher Platz" in the Old City and later studied in the Hebron Yeshiva, before leaving to go to England. Gabriel and Srulik went to school in the Old City in their early childhood but did not live there; they continued their studies outside the walls, in institutions that defined themselves in opposition to those of the Old City (Gabriel in the "Alliance" school, run by the *Alliance israëlite universelle*, a modern institution where the languages of instruction were French and Hebrew, and Srulik in the Rav Kook Yeshiva, the first Yeshiva in Eretz Israel where teaching was carried on in Hebrew; both studied, later on, in the Teachers' College).

On the other hand (or on the other side), the newer, modern neighborhoods of the Jewish city are almost entirely ignored: Rehavia and Talpiot are mentioned only once (*Nin-Gal*, 120, 203),[8] and Beit Hakerem, Kiryat Moshe, and Bayit Vagan are never mentioned. Not only do we not find any character in the novel who lives or otherwise belongs to these new Jewish neighborhoods (Boulos Effendi lives in a new Arab neighborhood, Talbiyeh), but out of the many passages describing the panoramic view that the narrator (or Gabriel, or the British painter Holmes) enjoys from an elevated observation point, only one shows the viewer facing westward and seeing, beyond the Old City, "the houses of the new city" (*Countess*, 91–92; the passage is repeated verbatim in *Ghosts*, 20–21).

The new neighborhoods the narrator and characters so systematically ignore belong unmistakably and unambiguously to the secular, Zionist, modern "New Yishuv." The location of the novel on the other side of a geographical-cultural divide may suggest that the novel depicts the world of the "Old Yishuv." If by the "Old Yishuv" we understand families who had lived in Palestine for generations, as opposed to the recent immigrants of the "New Yishuv," then the novel indeed depicts their world. But insofar as the term "Old Yishuv" is used to refer (as is often the case) to the ultra-orthodox community, living on the whole on "Haluka" money and mainly occupied by studying the Torah, then this is clearly not the world of the novel. The world of the novel does not fit easily within the categories of either the Old or the New Yishuv. Its members are native born and have roots in orthodox Jewry in the Old City and outside of it; but by the time of the events depicted by the novel, none of them leads the typical life of the orthodox Jew, though (with the possible exception of Lea Himmelsach) they do not seem to belong with the secular-modern-Zionist-socialist world either.[9] One can interpret this in-betweenness as an accurate representation of social reality: some historians of the Old Yishuv have in fact claimed that "many of the distinctions used today to differentiate between the two camps—new and old, national and ethnic, productive and non-productive, to mention but a few—should be understood in the context of the New Yishuv's attempt to stigmatize and delegitimate the competing Old Yishuv sector," hence, should be abandoned as ideologically motivated simplifications.[10] Alternatively, one can argue that while this opposition may describe accurately the situation in an earlier period, by the 1920s the sharp distinction between the two camps lost much of its edge: with more and more Jews settling in other parts of the country, the Old Yishuv (based in Jerusalem) lost its influence, and the more progressive elements within it merged with the New Yishuv, leaving only a small minority of fanatical ultra-orthodox Jews.[11] But what is specific to Shahar's representation of this period is its evocation of a way of life which, while not diametrically opposed to what came to be known as the "New Yishuv," has not (or not yet) merged with it, and thus remains clearly distinct from it.

The larger geographical context of Eretz Israel is treated in a similar manner: the world of agriculture and of pioneers—that is, the heart of the Zionist enterprise in Eretz Israel—is almost entirely ignored. Two of the novel's characters (the narrator's friend, Aharon Dan, and Nin-Gal) lived for a while in a kibbutz which, in both cases, remains nameless; only once does the novel mention a kibbutz by name, and that has to do with an episode in the life of the adult narrator, after the Six Day War (*Countess*, 46). Of the *moshavot*, only two are mentioned, in passing—Zikhron Ya'akov, in relation to the well-known historical episode of Sarah Aharonson's capture and torture by the Turks (*Countess*, 148), and Petach Tikva, as the place where Fat Pesach has an inheritance dispute (*Tammuz*, 167). The Mikveh Israel school of agriculture is mentioned (*Tammuz*, 80) only in relation to the phantomlike figure of Giora Landau (Orita's son, presumably fathered by Gabriel, who never makes an actual appearance in the novel). Tel Aviv is barely mentioned (once, in the context of the same episode in the life of the adult narrator, after the Six Day War [*Countess*, 47], and another time as the place from where a nameless watchmaker must order spare parts [*Nin-Gal*, 188]); no important narrative event takes place there and we rarely hear of characters actually going there: in *Day of the Countess,* we are told that during the week preceding the riots, Gordon spent part of his vacation in Tel Aviv (141); in *Of Candles and Winds,*

Gabriel goes to Tel Aviv to gather information about the murder of Brenner, and on his way back to Jerusalem by bus he spots Dan Gutkin and Orita driving in the opposite direction (108, 111). The places mentioned most often within Eretz Israel, outside of Jerusalem, are Jaffa, Bethlehem, Hebron, Jericho, Safed, Nazareth, and Nablus—that is, places associated with ancient, biblical times and/or with Arabs (or both).[12] It is important to note that in Shahar's novel, in contrast to earlier works, such as Agnon's *Tmol Shilshom* (*Yesteryear*) or Ben-Zion's story "Haget" ("The Divorce"), Jaffa (the predominantly Arab city later swallowed by Tel Aviv) is not the opposite of Jerusalem.[13] Jaffa, in Shahar's novel, is not the place where new, Hebrew, secular culture is being developed but rather where Gabriel's father, the Old Bey—a remnant of the Ottoman Empire—lives with his Sephardi wife and where Louidor and Lea "discover" the existence of the Arabs. The places in Eretz Israel outside of Jerusalem mentioned by the novel are not so much opposites of Jerusalem as rather like it. Still, they remain marginal, and no important action or event occurs in any of them. Indeed, important experiences take place either within a closely delimited area of Jerusalem or far away, overseas—especially in France. This restriction is particularly striking in the case of characters who, we know, enjoy great spatial mobility, such as Orita or Dan Gutkin; though there are allusions to their travel to different parts of the country, none of them turns out to be narratively significant.

Space and Plot

The restriction of events and characters to a small area of Jerusalem and the nearly complete avoidance by the novel of the rest of the city and of other important places such as Tel Aviv and the farming settlements are particular to the *Palace* sequence, and we do not find them in Shahar's other works. A comparison with the short stories, which by and large predate the composition of the novel sequence, is particularly instructive.[14] The two volumes of short stories—*The Death of the Little God* and *The Pope's Mustache*—gather most, if not all, of the stories Shahar wrote. These stories can in some sense be considered sketches for the *Palace* sequence, since they include characters, themes, and situations that we find also, with variations, in the *Palace* novels. Thus, for example, several stories describe a familial situation similar to that of the Lurias' in the *Palace*: an older husband (often referred to by his wife as "the old lecher," or simply "the Old One") who is far away most of the time; a wife (mother or grandmother) who lives with an unmarried sister whom she treats more or less as a servant and whom she sometimes accuses of having had an affair with "the old lecher"; a son or a daughter who live with the mother (sometimes after a long stay abroad) and whom the mother accuses of being like the father, "a bone of his bones" (see "The Proposal," "The Old Man and His Daughter," and "First Lesson"). Gabriel resembles and acts like several uncles that figure in the short stories (Kalman, Lippa, and Zemach in "The Fortune Teller," "The Find," and "Of Dreams" [trans. into English as "Uncle Zemach"]). Gabriel Luria himself appears already in the story "The Pope's Mustache," where we also find Boulos Effendi. The narrator walking at night with a child who discovers the night sky (in "Midnight Story") is a reversal of a similar situation in the *Palace* where the narrator accompanies Gabriel (told also in "First Lesson," where the father takes the role of Gabriel). The little doctor from Ethiopia Street (in the story by that name) resembles Srulik, the little librarian; the pharmacist in "The Pharmacist and the Salvation of the World" foreshadows Dr. Blum, the pharmacist in *Summer*, and so on. But in terms of the representation of space, there are important differences between these stories and the *Palace*.

Whereas in the *Palace* novels the location of the main characters and events in a particular part of the city is indicated clearly and repeatedly, some of the short stories seem rather indifferent to location. Thus the story "Bruria" takes place in a mental hospital whose location is never specified. That a later story—"That Day"—mentions the story "Bruria" and tells us that the mental hospital was on Mount Scopus and was moved from Sheikh Jarach when the fighting began in 1948 (*Pope*, 196) does not alter the fact that for the telling of "Bruria" this seemed of no crucial importance. Some other stories either happen in a spatial vacuum or neglect to name the location (which we may or may not be able to infer from clues). Thus in "Midnight Story" the narrator meets the child on "a street," they go down "an alley" (*Little God*, 24, 27), and eventually reach the child's home without any more specific indications of location being given; the same is true of the stories "Two Porters," "Moshe's Last Days," "Of Human Nature," and "The Death of the Little God" among others. Other stories include spatial references but stop short of pinpointing exact locations. In "The Pharmacist and the Salvation of the World," the narrator refers to "our neighborhood," and the pharmacist says that in his youth the entire area "between Mea She'arim and the Schneller Wood" was still unbuilt (*Little God*, 61, 65; *News From Jerusalem*, 100, 105); in the "Border Boy," we hear that the boy and his family lived on the border between the Arab and Jewish areas in a neighborhood whose inhabitants moved to Katamon after the 1948 war (*Little God*, 75, 79); Ephraim's family in "Of Shadows and the Image" lives in a religious neighborhood, and his father directs an orphanage there. These details may suggest to us possible location(s), but the narrator stops short of naming places, of turning a generic or an abstract space (a religious neighborhood, a border) into a specific one (Mea She'arim, Abu Tor).

When we look at those stories whose location is not specified, or only vaguely hinted at, we realize that geographic specificity is not a necessary condition for (or consequence of) detailed description. Thus the apartment of the child and his parents in "Midnight Story" is described in some detail (*Little God*, 27)—indeed, in greater detail than the narrator's own quarters in the *Palace* sequence—even though its location in the city remains unspecified. Similarly, in "The Proposal," the apartment of old Shprintza, Pinik's mother, is described in detail, even though the only hint we have about its location is that it has a window facing Sheikh Jarach (*Pope*, 54; *News*, 258). Conversely, interiors and exteriors in the *Palace* novels often are only sketchily or partially described (if at all), and this in spite of the precision with which their location in space is indicated. The fixing of the characters' sphere of activities in a certain area that is geographically precise and socioculturally specific is not, therefore, the equivalent of a "realism" predicated on visualizing space (streets, buildings, interiors) or objects. The short stories are not more "realistic" or less "realistic" than the *Palace* novels; rather, we might conclude that their object of representation is somewhat different.

Some short stories do give precise spatial indications, and there we can see that, both severally and in the aggregate, the stories are not as partial to one area of the city as the *Palace* novels are. "On a Summer Evening," for example, starts with the heroine walking away from her father's apartment to wait for the young terrorist in the park off King George Street, near the Moslem cemetery; while waiting, she thinks of various episodes of her life, connected to the Zion cinema, Ben Yehuda Street, the central bus station on Jaffa Road, and Mount Scopus. After hearing the blast, she runs to Julian Street (today, King David's Street), where she meets the terrorist, who then disappears in the direction of Nahalat Shiv'ah; she then walks all the way to Romema (by way of Mahaneh Yehuda), and farther to Beit Hakerem, in the company of the British officer, who may or may not be aware of her involvement with the Underground. In "Of Dreams," Uncle Zemach, upon returning from England, settles in an apartment in Beit Hakerem, as is appropriate for a successful lawyer. His office is on Mamilla Street, in a commercial, downtown neighborhood, where his woman friend from Betzalel Art School still lives. He kills a rioter in Mea She'arim and teaches his nephew, the narrator, how to paint in the park off King George Street and in Nahalat Shiv'ah. The family has relatives who live in Nes Tziona, and other agricultural settlements, such as Petach Tikva and Zikhron Ya'akov, also are mentioned. In "Of Shadows and the Image," the location of the family home is only hinted at, but other sites are named: Ephraim meets the painter Varda for the first time near the Tombs of the Sanhedrin, and later on he takes several walks far from the city center, for example, to Talpiot. In "Of Small Sins," the boy-narrator, who lives in one of the new neighborhoods of Jerusalem, comes to spend the summer months

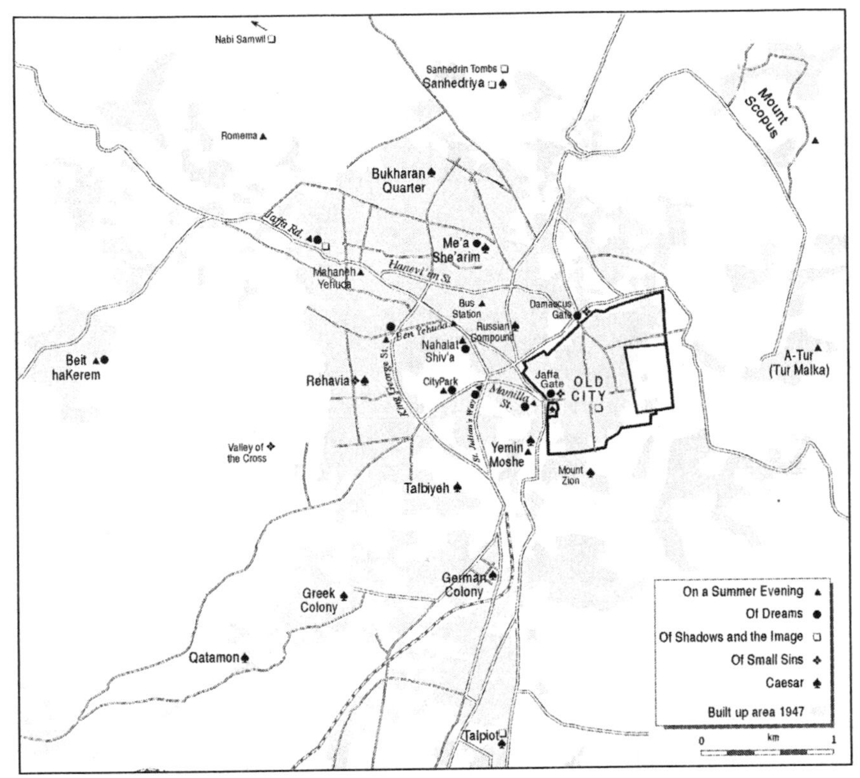

MAP 2. Jerusalem in the Short Stories

with his Uncle Zerach, who lives on a small street branching out from Ethiopia Street. After the incident with Reisale in his bookstore, Zerach goes out with the young student ("the daughter of a well-known ophthalmologist from Germany," *Little God*, 200), first to a café nearby, then to the restaurant Chez Simon, in the city's center, and finally to the Valley of the Cross, close to the new houses where the young student lives.

Even this partial list suggests that in these stories spatial diversity is, on the whole, in the service of social or cultural oppositions that generate the thematic content of the stories. The oppositions are various: in "Of Shadows and the Image," the opposition between the city and the open fields outside of it corresponds to an opposition between the restrictive life of the family, made even more rigorous by religious observance, on the one hand, and the freedom of artistic creation and the life of artists, on the other hand. In "Of Dreams," Zemach's apartment in Beit Hakerem represents a life of material and social success, as opposed to the world of childhood and art he betrayed; the opposition between Zemach and his cousin from Nes Tziona dramatizes the opposition between the sophistication of the city and the simplicity of the farming life. In "Of Small Sins," the new buildings where both the narrator and the young woman student lead their modern life and the kibbutz that Uncle Zerach's son is going to join stand in opposition to the old home and bookstore where Uncle Zerach lives his life, stuck in what he calls "an unsavory puddle" (*Little God*, 209). The story "Caesar" uses, most explicitly, spatial differences to narrate a story of social success. The narrator and his two brothers grew up in the "poverty and dirt of the northern neighborhoods" (*Pope*, 147) but went to school with the rich kids of Rehavia (in whose homes the narrator was introduced to the world of art). Amos, the narrator's brother, lived as a student in a room in the German Colony, but now, back from the United States with his diploma, he lives in the "most beautiful part of town," Talbiyeh (*Pope*, 129). The adult narrator does not belong either in the poor world of his childhood or in the world of social success represented by both his schoolmates and his brother; his stay in his brother's apartment is only temporary.

Against the background of such stories, where the variety of locations serves to dramatize oppositional structures and generate narratives of change, we can hypothesize that the spatial restriction of the *Palace* novels implies lack of interest in such structures and such a narrative. Rather than creating a plurality of opposed or competing places, the *Palace* novels center on one well-defined space—the area around Street of the Prophets. Some characters may belong to other spaces too (and those may be vaguely indicated, not mentioned at all, or unstable), but these spaces do not present an alternative or an opposition to the Street of the Prophets, since these characters' very entry into the story depends, as we have said, on their having a foothold at the novel's central space. Thus, for example, Elka and Ethel, Srulik's aunts, probably live near Sh'arei Hessed (*Voyage*, 15; 229) or in Nahalat Ahim (*Countess*, 220). But Elka's and Ethel's presence in the novel is determined by their regular visits to their nephew at the Bnei Brit Library, where they hold their "five o'clock tea," attended by the boy-narrator and by Gabriel (at different time periods, presumably). Bella is said to live in Mishkenot Sha-ananim, not far from Berl's house (*Tammuz*, 154), but as Fat Pesach's wife, she presumably lives with him, that is, near Café Cancan, between Melissanda Street (today Heleni Hamalka) and the Russian Compound (*Countess*, 111). She becomes a full-fledged character in the novel when she steps into Mrs. Luria's basement. Wertheimer lives, along with Brunhilde, in Mussrara (*Countess*, 34) but is also said (*Nin-Gal*, 155) to live in the same courtyard where later on Heinrich Reinhold, the hero of *His Majesty's Agent*, would live, that is, on Mamilla Street (next to the narrator, who, however, in the *Palace* novels, of course, lives on Street of the Prophets). However, we never see Wertheimer at his home; rather, we see him mostly in the cafés Gat and Cancan, where he sells his wares. Conversely, Berl Raban, whom we first meet in Dr. Landau's clinic and then in Mrs. Luria's basement, at the heart of Street of the Prophets, "acquires" in later volumes different homes: in *Nin-Gal,* he is said to live with his wife, Lea Himmelsach, in Mishkenot Sha-ananim (see, e.g., 85); in *Ghosts,* we find him living with his old uncle, somewhere near the American Colony (26). But neither location "sticks," and Berl's story remains firmly grounded in the area around Street of the Prophets.

The spatial configuration created by the *Palace* novels excludes certain common kinds of plot: they are not novels of transgression, where a protagonist might move from an initial home space to a foreign, forbidden space (e.g., from the city to the forest, or, as in the case of Ephraim of "Of Shadows and the Image," to the open fields); nor novels of *arrivisme,* where social advancement or other forms of success can be measured by spatial displacement (as in "Of Dreams"); nor are they, strictly speaking, novels of education, where the hero leaves family and home and goes to the "world," symbolized by the metropolis (and where the hero's education is measured by his changed understanding of either the "world," or "home," or both). It is true that Gabriel leaves Jerusalem for Paris and then comes back to Jerusalem, but as we have shown earlier, his life in Jerusalem prior to his departure is not clearly distinguished from his life there after his return, so that the possibility of a "Bildung" is ruled out. What concerns Shahar in the *Palace* novels is not so much the change in the life of his characters (success or failure) or the change in their understanding of themselves and the world but the depiction of the sociocultural world in which they all live, which in a sense they embody, and to which they remain, on the whole, faithful.

His Majesty's Agent, Shahar's other mature novel, written while the *Palace* sequence was already underway, shares with the *Palace* novels important themes and motifs, some of which receive similar spatial representation. Just like *The Palace of Shattered Vessels*, so *His Majesty's Agent* begins with the remembrance of an "originary" event—the appearance of the narrator's childhood hero, Heinrich Reinhold—here triggered by the reappearance of his "double," Yoël: "The sight of Yoël suddenly looming up out of the desert sand, like the reincarnation of a past buried in the depths of time, flooded me all at once with a wonderful sensation, the memory of one of the happiest days of my childhood—the day when I first saw Heinrich Reinhold" (12; 6). And here, too, the narrator and his family share living quarters with the main hero, Heinrich Reinhold/Yoël, in a house located on a border zone (on Mamilla Street), thus replicating the spatial arrangement at the heart of the *Palace* novels. The theme of betrayal, which appears in a minor key in the *Palace* novels (Gabriel's denial of his grandfather, Orita's "betrayal" of Gabriel, told in *Of Candles and Winds*), becomes the major theme of *His Majesty's Agent.*

Though the structure of betrayal remains the same as in the *Palace* novels and in some of the early stories—it can be mapped onto the family triangle of father-mother-(male) child—in *His Majesty's Agent* it acquires a prominence and an explicitness that it did not have in these other works as its various modalities inform the main events of the story: the betrayal of a male (child) by a loving woman (Heinrich's betrayal by his mother, by Tamara), a child's own betrayal of a loved father (Heinrich's involuntary betrayal of his father), and the father's fear of betraying his child (the bombing of the King David Hotel). The story of betrayal told in *His Majesty's Agent* almost intersects with that told in *Of Candles and Winds,* as the two works converge on one location: the King David Hotel. Indeed, Heinrich's daydream about a "honeymoon suite" in the King David Hotel (a daydream in which Tamara's betrayal is already prefigured—though he cannot decipher it—by the insistence of his mind to locate the suite in the section of the hotel allocated to the British military command) foreshadows the episode between Gabriel and Orita in the King David Hotel suite that Lord Radcliff left her and where her "betrayal" of Gabriel takes place. Gabriel merges with Heinrich as, toward the end of *Of Candles and Winds*, he recalls watching the sunrise from the balcony of the King David Hotel (as Heinrich did) and feeling, presumably, what Heinrich did, since the passages describing the two events are identical (except for two minor variations, as indicated below): "His heart swelled with joy at the image of a woman/his mother coming out of her room, erect and smiling, in a wide-brimmed hat and gloves that reached up to her elbows, wearing high heels and carrying a handbag and smiling mysteriously as she said to him, with impetuous gaiety, 'Come, sweetheart [*yakiri/havivi*), let's go out for a little walk'" (*Candles*, 152; *Agent*, 166; 170).[15]

In stating that the King David Hotel was only a few houses (and not a few blocks, as the English translation has it) away from his/Heinrich's house (214; 220), the narrator of *His Majesty's Agent* seems to move toward a concentration of the plot in one small part of the city, as he does in the *Palace* novels. The theme of betrayal (and its complement, the loss of control over one's life), however, does not require such limitation: betrayal can take place anywhere. And indeed, the plot of *His Majesty's Agent* spreads all over Jerusalem and beyond it: Heinrich lives on Mamilla Street and works at the King David Hotel, Tamara lives in Talbiyeh, behind Terra Sancta, and they first meet in the Augusta Victoria Hospital, on Mount of Olives. They go to Café Paramount as well as to Café Atara, on Ben Yehuda Street, they attend a play at the Edison Cinema, and Tamara spends a week in Galilee. Tamara's husband, Daniel, and the narrator's father, work in a bank on King George Street, but Heinrich first meets Daniel in Egypt and later runs into him in Haifa (in the house where Tamara grew up); he sees Daniel and his son in the Café Europa, opposite Schwartz's department store. After the bombing of the King David

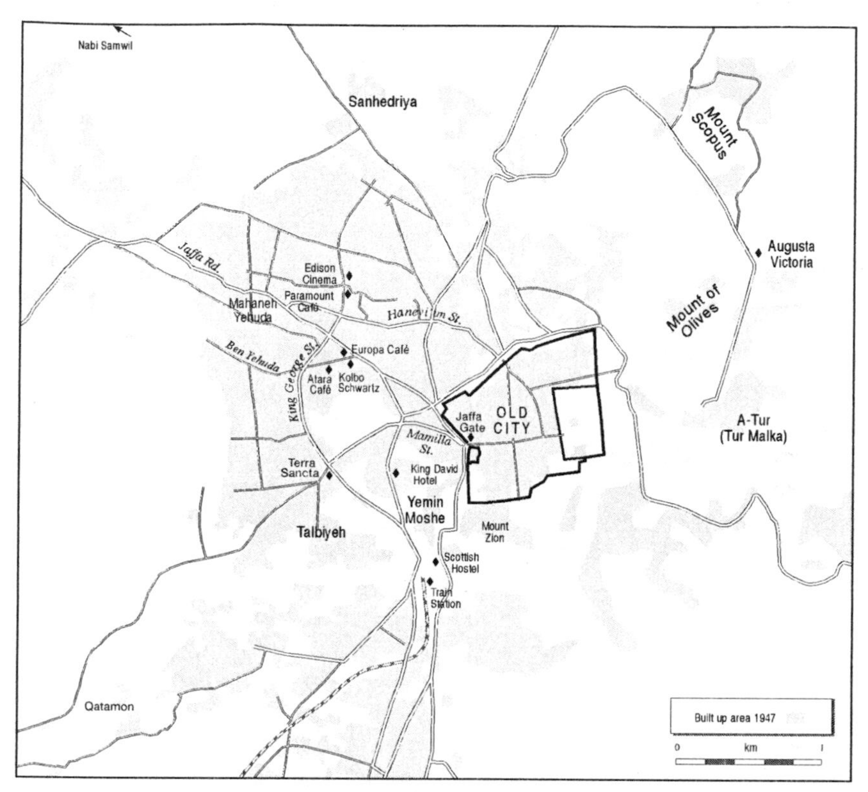

MAP 3. Jerusalem Sites in *His Majesty's Agent*

Hotel, Heinrich hides in the Scottish Hospice by the Railway Station and then makes his escape to Brussels. A considerable part of the novel takes place in the south, notably in the Sinai Desert, and later on across the ocean, in distant Los Angeles.

Practically each one of these places is the scene of some act of betrayal. In the *Palace* novels, on the other hand, betrayal does not spread and pullulate; it is contained. Though Orita's "betrayal" of Gabriel can be seen as the event that has structured his entire life (as we argued in chapter 2), this originary event is in some sense confined to the edges of the novel: relegated to the last volume, it recounts what took place prior to the events told in the first volume. The belated exposure of the reader to this important episode does not turn around his or her understanding of the characters involved and of the world represented in the novel; it has no major impact on the world of Street of the Prophets.

HETEROTOPIA

The area around Street of the Prophets that is at the center of the *Palace* novels played an important role in Jerusalem of the early twentieth century.[16] In the second half of the nineteenth century, when the first neighborhoods outside the walls of the Old City were built and the "new city" started to grow, Jaffa Street—the road that connects Jerusalem to the port of Jaffa—became a thoroughfare, and on its two sides, shops and businesses were built. Street of the Prophets, which runs north of Jaffa Street, from the neighborhood of Mahaneh Yehuda to Damascus Gate, did not become as important an artery. On the other hand, perhaps because of its location on a small ridge where the air was considered better, it became a desirable place of residence where the city's "high society" lived. Many consulates established themselves there, and since in the second half of the nineteenth century foreign nationals (of major European countries and the United States) enjoyed extraterritorial privileges vis-à-vis the Ottoman regime, the consulates were in fact small seats of government abroad. "Street of the Consuls," as the street was called then, connoted not only social prestige but also political power. The current name of the street, given by Sir Ronald Storrs at the beginning of the British Mandate, is suggestive of another important aspect. It is likely that this name was given to the street because of its proximity to the tomb of Nebi Ukasha, where, according to local tradition, the prophets of all three monotheistic religions were buried.[17] Indeed, until 1948, the area around Street of the Prophets was not exclusively, or even predominantly, Jewish (and thus different from the new Jewish neighborhoods built outside the walls, including those nearby, such as Mea She'arim, Zikhron Moshe, Beit Israel, or the Bukharan quarter). Not only did Street of the Prophets border on the Arab neighborhood of Mussrara, but the "Abyssinian Quarter" located in its middle section (bordered by the Street of the Prophets, Abyssinian Road, Bnei Brit Street, and Hazanovich Street) was built mainly by the rich and influential Arab family, Nashashibi (who competed with the Husseini family for control of the city). The Christian presence in the area came not only from the consulates but also from the churches and especially from other institutions, such as schools and hospitals, run by Christian missionaries. Whereas the new neighborhoods outside the walls, especially those built by Jews, were by and large ethnically and culturally homogeneous (separate neighborhoods for Sephardi and Ashkenazi, and within this division, separate neighborhoods for Hungarians or for Yemenites, Kurds, Bukharans, etc.) and often constituted organized communities, with their own institutions and bylaws, the population in the area around Street of the Prophets was heterogeneous and, despite the presence of many public institutions in it, was not an organized community.

The presence of foreign powers in the area is largely responsible for the grandeur of many of its buildings, which, in turn, made it into one of the most elegant streets in Jerusalem of the early twentieth century. At the corner of Street of the Prophets and the present-day Shivtei Israel Street (Hebrew for "Street of the Tribes of Israel," St. Paul Street during the British Mandate), which marks the southern edge of the area relevant to the novel, stands the elegant Italian Hospital (built 1911–1917) and, across the street from it, the castle-like building "Mahanayim," built in 1885 by the Swiss banker Frutiger, which served at one time as the residence for the High Commissioner, Lord Plumer. At the other end of Street of the Prophets, near Mahaneh Yehuda, was the English Hospital, founded by English missionaries. Between the two, we find the large building of the Ethiopian Consulate (built 1925–1928); the Probst House, built (in 1903) by the German Protestant Church on the grounds where the camp of the German Kaiser had stood, when he visited Jerusalem in 1898 (and where Sir Ronald Storrs, the first governor of Jerusalem, lived for a while); the Abyssinian Church (1874–1893), on Abyssinian Road, close to the corner of Street of the Prophets; Tabor House (1882–1889), built by the architect Conrad Schick, as his private residence; the Saint Joseph monastery (1887); the German Hospital (1894); the Evangelical Church; and the Pasha house (situated between Street of the Prophets and Jaffa Road), a house built by the Greek Orthodox Church at the end of the nineteenth century, which served as the residence for the "Pashas," the governors of Jerusalem during the Ottoman rule.

But the Jewish presence in this area was far from negligible. Not only do we find a fair number of imposing buildings, housing important Jewish institutions, such as the Bikur Holim Hospital, the Rothschild Hospital, the Laemel School (on nearby Yesha'ayhu Street), the Bnei Brit Library (on Bnei Brit Street), and the Kamenitz Hotel (the most elegant and modern hotel in Jerusalem at the end of the nineteenth century, located between Street of the Prophets and Jaffa Road, near the English Hospital), but the area as a whole was a center for the new cultural life of Jerusalem in the first decades of the twentieth century. In his autobiography, *Derekh shofet bi-Yerushalayim* (*The Career of a Jerusalem Judge*) Gad Frumkin calls Abyssinian Road "the Latin Quarter of Jerusalem" because of the high concentration of schools, teachers, and students in that small area.[18] A quick look at the schools that found their (temporary) home there suggests, again, the mixed nature of this "new culture": the Laemel School, where students received both Jewish and general education and where the teaching was done in German; the Teachers' College, which trained teachers for modern schools; the art school, Betzalel; the Tahkemoni School for Boys, a Sephardic, traditional school that nevertheless inculcated Zionism and Hebrew culture; and the Ma'aleh School, an Ashkenazi religious school. The reference here to Gad Frumkin is far from arbitrary: as the only Jew to have served as a supreme court judge in the British Mandate administration, he is the easily identified model for Shahar's Judge Dan Gutkin. But though Judge Frumkin did indeed live on Abyssinian Road and later on Street of the Prophets, near the Italian Hospital, by 1924, like many others of his class and education, he left this neighborhood to move westward (in his case, to Rehavia). The same is true of many institutions: the Betzalel School moved to Shemuel Hanagid Street in 1908; Hagymnasia Ha'ivrit (the Hebrew Gymnasium), founded in 1909 in nearby Zikhron Moshe[19] and located, between 1915 and 1921, in the Bukharan neighborhood,[20] moved to Rehavia in 1927; the Teachers' College, first housed on Abyssinian Road, moved to Zikhron Moshe, where it operated in different locations until 1928, when it moved to its permanent home in Beit Hakerem;[21] the National Library, housed from 1920 to 1930 in the Bnei Brit Library, moved to Mount Scopus, as did the Hadassah Hospital, housed from 1918 to 1939 in the Rothschild Hospital. Needless to say, though the Consulates may have stayed for a while on Street of the Prophets, they lost their power when the war broke and with the establishment of the British Mandate. As we can see, this exodus did not occur all at once: the Hadassah Hospital remained in the area until 1939; the Evelina de Rothschild school for girls remained in the "Mahanayim" building (at the corner of the Street of the Prophets and Shivtei Israel Street) until 1948; and the Edison movie theater remained the largest public hall in Jerusalem and hence was a favorite venue for major musical and theatrical performances until the construction of Binyanei Ha-uma in the early 1960s. Nevertheless, one can say that by the mid-1930s—the presumable time of the events at the center of the novel—most of the institutions and individuals that gave the area around Street of the Prophets its social and cultural prestige relocated to the newer neighborhoods—especially Rehavia.

We have noted elsewhere that the description by Shahar of the "Bloody Events" of 1936 is actually more germane to the 1929 riots. We now can make an analogous point about the sociocultural milieu in which his characters live. Especially through the figure of Judge Gutkin, Shahar attributes to Street of the Prophets a prestige that it has in fact lost by the mid-1920s: the concerts and balls he places at the Gutkins' and Lurias' on Street of the Prophets during the 1930s, would have taken place in "reality," at the Frumkins' and Yellins' in Rehavia. But Rehavia was not simply a newer version of Street of the Prophets: though it became the preferred residence for Jerusalem's Jewish intelligentsia and a center of social interaction between leaders of the Jewish community and officials of the British administration, it did not have the ethnic and religious heterogeneity of Street of the Prophets. It was a predominantly secular, Jewish-Zionist neighborhood, a fact underlined by the presence of the "National Institutions" [*mossadot leumiyim*] as well as of "*Me'onot Ha'ovdim*," a workers' cooperative housing complex.

It is important to stress that Shahar does not simply transpose a "reality" of the 1920s to the mid-1930s. His story covers both periods, since the narrator tells us both about his relations with Gabriel and Srulik when he was a young boy (mid-1930s) and about Srulik's and Gabriel's younger days (in the 1920s), before both left Eretz Israel. As we have shown elsewhere, these two time-periods tend to blur, so that the reader may often perceive events occurring after Gabriel's return as having taken place before his departure. The novel's references to the Bnei Brit Library as a lending library for young people, to the Edison movie theater, and to the Rose Garden, all related to the childhood and adolescence of the boy-narrator, make perfect sense in terms of his world, the "reality" of the 1930s.[22] The references to the Gymnasia and the Teachers' College make sense in terms of the 1920s (when Srulik, Gabriel, and Srulik's sister, Rina, were all students) but are anachronistic in terms of the narrator and his contemporaries.[23] The presence of Dan Gutkin on Street of the Prophets during the narrator's childhood (i.e., in the mid-1930s) seems anachronistic and is a cause or an effect of the blurring between the boy's experience and that of his admired older role models. A similar effect may be observed in the case of Dr. Landau's clinic. To anyone familiar with Jerusalem's history and folklore, Dr. Landau immediately calls to mind the legendary ophthalmologist Dr. Albert Ticho, who lived and worked on Harav Kook Street well into the 1950s. It is interesting to note though that the location Shahar gives for Dr. Landau's clinic all through the 1930s (on St. Paul's Street, near the police station) is that of Dr. Ticho's first clinic, where he worked until he was attacked by an Arab in November 1929.[24] The spatial concentration of the novel would not have been impaired by locating the clinic on the nearby Rav Kook Street; placing it where he does, Shahar both slightly disguises his historical model and blurs the difference between the 1920s and the 1930s.[25] We can say, therefore, that Shahar's selective anachronism results in a temporal "telescoping," an analogue to the rhetorical effect whereby the arena of the action is made to seem an even smaller, denser place than it actually is.

By partially collapsing the 1920s and the 1930s the novel stretches the moment when the area is on the verge of decline and so can tell the story of two or three generations without constructing it as a story of cultural-historical change. Thus it locates the events of the novel in an urban area that is both central and a border zone, both marginal (by its ethnic and religious heterogeneity and in relation to the Zionist enterprise whose presence in Jerusalem—problematic in itself[26]—is located elsewhere) and of great cultural significance. All this with the retrospective knowledge—never allowed to impinge on the description of events—that this world will not survive, that, indeed, it is already on the wane. This does not mean, of course, that the narrator pretends that things have remained unchanged, but the allusions to changes in the neighborhood occur in passages where the adult narrator speaks of his experiences in the "present of writing." Thus, for example, he might tell us that at the time of writing the Café Gat no longer exists, but in describing characters and events at the Café Gat, he does not intervene, as narrator, to comment on its impending ruin, nor does he let on that, historically speaking, it has already lost its prestige. Our point is that rather than trace historical change, Shahar's novel sequence is geared toward the recreation of a lost world. It represents a certain form of life, marked by heterogeneity and in-mixing, by a coexistence unlike that of an organized community, one that enjoyed social and cultural prestige for a while, before losing out to more uniform, homogeneous, and organized forms of life.

The social world emerging from Shahar's *Palace* novels resembles what Michel Foucault described under the name "heterotopia."[27] Whereas utopia is an ideal space existing nowhere, in which social reality is mirrored/reversed (all of its ills are cured), heterotopia is an actual space where society's unconscious (that which does not fit on its ideological map) is materially present.

A full assessment of what renders Shahar's representation of Jerusalem different, if not unique, is possible only in a comparative context. This obviously leads far beyond the limits of this book. One brief example may suggest the direction in which such a comparison may go. Amos Oz's novel *My Michael* (first published 1968) is set in a Jerusalem that would be quite familiar to the characters of Shahar's novels. Though its story takes place in the early to mid-1950s (i.e., after the 1948 war and the division of the city between Israel and Jordan), most if not all of the sites mentioned in it existed already in the mid-1930s. And these sites are many: the novel mentions about 120 particular places in Jerusalem, from neighborhoods to streets to landmarks and particular buildings (cafés, stores, office buildings, and so on). This specificity (one of whose functions is to anchor the inner, mental drama of the heroine in a particular sociohistorical context) is, however, counterbalanced by repeated references to the city of Jerusalem as a whole ("Jerusalem" is mentioned in the novel over 100 times, often several times on the same page). These repeated references to the city as a whole are motivated, in part, by the fact that Jerusalem often is seen from the outside: many of the novel's characters live elsewhere, and some travel to and from the city. But most of the references to Jerusalem as a whole are actually made by characters of and within the city. A few examples will have to suffice.[28] "In winter, at night, the buildings of Jerusalem look like gray shapes against a black backcloth. A landscape of suppressed violence. Jerusalem knows how to be an abstract city: stones, pine trees, and rusting iron" (15; 18); "this isn't a city . . . it's an illusion. We're crowded in on all sides by hills. . . . All of a sudden the city seems very insubstantial [*rofefet*]" (20-21; 26); "When it's been raining Jerusalem makes one feel sad. Actually, Jerusalem always makes one feel sad, but it's a different sadness at every moment of the day and at every time of the year" (21; 26); "your Jerusalem is backward" (30; 40); "Jerusalem is a remote city, even if you live there, even if you were born there" (65; 92); "There is no end to Jerusalem" (75; 107); "Jerusalem is a burning city" (76; 109); "Can one ever feel at home here in Jerusalem, I wonder, even if one lives here for a century? City of enclosed courtyards, her soul sealed up behind bleak walls crowned with jagged glass. There is no Jerusalem" (77; 110), and so on.

These few examples suggest that characters in the novel, while aware of the specificity of particular parts of the city, also tend to regard it as a totality to which they seem to attribute an "essence." The attributes that make up this essence are here, for the most part, negative: the city is "burning," "backward," suffused with "suppressed violence," makes one sad. Yet another set of characterizations—the city is "abstract," "remote," "insubstantial"—suggests another kind of negativity, going almost so far as denying the city's very existence. This kind of ontological negativity suggests that the Jerusalem alluded to in these particular remarks is not the "real," "material" city (which obviously does exist) but an idea, or an ideal, of the city, which fails to manifest itself. The vision of the city as a totality, then, oscillates between longing for (or mourning over) an absent ideal and, its correlative, a dissatisfaction with a present reality. It oscillates, in other words, between the city as utopia and the city as dystopia.

This type of meditation about Jerusalem often personifies the city, and this personification suggests that the characters identify with the city or see the city as an external manifestation of their own inner world. Thus the second paradox about the view of the city as a totality is that it is thoroughly subjective and yet is pronounced as a universal, eternal truth about the city. This paradox is not unique to Oz's novel; it may also be found, in a particularly explicit form, in a short statement in A. B. Yehoshua's novella, "Three Days and a Child": "One has to take a clear stand about (*keneged*) Jerusalem. One cannot pass through in silence. I claim that Jerusalem is a hard town. A harsh town, sometimes. Don't trust its modesty, its gentleness that isn't gentle. Look at its sealed stone houses."[29]

Though in interviews Shahar was not averse to "taking a stand" about Jerusalem, presenting his subjective relation to the city as a generalized statement about the city's dystopic/utopic "essence,"[30] in the *Palace* novels neither the narrator nor the characters indulge in this kind of aphoristic pronouncement. The city, as we have shown, is never projected as a totality, and the part of the city that is the main setting for the novel's action cannot be made to stand for the whole because of its irreducible heterogeneity and otherness—its "hetero-topic" nature. As we shall show in the next chapter, neither can the characters (who in some sense embody this part of the city) be made to stand for a collective. From this it follows that they cannot consider their subjective relation to this part of the city a general truth about the city as a whole. Thus Shahar's Jerusalem, neither a utopia nor a dystopia, is also never a "symbol."

An Urban Idyll

The Jerusalem of the British Mandate period was more than a provincial town and less than a metropolis. During the thirty years of British rule, its population increased steadily (from about 50,000 in 1917 to about 90,000 in 1931 and about 160,000 in 1947).[31] The relative weight of the Old City diminished as most newcomers and many old residents settled in new, modern neighborhoods; this shift was particularly strong among the Jewish population (the number of Jews living in the Old City decreased from about 19,000 in 1900 to less than 2,500 by 1947).[32] The city recovered its long-lost status as the capital, and the British put considerable resources into modernizing it (water system, sewage, railroad, new roads, etc.) while also preserving its historical character. The population remained diverse (all visitors comment on the variety of clothing and customs), with the British themselves introducing yet another element into the cosmopolitan mix. The presence of the British as well as the large influx of highly educated Jews (primarily from Germany) and the opening of the Hebrew University on Mount Scopus (in 1925) all contributed to the creation of a polyglot cultural elite in the city. With the opening of the King David Hotel in 1930, the city could boast a grand hotel, worthy of foreign dignitaries and celebrities. The city's elite led a busy social life, of the sort one led in the big cities of Europe, with "salons" and "at homes"; the number of cafés, restaurants, and movie theaters increased.

Though Jerusalem was no longer a rundown Oriental town in the backwaters of a crumbling empire, it was not exactly a modern metropolis either. To a large extent the city remained determined by its past—a traditional, conservative town par excellence. This was very much the view of the Labor-dominated Zionist mainstream, which tended to regard Jerusalem as provincial and backward, the bastion of conservative, if not downright reactionary, forces, as opposed to the budding real metropolis, Tel Aviv.[33]

If we assume that the time/space of a novel is never simply a given (as a naively mimetic approach would have it) then we need to ponder the implications for the *Palace* sequence of the hybrid nature of its time/space, or—to use Bakhtin's term—its "chronotope." According to Bakhtin, the chronotope is the organizing principle of a narrative, toward which "all the novel's abstract elements—philosophical and social generalizations, ideas, analyses of cause and effect—gravitate . . . and take on flesh and blood"[34]; he uses this notion primarily to distinguish between narrative genres. Following Bakhtin's lead, we propose that some aspects of Shahar's novel sequence make sense in terms of a "mixed" chronotope: it has elements that belong to the tradition of the "provincial novel" (which Bakhtin briefly describes as one of the novelistic developments of the idyll in the eighteenth century[35]), while other elements are better understood in terms of urban literature (or, more specifically, the "urban novel"), theorized by many critics, from Walter Benjamin to Franco Moretti.[36] In this mixture of elements from two, ostensibly incompatible, worlds and genres, the constitutive motifs and structures of each genre impinge on those of the other and change them; together they create a hybrid form that we can call "an urban idyll."

Idyllic time is everyday time, repetitive or cyclical in nature, detached from the "progressive forces of history"[37]; idyllic space is a delimited locale in which the characters are "at home." Their combination into the idyllic "chronotope" is clearly a feature of Shahar's *Palace* novels, but the idyllic chronotope is modified by, and in turn modifies, elements that pertain to the urban novel. The privileged space of the modern urban novel is neither private (home) nor public (forum, public square) but a space in between the private and the public, exemplified by cafés, theaters, and shops.[38] It is in these spaces that the modern urban experience par excellence—the passing, chance encounter—takes place. Time in the modern urban novel is discontinuous, marked by happy coincidences and missed opportunities; space is open, infinitely available, and yet limited by partial exclusions and inaccessibilities.[39] Characters in the modern urban novel are always mobile, in search of that which escapes them (in time) or is inaccessible to them (in space).

As we have seen, characters' centrality in the *Palace* novels does not depend on their mobility but on the extent to which they can be firmly located in and identified with a limited, privileged space. On the whole, they restrict themselves to their small world and do not explore other areas of the city. Gentilla Luria goes to the Red Ear's grocery store, to Gutkin's house, and to Dr. Landau's clinic; the latter moves between his home and workplace nearby; Srulik shuttles between his home, the Teachers' College, and the Bnei Brit Library, all within the same neighborhood; Gabriel, it is true, roams around, going to Mount Scopus and the Tombs of the Sanhedrin (and in that he anticipates and doubles the boy-narrator), but otherwise he seems mostly to stay at home or hang out at the Café Gat down the block. Even important events in these characters' lives do not take them far away: when Orita Gutkin marries Dr. Landau, she moves only a few meters away from her father's house, just as Gentilla, when snatched by the Old Bey from her school, is settled by him in a house just up the street. Gabriel comes back from his long years in France to his father's house (in a chapter entitled "The Return of the Prodigal Son" [Greeting the Returning Son—*Kabalat hapanim laben hahozer*]), and the narrator, coming back from Paris, hurries to the old neighborhood, to the "basement of his childhood" (*Ghosts*, 20). Both Srulik and, later on, Tammuz come back to Jerusalem. These returns to the father's house, to childhood, to one's true identity, show the enduring validity of the small world, its being the characters' true "home."

This principle may be confirmed by a counterexample. As we have shown before, the area around Street of the Prophets "attracts" characters that "originate" in other areas and become characters in the novel by entering this small world. The only character who never gains a firm foothold in the area of Street of the Prophets is Lea Himmelsach. This does not mean that she does not turn up there with alarming frequency, but rather that her link to that area does not carry greater narrative weight than her link to other spaces. Lea is, we may say, "spatially promiscuous" (but, it is important to emphasize, even she, a highly mobile character and in many respects an "outsider," never ventures either into the new western suburbs or into the Old City). She first lived in Sanhedria and then moved all the way to the other side of town, to Mishkenot Sha-ananim; she sits in Café Peter in the German colony, in Café Atara on Ben Yehuda street, as well as in Café Paramount and Café Gat; she attends concerts in the Edison theater and often visits the main post office on Jaffa Street; she goes for a walk with Daoud in the Schneller Wood and with her editor in the Rose Garden; she twice "mounts the barricades" near the Tombs of the Sanhedrin; she enlightens the Arabs in historical materialism, first at the home of Gabriel Luria and then in the Bnei Brit Library; she receives Betzalel students at her home and opens an exhibition in Nahalat Shiv'ah; she goes with her friend, Anastasia Wissotzky, to Shealtiel's bookstore, visits Judge Gutkin at his home, and confers with Dr. Zondack in his hospital, Bikur Holim. She seems to be all over the place but does not belong in any one place. She considers herself a cosmopolitan and Gabriel a backward provincial from the Old City (*Nin-Gal*, 144), perhaps with some truth, but the novel's valorization of identification between individuals and a specific space turns her spatial mobility into a negative trait. Lea Himmelsach is undoubtedly the character most despised by the author among the entire population of the novel sequence, the object of vitriolic satiric treatment.

The correlation between person and place, the being-at-home-in-the-world that is the object of the narrator's nostalgia, curiously coexists with the novels' representation of several characters as homeless: Berl and his brother Haim Longlife grew up in an orphanage (*Countess*, 154); Haim Longlife does not seem to have a permanent home and at various periods is hiding from his creditors in different places. Elka and Ethel were orphaned in their childhood and were "left alone in the big house," prey to neighbors and "friends" who tried to take advantage of them (*Voyage*, 29–30; 246). Shoshi, who also grew up in an orphanage, is obsessed with the desire to have a place of her own, but when she finally gets what she wanted (her husband, Reb Yitzhok, purchases a house and registers it in her name), she feels "the taste of dust and ashes in her mouth . . . Shoshi's house exists and stands, but Shoshi herself is dead and gone" (*Countess*, 222).

The depiction of orphans and homeless people functions as a "realistic" counterweight to the idealizing tendency inherent in nostalgic representation, but it is important to note that homelessness in Shahar is not the result of changes in (or the loss of) the old, idealized world-home of the narrator's childhood. Homelessness and orphanhood are not here the signs of the disintegration of an old, traditional, stable world (the world of the "provincial novel"), of the alienation that presumably characterizes life in an urban center. Historically speaking, they seem appropriate elements in a realistic description of a turn-of-the-century Jerusalem, backward, poverty stricken, and dependent on philanthropic support. Realism and idyllic/idealized representation in Shahar cannot be mapped onto the oppositions of new versus old, modern versus traditional, urban center versus provincial town.

The affinity between the *Palace* novels and the modern urban novel is most obvious in the novels' depiction of social interaction among characters as taking place, on the whole, in spaces that are neither private nor public (in the sense of devoted to public affairs). With the important exception of the Luria house (to be discussed shortly), the preferred spaces of social interaction in the *Palace* novels are cafés, hotels, a library, and a clinic. Whereas this kind of space often is used in urban novels to evoke an experience of anonymity and the tension between availability and inaccessibility, between "physical proximity and mental or social distance,"[40] in Shahar's novels, these archetypal urban spaces have a small-town character: everybody knows everybody else in the Café Gat or Cancan and at the Bnei Brit Library. At the same time, what characterizes these spaces is their nonexclusivity: the familiarity is not the result of homogeneity. Practically anybody may enter the lobby of the luxurious King David Hotel (though only a Lord Radcliff can afford a suite there); Dr. Landau's eye clinic brings together poor Arab fellahin and the old Bey's wife; and the Bnei Brit Library is open to Orita and Gabriel, as well as to marginal figures such as Srulik's aunts, Ethel and Elka, and street bums (who are driven out only later on, in the days of the more "progressive" and efficient librarian, Devora Kalmanson). At first there seems to be an opposition (as well as a competition) between the two cafés—Gat and Cancan: the first serves "high society . . . British gentlemen and Arab effendis" (*Voyage*, 112; 340), whereas the other caters to "the leaders of *Plugat ha'avoda* [labor detail]" (*Voyage*, 110; 338); the first is run by the exotic Yossef Shwili, "the best barman in the Middle East," whereas the other is operated by the prosaic Fat Pesach; the first is patronized by Orita and Gabriel—handsome and young—and the other by Yaeli and Berl, not so handsome and not so young. But the novel, as we have shown, does not depend on such oppositions for its plot or themes and therefore they are subsequently dropped or blurred: Berl wrote his poems at the Café Gat, Gabriel is among the customers at Café Cancan. This does not mean that the novel is blind to socioeconomic differences; far from it. The childhood poverty of some of the characters (Gentilla Luria, Srulik, Oded) is dwelt upon at some length, and the social marginality of Rosa or Haim Longlife is central to their characterization. Orita Landau is clearly different from Lea Himmelsach or

Shoshi Raban, and only the Gutkins and the Lurias are ever invited to the receptions held by the High Commissioner. Still, social differences per se are not one of the novel's chief interests. Though it insists on the plurality and heterogeneity of its human world, it does not link this heterogeneity to any agonized consciousness of difference, invidious comparison, or sense of deprivation and envy. This may be interpreted as simply a symptom of Shahar's idealizing nostalgia, but again it is important to point out that if the world he represents is one where the sense of alienation and exclusion is nearly absent from the characters' experience, it is not because this world is homogeneous and conformist. The object of Shahar's nostalgia is not a "traditional" society where everyone has his or her place (as opposed to the modern mass society of alienation and exclusion) but a world that tolerates plurality and allows each person to pursue his or her individual, idiosyncratic project.

The most important place of social interaction in the novel, however, is the Luria house. Most of the characters mentioned in the novel are in some way associated with this space, which also is the site of two (of the few) large gatherings described in the novel (Brunhilde's concert and Lea's first lecture on dialectical materialism). However, only two parts of the Luria house are of narrative importance: the verandah and the basement.[41] Indeed, the interior of the house—the living quarters of the narrator and his family or of Gabriel—are not even described. This is equally true of the interiors of other houses (e.g., Gutkin's or Landau's). The verandah, where most social interactions in the Luria house happen, is a liminal space between inside and outside, private and public. It is an ambiguous space in yet another sense. The initial reference to the house specifies that the narrator's family occupied its upper part, and that Mrs. Luria kept for herself only the part "under the stairway"; the verandah is situated over her part of the house (*Summer*, 23; 19). Though the verandah is nominally included in the space rented by the narrator's family, and though we see him lying there, reading, it also is the center of the Luria household: this is where the Old Bey used to sit in his red chair, where Mrs. Luria receives guests such as Dan Gutkin, and where Gabriel shaves every morning. This contradiction may be explained by the implicit identification between the narrator and Gabriel Luria.[42] The verandah is the space of social interaction but also the locus of identification—where the experiential spheres of Gabriel and the narrator merge. In opposition to the verandah, the basement is a concealed, private space, but insofar as it is the place where both Gabriel and Berl retire to write, and where both lead their clandestine love affairs, it too is a space where characters merge rather than simply interact.

Certain forms of identification in Shahar seem to overcome the sense of inaccessibility or exclusion so prevalent in the modern urban novel. Thus one of the most highly invested objects in his Jerusalem urban scape—the stone fence—does not function, contrary to our expectations, as a sign of exclusion.

The stone fences for which the narrator (as well as Gabriel) often expresses his fondness (see, e.g., *Summer*, 78, 130, 213; 64, 114, 201; *Countess*, 31–32) characterize old Jerusalem, as opposed to the modern one (*Summer*, 130; 114). Although the narrator comments on the beauty of the pink Jerusalem stone, especially in opposition to the ugly, gray cement ("I feel like laying my cheek on the hewn stone and drinking its color. A block of concrete fills a hole in the fence with gray opaqueness that does not radiate anything and I say to myself: 'The stone is alive and the cement is dead'," *Countess*, 31), what really attracts him to stone fences is that they enclose a mysterious, secret world (see, e.g., *Summer*, 213; 201; *Countess*, 32). The analogy, however, between the fence and the cover of a book, between the houses behind the fence and works of literature, suggests that this mystery *can* be penetrated, that the concealed world lying behind the fence is not inaccessible. Watching the stone fences on his way to the library, the narrator reflects:

> These thick, opaque, stone walls, entirely surrounding the life stored up inside them, were like the stiff covers of the books come back from the binder's; standing side by side, they presented a closed, uniform face while each and every one of them sheltered a separate flow of life, unique and distinct in its color and sound and flavor and individual twists and turns. I longed to enter the gates in the garden walls, just as I was eager to open the covers of the library books, because I yearned for the wonderful, unique world of the life hidden behind their blank, protective outer coverings. (*Summer*, 78, 64. For the analogy between houses and books, see also *Countess*, 32)

Turned from a reader into a writer whose literary practice depends to a large extent on his ability to enter the minds of his characters, the narrator of the short story "First Lesson" sees himself as "a kind of medium" and compares himself to a fence (albeit a wooden one): "If this fence were to write down its sensations they would surely resemble my own" (*Pope*, 248; *News*, 216). The fence here is not the cover of a book, dividing the imaginary world from the real one, but rather the narrator himself situated in a border zone "between the inside world and the outside world" (*Pope*, 247; *News*, 216), between his own consciousness and that of others.

Identification with the other can, of course, reduce its otherness, eliminate the mystery; at its limit, it can turn the plurality and heterogeneity of the novelistic world into a merely apparent one (different cover, same story, so to speak). While Shahar does not seem particularly interested in the epistemological question of knowing the other *qua* other, he does show awareness of the violent potential of the act of identification (as our discussion of an episode from *Nin-Gal*, in the next chapter, will show). In terms of the representation of Jerusalem, otherness and violence come together at the border—another highly invested element of the cityscape—especially as this becomes the militarized, impenetrable cease-fire line at the heart of the city. As we can expect by now, the border for Shahar is not a site where an inaccessible or even a forbidden world might be within sight but permanently out of reach. Though the novel spans the period between the early 1920s and the late 1980s we never see the narrator or any other major character stationed behind barbed wire, longing to revisit old places (such as Mount of Olives or Mount Scopus), now across the border in Jordanian East Jerusalem, nor do we find him expressing joy when these sites become accessible once again after June 1967.

Yet the border is an important element in his narrative. The Street of the Prophets is described as a border zone, beyond which lie the potentially violent worlds of the Arabs and of the Jewish ultra-orthodox. The narrator also takes pains to point out that several locations, which to readers of short memory may seem unmarked in the continuous Israeli space of Jerusalem were at one time (between 1948 and 1967) zones of violence on a dangerous frontier (see, e.g., the description of Yaeli Landau's apartment in Abu Tor [*Tammuz*, 44], the description of the vocational school Meretz where the adult narrator and Aharon Dan teach [*Nin-Gal*, 9], or the description of the room in Independence Park, where the narrator spends time doing guard duty with Rahamim [*Nin-Gal*, 87]). What lies behind the border is not some otherness tantalizing by its combination of proximity and inaccessibility, but one felt as posing a threat to the (heterogeneous, pluralist) world cherished by the narrator. However, the converse also is true: as we shall see in the next chapter, this violent "other" is the other who lost his or her individuality by being absorbed into a homogenizing group—a mob. Its coming into being in the political-historical arena coincides with the reduction of the idealized heterogeneity of the childhood world and its forcing into a specular opposition.

Chapter 4

Otherness, Identity, and Place

Shahar is not often thought of as an author who deals with the "Arab question," and studies dealing with the treatment of this topic in Israeli literature hardly ever mention his name.[1] It is true that the narrative of *The Palace of Shattered Vessels* does not seem, at least at first sight, a particularly hospitable context for the discussion of political and ideological issues. Yet the narrator's repeated insistence that the day on which the "Bloody Events" of 1936 began was a crucial one in his life, a day that "divided time and the world in two," while puzzling in itself, suggests that the Arab-Jewish conflict is not absent from his novel.[2] Another narrative detail that invites further study is the close, detailed, and increasingly sympathetic development in the novel sequence of the character of Daoud Ibn Mahmoud, Judge Gutkin's chauffeur. Even more significant than the events of 1936 or the character of Daoud are recurrent patterns of representation bearing on questions of identity, in relation both to ethnic and national affiliation and to territory or place. In the latter part of this chapter, we offer analyses of several passages where Shahar tackles national-historical issues head on; we also provide a brief discussion of the presence and implications of the Canaanite ideological paradigm in his work. In following this itinerary, we identify a fundamental ambiguity, even a contradiction, in Shahar's treatment of these issues. While at a "personal," "phenomenological" level, Shahar adopts a flexible, pluralistic attitude toward questions of identity, the closer he gets to an explicit thematization of the Jewish-Arab conflict, the more he tends to slide into a rigid, nationalist position.

Fluid Identities and Violent Mobs

Shahar's fictional recreation of the events of 1936[3] centers around three separate killings: of a Jew, an Arab, and a British policeman. While this seems to suggest an allegorical, almost mechanical, representation of the political conflict, the picture is complicated by the observation that at the scene of their death, all three appear out of character and are in some sense misrecognized. Thus the boy-narrator, hearing from Dr. Zondack that the mob is coming out of the mosques and approaching the nearest Jewish neighborhoods, comes running into the street only to see Gabriel Luria sitting by a dead rioter whom he has apparently just killed. When the British policeman, who arrives within minutes, turns the body over and reveals its face, the boy and Gabriel are shocked to discover that it is none other than Daoud Ibn Mahmoud, until very recently Judge Gutkin's loyal chauffeur. Neither Gabriel nor the boy-narrator had at first recognized Daoud who, unaccountably, is dressed in traditional Arab clothes. The question uppermost in the boy's mind at the moment of recognition is "why all of a sudden he [Daoud] decided to disguise himself as a Bedouin or a fellah from el-djabel" (*Countess*, 138). The policeman tells Gabriel that William Gordon, the chief of the Mahaneh Yehuda police station, also has died in the riots. Having returned to Jerusalem from a leave just as the crowd started gathering, Gordon hurried, still in his civilian clothes and armed with his camera, to the Damascus Gate. There he was seized by the mob as a Jewish spy and killed on the spot (*Countess*, 139–40). A few days prior to the outbreak of the riots, another character, Louidor the Silent, was caught and killed in Wadi Kelt, outside of Jericho, by "Arab thugs from Abu Issa's gang" (*Countess*, 111).[4] When two Arab shepherds tried to stop the killing by saying that Louidor was a "Jewish holy man," the murderers replied that he was a "Zionist spy" (ibid.). Two days earlier, the boy-narrator was astounded to hear from Berl that the "*willi*"—or "Moslem holy man"—they both saw near the Jaffa Gate was none other than Louidor; he then remembered hearing that Louidor had been seen in Ramlah dressed in Bedouin garb, and that Mrs. Luria refused to believe that this was, indeed, Louidor (*Countess*, 94).

The error or misrecognition in each of the three killings raises some doubts about the "true" identity of the victims, as well as some uncertainty about their own loyalties and affiliation to a group. The most obvious case of divided loyalties is that of Daoud, who up until this point in the story regarded Judge Gutkin as his adoptive father, was passionately, though respectfully, in love with the judge's beautiful daughter, Orita, admired Gabriel Luria as he had admired his old father, and seemed a staunch supporter of the British Empire (*Countess*, 50).[5] Daoud's sudden conversion to Arab nationalism is never clearly explained in the novel (just as the even more unexpected conversion to Calvinism by Srulik never is). The most likely explanation is that it was a defensive response against the provocative intimacy of Jewish women (Orita, who invites him to dance with her in the street [*Countess*, 45–46], and Lea Himmelsach, who seduces him when they go out for a walk [*Ghosts*, 184–88]). As to Gordon, the early volumes of the novel tell us little about him other than to note that he was much more interested in his hobby—photography—than in his work as a police officer. His lack of zeal for his work may have stemmed from his being torn between loyalty to the British and sympathy for the Jewish cause. The very choice of the name "Gordon" suggests this ambiguity. On the one hand, it is a Scottish name, borne by numerous servants of the British empire, notably General Charles George Gordon (1833–1885), who distinguished himself in China, Africa, and India. On the other hand, it is a Russian-Jewish name, borne by several prominent Jewish figures: Yehuda Leib Gordon (1831–1892), a poet, critic, and journalist, a key spokesman of the *Haskala*; the biblical commentator, Shemuel Leib Gordon (1865–1933); and, most importantly perhaps, the major ideologist of the Zionist Labor movement, Aharon David Gordon (1856–1922).[6] In Louidor's case, the confusion of identities is even more remarkable: a Jew who left Europe under the conviction that his like would always be despised among the Gentiles, he arrives in Palestine only to find out, to his dismay, that the land is full of Arabs rather than empty. He then concludes that the only solution is for the Arabs to evacuate the land. Since as long as he remains a Jew he cannot, in good faith, urge them to leave, he converts to Islam and turns into an itinerant preacher.[7]

Thus even at a moment of extreme polarization—the violent confrontation between Jews and Arabs and Arabs and British in 1936—the novel does not present us simply with a conflict between groups or between individuals who plainly stand for these groups. Shahar's representation of the relations among individuals belonging to different ethnic and religious groups in Palestine under the British Mandate cannot be read as a plain national *allegory* (as is the case, for example, with some of Benjamin Tammuz's narratives dealing with the same time period, such as *The Orchard*), since his characters resist neat categorization and opposition to other neatly categorized characters. This, of course, does not mean that his fictional depiction of the 1936 riots does not address this political conflict in a meaningful way.

Daoud, Louidor, and Gordon are not exceptional characters in the novel; indeed, we can say that what characterizes many members of the small community described by Shahar is that their identity is somewhat indeterminate. These three characters, however, seem to pay with their lives for their failure to define themselves unambiguously as belonging to one particular group.[8] The time before the world was "split in two" is presented as a time when hybrid identities and shifting alliances were possible, before clear-cut divisions, identities, and group affiliations asserted themselves in moments of violence. In *The Palace of Shattered Vessels*, then, the 1936 riots mark a mythical moment in which a prepolitical world of private and free individuals is violently articulated by a nationalist logic into clear-cut identities with public and political validity. But 1936 also marks the end of the narrator-protagonist's childhood, and the infantile world he must take leave of is overdetermined (as we have argued in chapter 1) by the curious logic of the uncanny, where the boundary between discrete identities is porous, and chunks of experience can migrate from one person to another. In the resulting narrative developments, the challenging of rigid, unitary, and impoverished conceptions of the self on the thematic level will therefore echo the fusion between distinct characters on the narrative level. By collapsing together a "historical" and a "biographical" event, the world of childhood—the object of the adult narrator's nostalgia—appears as a nonpolitical paradise and the world of pre-1936 Palestine as a mythical, undifferentiated wholeness, before the "breaking of the vessels." From this perspective, the violence of being interpellated by a group, which limits the freedom of individuals to define themselves and which the narrator repeatedly deplores, takes on a more ambiguous connotation insofar as it may be associated with the need to resist the seduction of the uncanny and live up to the standards of common sense required by the adult world.

Again and again the novel depicts persons whose belonging to a group is "unorthodox" and who pay the price for their failure to conform. Mrs. Luria's father, the skilled carpenter from the Old City, is driven to extreme poverty by the synagogue officials who withhold his wages; he accepts, in his desperation, a commission to make wooden crosses for the Russian Monastery on Mount of Olives. This brings about his being stoned by the synagogue officials, who even go so far as setting his house on fire (*Summer*, 90–93; 73–76). Srulik, who has converted to Christianity and returned to Jerusalem as a Calvinist missionary while still considering himself a loyal Jew (*Summer*, 122; 106), is attacked by a crowd of ultra-orthodox Jews demonstrating against missionaries. Immediately upon seeing him, they "began spitting in his face and cursing and reviling him and some of them even went so far as to lay hands on him, slapping his face hard on both cheeks, pulling the spectacles from his nose and tearing his coat" (*Summer* 127; 111). Konstantin Shapiro (a Jewish poet in Russia admired by Louidor's father), who dreams of Jewish revival in the land of Israel, is punished by his orthodox father and thrown out of his home for reading Hebrew poetry and smoking on the Ninth of Av. Years later, having converted to Christianity in order to marry the daughter of the woman who saved him in his hour of need, and having become a successful photographer, he sends money to Hovevei Tzion, only to be rejected once again when his donation is refused (*Countess*, 97–99).

The clearest examples of group violence against individuals in Shahar's novels come from the world of ultra-orthodox Judaism. This, however, is not so much because Shahar has a particular score to settle with this extremist faction, but because he seems to consider all groups extremist: to command allegiance, groups have to insist on sharp demarcations that destroy the possibility of mixed identities shuttling back and forth between loosely defined, partially overlapping, collectivities. The violent call of religious institutions and sects is opposed to genuine religious experience which, in Shahar, not surprisingly, tends to be of the mystical variety, where, precisely, distinct identities are lost. Freeing himself from the clutches of the crowd during the "coronation" of the Sephardic Chief Rabbi, the boy runs away, out of the city, to Mount Scopus, where he commands a view over the whole city: "Everything seemed clear and self explanatory and having its cause within it as if I were not one child, a little creature looking at the space surrounding him, but on the contrary: Jerusalem itself with the mountains around it, and with the space that surrounds the mountains and the sky, all these were inside me and it was my body that was encircling them, and from it they originated and in it they existed" (*Countess*, 91–92).[9] In this moment of merging with the entire landscape, the child finds the meaning of the word "God" in a mystical experience that is explicitly contrasted to the rituals instituted by religion to impose distinctions between members of the group and others. The individualism Shahar opposes to group allegiance is not that of a rigid personal identity within well-defined boundaries; such rigidity is, on the contrary, the hallmark of group self-definition. His individualism has to do, rather, with the potential fluidity of self-identity and with the refusal to be permanently bound by a finite profile. In other words, Shahar does not see individuality as it is commonly defined: a coherent essence or a unique set of features that sets a person apart from everyone else. What is important for him in the notion of individuality is the freedom of self-fashioning, seen as the potential to be many different things.

Given his view of the inherent violence of the collective in relation to individuals, Shahar tends to describe groups as crowds, indeed as a violent mob, endangering the freedom of the individual (the freedom not to be determined by the group) and inspiring fear. On the eve of the "enchanted day," the boy finds his way to the Jaffa Gate, where a crowd has gathered around an Arab "*willi*" who may or may not be Louidor. The narrator comments that even though there was no hint of violence in the crowd, nothing to indicate brewing trouble, he experienced fear and wanted to run away, since in his experience all crowds end up violent (*Countess*, 81). He lists examples, ranging from his own experience a week earlier during the "coronation" of the new Sephardic Chief Rabbi to a story he heard from his grandmother about events that took place in the Nativity Church during the visit of some important Ottoman dignitary there (*Countess*, 81–90). The violent potential of crowds is thus represented as affecting Jews as well as Arabs, Christians as well as Moslems.

From this perspective, the violence of the 1936 riots would be just one instance of crowd behavior, one that happens to pit Jews against Arabs. This line of thinking gains some support from the fact that the traumatic witnessing of violence by the ten-year-old boy-narrator in the summer of 1936 resembles other traumatic events witnessed by the two other participants in the scene, that is, Gabriel and Daoud. The boy, we recall, sees Gabriel crouching, dagger in hand, by the body of Daoud. It is very likely that this Daoud Ibn Mahmoud is the same Daoud Ibn Mahmoud who, in an earlier volume, was said to have witnessed his father's murder with a dagger that could be the same as the one now used by Gabriel (*Summer*, 104–105; 88–90). Gabriel, too, at age ten, was witness to a scene of violence when, on the same day that Mahmoud Effendi (who may be Daoud's father) is killed, he and his own father (who later bought the dagger that killed Mahmoud Effendi) are nearly trampled by an Arab mob not seeking to kill but demanding "Baksheesh" (*Summer*, 215–17; 204–207). The slight uncertainty that the narrator maintains about the two Daouds and the two daggers being the same (see, e.g., *Summer*, 113, 117; 98, 100) is yet another manifestation of the poetics of flirting with the uncanny.[10] What the boy-narrator witnesses is also what Daoud and Gabriel have witnessed because, as we have said, in the boy's world of fluid identities, experiences "migrate" among different subjectivities in the same way that objects can circulate. This latter point is made explicit earlier on, when the boy hears for the first time the story of Mahmoud Effendi's murder and the purchase of the dagger by the old Bey, Gabriel's father. He himself has just stolen a dagger from the old Bey's cellar, and after hearing the story, he feels he must return it, not for "fear at the curse that lay on this dagger, but rather by a . . . feeling that when I had stolen it from the damp cellar floor and placed it in my warm trouser pocket I had broken into the framework of a life that was not mine . . . as if I had forced my way into a holy shrine and violated its sanctity by my presence" (*Summer*, 111–12; 96–97). No matter how guilty the boy feels about this transgression, it is clear that the narrative depends, to a large degree, on precisely such crossings of boundaries and a melting of personal identities.

Though the 1936 riots are, in some sense, but one example of crowd behavior, it does not follow that the "Arab" is purely one semantic filler among others for a general notion of "group violence." Rather, in the representation of the continuum of ethnic and religious identities in Palestine, and the way they repeatedly get differentiated and polarized, the Arab occupies a specific, though paradoxical, position. As we have seen, ultra-orthodox Ashkenazi Jews are the narrator's prime example for the assault of groups on unorthodox individuals. To the extent that Arabs in the novel are involved in acts of violence they are, implicitly or explicitly, likened to these Ashkenazi zealots. That the Arabs, in Shahar's depiction of 1936, are repeatedly said to have emerged out of the mosques where they have been incited to violence by Islamic preachers makes them another example of religious intolerance and thus similar, rather than opposed, to the Ashkenazi Jews. The narrator himself draws our attention to this similarity when he tells of the "holy wars" waged by Reb Itzhok against "transgressing" Jews (*Countess*, 85–88), for instance, when he attacks a young couple (probably Kibbutzniks) strolling outside of his store in what he considers inappropriate attire. In the later volumes of the *Palace* and in the posthumous fragment *To the Mount of Olives*, the analogy between the Arabs and the ultra-orthodox Jews is even more explicit, in keeping with these volumes' tendency to show the Arabs in a unidimensional way.[11] Nowhere does this analogy receive a clearer representation than in an episode of *To the Mount of Olives*, where an Israeli reporter, returning by car from an interview with a Palestinian leader, is first shot at by Palestinian terrorists and then stoned by some orthodox Jews (10–18, 41). However, in the earlier volumes of the novel, we find also a different constellation: the Ashkenazi Jews, who are always driven to aggression by their religious zeal, are opposed to the Sephardic Jews, who are seen by the narrator as moderate and tolerant (*Countess*, 89), and the Sephardic Jews are culturally likened to the Arabs. Thus, at least in the earlier volumes of the novel, the Arab is both a figure of dichotomization and violence, similar in this to the Ashkenazi Jews, and a figure of fluidity and moderation, like the Sephardic Jew.

In a general way, Shahar's characterization of the Oriental, whether Jew or Arab, draws on stereotypical attributes and properties that clearly come under the critique of Orientalist discourse. This critique, of course, remains valid, even when the attribution of stereotypical characteristics to the other is felt as sympathizing or otherwise positive. What makes Shahar's use of such stereotypes peculiar is that he highlights the continuity between the oriental Jew and the Arab, whereas a prevailing tendency in elaborations of mainstream Zionist narrative has been to drive as wide as possible a wedge between them. The continuity between oriental Jew and Arab can be seen in the characterization of Yehuda Prosper Bey, Gabriel's father.

Like his friend, the Christian Arab Boulos Effendi, Yehuda Prosper is a merchant dealing in antiquities and art objects. The basement where he used to store his treasures in the heyday of his career is described in terms that remind us of an oriental bazaar or a palace from the *Thousand and One Nights*: covered with carpets, with swords and javelins sparkling on its walls, and its armoires bursting with jewels and rich materials (*Countess*, 122). The old Bey also resembles another important Arab character, the Moslem Mahmoud Effendi. As we have seen, these two characters are associated through a dagger, but another link between them is that both are bigamists. Mahmoud Effendi is killed when he comes to Jerusalem to buy a gift for his third wife, a young girl named Dunya (*Summer*, 104–105, 217; 88–89, 206). The elderly Bey, married and the father of five, seduces the beautiful sixteen-year-old Gentilla, whom he then establishes as his "Jerusalem wife" as opposed to his Sephardic "Jaffa wife."[12] This new matrimonial relation hardly stops him from having other affairs, notably with Pnina, his Jerusalem wife's sister. This bigamy cum adultery, this excessive sexuality, is repeatedly linked to the Bey's orientality, to his being, as his Jerusalem wife repeatedly calls him, "an old Turkish lecher."[13] In a passage that reports (in free indirect discourse) Mrs. Luria's nostalgic reminiscing about the old days when she was first married to the Bey, a causal relation is even established between the old Bey's lust and the Ottoman rule over Palestine: "As long as the Turks ruled the country, until the breaking of the war, his lust knew no boundaries" (*Countess*, 122).

The scene of the Bey's desire for her in the early days of their marriage—the basement filled with exotic treasures—is not only an oriental bazaar, but also a sexual paradise and therefore a specifically Moslem paradise. Shahar is keen on observing that what distinguishes the Moslem paradise from its Jewish or Christian counterparts and makes it superior to them is the presence in it of sexuality—that is, of the material body. In the last volume of the *Palace, Of Candles and Winds*, Gabriel reflects that the Jewish paradise, replete with choice foods, odorous flowers, and precious jewels, goes only halfway toward acknowledging the body, since it does not allow for sexuality; this is precisely what the Moslem paradise does do by providing young virgins for the justly deserved pleasures of the righteous (*Candles*, 34–38). It goes without saying that this is a male chauvinist fantasy from which Shahar as author is not exempt. While this may be one of Shahar's ideological blind spots, his adamant refusal to condone the rejection of or abstraction from the physical, which we see in his characters' preference for the Moslem paradise, stems from the complex problematics discussed in the first chapter. The old Bey's association with beautiful material objects and with sexuality, which codes him as "oriental," closer culturally and temperamentally to his Arab neighbors than to his Ashkenazi Jewish ones, also makes him a kin spirit to the narrator/author.

In the scene referred to earlier, where Mrs. Luria remembers the happy days in the basement, we read that "the old lecher" would cover her naked body with jewelry because he had "oriental fantasies." The tendency to "fantasies," "imagination," and "dreaming" is attributed repeatedly by Mrs. Luria to her husband and is explained by his being Oriental: "The old man was Oriental, all Orientals are full of fantasies. All his life the old man was immersed in oriental fantasies" (*Summer*, 51; 42).[14] At the same time Mrs. Luria insists that the old man was also a shrewd merchant, anchored with both his feet in the world of reality (*Countess*, 28). Moreover, to the extent that "oriental fantasy" denotes the propensity to take leave of solid reality, indulge in dreams rather than act, it tends to blur with what Mrs. Luria calls "Jerusalem daydreaming" [*batlanut yerushalmit*], whose clearest manifestation is the absorption in the study of scriptures. The Bey himself is "guilty" of this when, toward the end of his life, he becomes obsessed with "Our Master Moses." When Mrs. Luria rages against her husband for his excessive interest in "our Master Moses"

(*Summer*, 40; 32–33), she indirectly accuses him of neglecting her both because of his retreat to the world of the spirit (his absorption in scriptures) and because of his sexual appetite (the title of the chapter, "Moses and the Ethiopian Woman" reminds us of Moses' own sexual excess and suggests that the old Bey's interest in him may derive from their similarity in this respect). What characterizes the old Bey, then, is his duality (his strong investment both in material objects and in the world of spirit, both in sexuality and in religion) as well as his ability to shuttle back and forth between two opposed worlds (the world of the imagination and that of reality). It is in this sense that the Bey, and through him, the "Oriental," is different from the Ashkenazi Jew: whereas the Ashkenazi Jew is seen as being keen on keeping a distinct identity, forever requiring separation and polarization, not tolerating any in-mixing (hence, his function in the novel as the figure for intolerance and violence), the Oriental becomes the figure for moderation and tolerance because of his ability to occupy and move between different worlds. In this sense, the death of the old Bey a short time before the eruption of violence between Jews and Arabs in 1936 acquires a symbolic meaning: it announces that a certain way of mediating between supposed opposites has ceased to be possible, replaced by the violence of polarization.

The Portrait of the Narrator As an Arab Chauffeur

The *Palace* sequence includes over fifty odd characters, and their ranking as "main" and "secondary" is not obvious: characters who appear marginal in one volume may turn up to claim centrality in another. Thus it should not surprise us that Daoud, a rather minor character in the first two volumes of the novel, killed off at the end of the third, reappears in the fifth volume as a full-blown character. One of the signs that a "secondary" character has become a "main" character is that he or she stops being merely an object for others (including the narrator) and is allowed a voice of his or her own and an interiority—usually by being given a monologue (addressed to someone else or to oneself, depending on whether the narrator can give plausible motivation to its being heard or not). There are some important exceptions to this rule: thus Gabriel Luria, by all accounts a major character from the moment he appears on page one of the novel, is not given voice, inner feelings, and thoughts until the last part of the first volume; it is even possible to argue that we never really get to know him intimately until the very last volume, *Of Candles and Winds*. This may be motivated by Gabriel's being, in a sense, a mystery for the narrator, being different from, indeed superior to, other characters precisely because of his mysteriousness. Likewise, Orita, another character of great significance in the overall economy of the plot, is given voice only seldom, whether in dialogue or in interior monologue. A possible explanation is that she is posited as the object of desire par excellence—a woman desired by all but possessed by none, whose loving gaze or "light" [*or*] gives life and whose contempt is death—and therefore has to be kept precisely as an object for others. These exceptions do not alter the common principle according to which a major character is one to whose inner world we are given massive access. Such a character is Daoud.

In *Summer in the Street of the Prophets*, we are introduced to Judge Gutkin's Arab driver, who remains nameless (101; 84); a few pages later, the judge himself tells the story of the murder of Mahmoud Effendi, who came to Jerusalem with his youngest son, Daoud, his favorite ["*bno yakiro veyeled sha'ashu'av*"] (105; 88). The identity between these two is not certain, but one thing is: Daoud Ibn Mahmoud, the Arab driver of the old judge, will be killed (117; 100). Death is a fairly common occurrence in Shahar's novel, and the use of narrative anticipation (prolepsis) fits well with the novel's deemphasizing of linear development and suspense. And yet it is rather peculiar that with Daoud barely mentioned, and before we even hear him speak, we are already told that he is going to die.

A Voyage to Ur of the Chaldees mentions Daoud several times, always as the driver of Judge Gutkin (38, 92, 171, 181; 253, 316, 405, 417), and the last mention develops into a full-fledged interior monologue (182–89; 418–27). This monologue attributes to Daoud many of the features of the subservient native, thus casting him in an image typical of an Orientalist or a colonialist discourse: he is shown as being obsessed with honor (as opposed to having moral standards); his job is to serve a colonial official, and he identifies with this job and the apparent power it delegates to him from his colonial masters; he is childishly enamored with the external, trivial paraphernalia of his status (uniform, hat, official car) as well as with the gadgets and symbols of Western civilization (cigarette lighter, camera). The main incident narrated in this monologue—the story of the "great reception" at the High Commissioner's residence—shows Daoud as being totally determined by his relation to his colonial superiors, so much so that having failed to salute the car of the High Commissioner because he could not find his hat in time is said to affect him as a major tragedy. This is not so much an interior monologue as it is a "character sketch" intended to conjure up a type—the Arab chauffeur in the service of the British Empire. The tone is not satirical but rather sympathetically condescending—Daoud is childishly and innocently vain and capable only of trivial concerns. The narrator does not "other" him by marking his language; Daoud's inner speech appears uniform with the language of the general narrator. Characters within Daoud's monologue are presented as having their own idiom—literally, as when Gordon (reported by Daoud) addresses him in English; on the other hand, when Daoud (always within Daoud's monologue) addresses Orita, the text presents his utterance in Hebrew ("*le-an gvirti*?" [Where to Madame?]), adding that he said it "in English" (182; 419). Arab words in his monologue are few (*mastoura, rassia*). Only in the very last lines, when Daoud comes out of his monologue to address Orita, thus merging back into the main narrative, does his Arab idiom and pronunciation (calling Gabriel "Ibn Yehuda" and saying "Bariz" for "Paris") become pronounced. The neutrality of the language is here another sign that even though the passage is cast in the form of "interior monologue," we are not quite "inside" Daoud but rather we read the narrator's portrait of him.

Daoud's first appearance in *Day of the Countess*—the volume in which his death is described for the first time—is in a scene with Mrs. Luria in which both deplore Yaeli Gutkin's attraction to Berl. Before Daoud leaves, Mrs. Luria shows maternal concern for him when she gives him a scarf to wrap around his neck. The narrator concludes the scene by remarking that Daoud was closer than anyone to Mrs. Luria "in his taste and in his views of good and evil and the beautiful and the ugly and the proper road for man to choose for himself" (21), explicitly opposing Daoud to Gabriel. Mrs. Luria is Gabriel's mother, but she also acts, very often, as the boy-narrator's mother.[15] The scene we have just discussed reveals, however, that *her* "favorite son" may be Daoud, who thus becomes the "good double" of both the narrator (they share the same name, David = Daoud) and Gabriel.

The next scene in which Daoud appears is the gathering in the Café Gat on the "enchanted day" (*Countess*, 40 ff.). Daoud and Gordon are opposed to each other (as they were in Daoud's interior monologue in *Voyage*), and we are told that both will die on the same day, a week later. Though Daoud's taste is described by Gordon as "kitsch," the narrator points out that most of the people who frequented the Café Gat—senior government officials, consuls, army officers, and so on—shared Daoud's taste. Daoud is not here to personally exemplify "Arab taste." Watching Gabriel play the violin on the street and later on watching Orita dance and then pass Gabriel's hat as if to collect money, Daoud is beside himself with shame. But his sense of honor and decorum is no longer focused on buttons and hats. Daoud's shame at Gabriel and Orita making a spectacle of themselves is fueled by his memory of another scene, where some Egyptian kids made a spectacle of themselves in an especially offensive way and caused a British soldier to say, "All Arabs are pimps and shameless monkeys" (45). When Orita invites Daoud to dance and he practically flees, the narrator intervenes to create an analogy between this scene and a scene from his own experience after the Six Day War, involving both himself and an Egyptian prisoner (46–47). The coherence of the entire sequence thus rests on analogies that juxtapose Jews and Arabs as well as national pride and honorable male behavior in the face of female provocation.

Exhibiting male self-control in a typical Shaharian scenario, Daoud is no longer the "subservient native" of Orientalist, colonial discourse but rather a double of the narrator. This is his function also in his last appearance, in the novel's last volume, *Of Candles and Winds*. There Daoud appears in Gabriel's dream (or daydream) of the scapegoat, which closes the volume and the whole novel sequence. This dream elaborates on the same scenario of seduction and betrayal of the male subject by a "loving" woman, whose archetype is the mother. As we have seen in chapter 2, this betrayal often is linked in Shahar to the father's inability to protect his child (with the male subject sometimes playing the role of the father and sometimes the role of the child, thus showing the strong identification between father and male child "against" the mother). In his scapegoat dream, Gabriel, feeling guilty for deserting his son by Orita, comforts himself with the thought that Dr. Landau will take care of his child and protect him against the bad mother, only to discover to his dismay a danger from an unexpected direction: Bella turned from a loving woman into a monster and is about to throw the child into the abyss. Whereas Gabriel tries to save the child, Daoud enters the dream as his bad double and is seen leading the child-scapegoat to the top of the cliff.

No longer the stereotypical native of earlier descriptions, Daoud is, both in *Day of the Countess* and in *Of Candles and Winds*, the mirror image (same and opposite) of either the narrator or Gabriel. This is important to note, especially as it affects our reading of Daoud's appearance in the riots in *Day of the Countess*. Had this event followed his character sketch as the "subservient native," his participation in the riots could have been read as merely one more element in this portrait: the subservient native would, of course, turn against his master and benefactor on the first opportunity. Such a reading of Daoud gets complicated by his role as a double. At the same time, we should note that Daoud's complexity and depth (his increasing distance from a stereotype) seem to grow in proportion to our certainty of his death: when Daoud reappears in the last part of *Day of the Ghosts*, we have not only been told he will die, but we have actually read the scene of his death, and it is at this point that we are presented with his longest and most complex interior monologue (which will be followed by a retelling of his death).

The appearance of Daoud in *Day of the Ghosts* parallels, in some respects, his appearance in *Day of the Countess*: if in the former he is alarmed by Orita, who invites him to dance with her in the street, in the latter he is repelled by Lea Himmelsach, who seduces him into a sexual encounter when they go for a walk in the Schneller Woods. Both scenes are followed by the appearance of Daoud as a rioter in traditional Arab garb; by the principle of *post hoc ergo propter hoc*, it is thus suggested, in both cases, that his behavior is the result of his encounter with female permissiveness (thus elevating a male psychodrama into a political *prise de conscience*). The intensity of the scene, however, has increased considerably in the second telling. Whereas Daoud flees from Orita in a mixture of dismay, fear, and anger, Lea's seduction is followed by his sodomizing her and berating her as a "Jewish harlot" who has caused him to betray both Berl and Orita (*Ghosts*, 186–88). The degree to which the narrator sympathizes with Daoud's behavior is indicated not just by his fairly obvious hostility to the character of Lea (whose depiction is almost exclusively in the mode of virulent satire) but also by the fact that in *The Nights of Lutetia* he himself, in his role as the adult David Shahar, treats the pretentious and hypocritical American poet, Helen Morely (a near replica of Lea), in quite the same way. Still, Daoud's outburst of verbal violence is quite striking (since up until this point, he was characterized by a delicacy of language and conduct) and unparalleled in the novel. It may be that Daoud is given this freedom of expression because he is "an Arab," an other, or because he is going to die, or both.

Daoud's interior monologue in *Day of the Ghosts* does not start, however, as a response to Lea's sexual provocation but rather as a critique of her opinions and, more specifically, of her insistence on "honesty" and "truth." But the texture of the passage suggests that this is not simply a matter of difference of opinions. Whereas Lea presents abstract, general arguments, Daoud is unable or unwilling to state his position theoretically; instead he will tell stories that may or may not have an allegorical sense. He thus manifests his disconnection from knowledge/power as proficiency in manipulating concepts, definitions, and distinctions, and his favoring what might be called "narrative knowledge."

In his monologue Daoud does not so much argue with Lea as counter her abstract discourse with a series of stories. He starts with Jamilla's story about Rabah Effendi and the apricots (154–55; told also in *His Majesty's Agent*); he then tells the story of his father's murder (using the very same words as Gutkin in his narrative of this event; compare *Summer*, 105–106, and *Ghosts*, 156–57); he complements the narrator's account of Brunhilde's death and the role Lea played in this (158–59); he tells the story of Talmi, Sabudik, and the gold coins (159–62), to which are added several other episodes concerning Talmi; and he also tells the story of the Beirut driver and the nurse, Mildred (172), and the story of the reception the judge gave when he was appointed Officer of the British Empire (using the same words as the narrator's own account of this event; compare *Voyage*, 65, and *Ghosts*, 176–77). In telling these stories, Daoud "quotes" the characters' words, even when it is not clear (and sometimes quite unlikely) that he himself was present during the conversation. Thus he "quotes" the words Sabudik uses to flatter Talmi into letting him sell the gold coins for him (160–61), the conversation between Professor Zondack and Lea concerning Talmi's illness, including Zondack's thoughts (168–69), and Talmi's reaction to the announcement that he is about to die (170). In describing his own reactions to Orita's invitation to go for a walk, Daoud uses the exact same words attributed by the narrator to Srulik on a similar occasion (compare *Voyage,* 60, and *Ghosts,* 177–78).

In the imaginary dialogue between Lea and Daoud, the narrator (who here stands probably for the author) is much closer to Daoud than to Lea, not only because of his distaste for the character of Lea and the hollow dogmatism of the conceptual mode she exemplifies, but also because, after all, he too is primarily a storyteller. To the extent that abstract reasoning is coded as Western and storytelling as Oriental (childish, premodern), the narrator is Daoud's fellow practitioner of the art of the Orient. Moreover, as a storyteller, Daoud resembles the narrator, not only because he "quotes" the narrator's words but also because of his ability to merge with other characters, enter into them, speak for them—to be, like the narrator, a "medium." The sympathetic view of Daoud, established by their both sharing the typical Shaharian "male" position (and possibly also the "nationalist" stance), becomes here something more specific and more intimate: Daoud "doubles" the narrator not as a mirror image (same and/or opposite, good and/or bad double) but by exemplifying the narrator's literary values: the porousness of the speaking self, its receptiveness and readiness to be (imaginatively) "inhabited" by the other. It is primarily on these grounds that Daoud differs from Lea, and it is primarily on these grounds (rather than as a feminist or a Marxist[16]) that Lea is condemned.

Exchanging Clothes, Exchanging Places

We have seen that the narrator depends for the creation of his world on identification with others, and that this identification presupposes a self whose identity is not rigidly defined but is, rather, fluid and permeable. The narrator dramatizes moments in which individuals are "interpellated" (or co-opted) by a group and thus acquire a rigid identity as moments of violence and loss. However, the narrator also shows awareness that identification with the other is potentially aggressive, since it implies, at the limit, taking the other's place. This broad issue is addressed in the novel in phenomenological and even metaphysical terms that do not relate directly to, or derive from, a specific political situation or specific power conflict, but it also intersects in interesting ways with a more explicit thematization of the national question and of the Jewish-Arab conflict over the land or "territory."

A scene from *Nin-Gal* can serve as an example for the novel's exploration of the relation between place and subjectivity in the broadest terms. On his first day in Paris, the adult narrator remembers Nin-Gal, a young girl he was in love with in his youth and who died mysteriously soon after their brief acquaintance. His memory of Nin-Gal is triggered by his encounter with Thomas Astor (who may be Tammuz Ashtarot, Berl's son and Nin-Gal's brother). On that same day, he also runs into Arik Wissotzky (now known as Eric), who was his classmate for a year before he and his mother left Palestine for Paris, where they have been living ever since. The strongest memory the narrator has of Eric is that of attending his birthday party and dancing with his mother, the beautiful and unconventional Anastasia. The memory of Nin-Gal intersects with that of Anastasia when the narrator tells of the visit he and Nin-Gal made to Rosa's apartment, which happens to be the same apartment Eric and his mother inhabited during their year in Jerusalem.

Rosa, an old cleaning woman and laundress, has appeared in *Day of the Countess* as Louidor's "confidante" and will reappear in *Day of the Ghosts* as a member of the audience—an unsympathetic one—of Lea's lectures on historical materialism. In the scene from *Nin-Gal,* she appears as Nin-Gal's motherly friend, hosting the young couple for dinner. While Rosa prepares the meal, Nin-Gal and the young narrator dress up in old clothes found in her chest of drawers.[17] Insofar as Rosa is a mother substitute (compensating for the bad mother, Lea Himmelsach, Nin-Gal's natural mother), one might expect dressing up in old clothes found in her house to be a reliving or an imitation of a family past. The clothes in question, however, are not Rosa's own old clothes; they were left in the apartment by the former resident, Anastasia Wissotzky, and even she was not their actual owner, since these are costumes she borrowed for use in her drama club. Furthermore, in their "semantic" content, these costumes represent an "elsewhere"—an imaginary, romantic, Christian Europe, full of princes and princesses, the phantasmatic, unattainable "other" of Jewish Europe as well as of provincial Palestine. Rather than repeating a past, the dressing up can be seen, then, as taking the place of an other; as such, it is analogous to Rosa's occupation of Anastasia's apartment, and both may be considered analogous to the transmigration of souls (a topic the novel sequence often alludes to) or to possession.

Indeed, as the scene continues to unfold, the spectacle of the young people dressed up in the old clothes makes Rosa recall the distant days in which she was as young and beautiful as Nin-Gal and was loved by her fiancé, all too soon gone away for a soldier, never to return. Rosa then dances with Nin-Gal, with the narrator now assuming the role of spectator to whom this spectacle suggests the old woman's desire to possess the body of the young girl, thus becoming again the young girl she once was (or imagines to have been)—but at the necessary and terrible cost of Nin-Gal's demise. In that sense, this episode resembles the spectacular scene of the "evil eye" in *His Majesty's Agent,* where the mother's identification with the image (in the mirror) of her young and beautiful daughter is said to lead to the child's death by fire (again, according to Heinrich's understanding of the burden of Jamilla's story). The entire episode from *Nin-Gal* is thus clearly inscribed within the pattern of analogy often drawn in the novel between house, clothing, and body as receptacles for the human person. One important aspect of this pattern is that such a receptacle may appear as a place successively occupied by different residents. Needless to say, this pattern has the potential of occasioning a conflict between two parties over the possession of a particular place.

The relation between inhabiting the place of the other (house, body, clothes) and assuming an "imaginary" (phantasmal, idealized) view of oneself we have seen in the scene from *Nin-Gal* leads naturally and surprisingly to the much larger and differently charged national question. Can Zionism, the acting out of the fantasy of a return to Zion, be considered analogous to the old woman's coveting of the young girl's body? Surely putting it this way would be a far cry from Shahar's intentions (certainly from his personal political views), but we believe that the structural analogy is not without relevance. The idea of inhabiting the national/territorial body as a way of regaining the (mythical) glory of the past animates the following passage where the boy-narrator describes the view from the window of his childhood home:

> On summer afternoons I would stretch out full length on the round windowsill—the walls were so thick—and look out toward Tur Malka at the top of the Mount of Olives and the section of the Old City walls facing the crowded square in front of the Damascus Gate. Horsedrawn carriages stood side by side with the Arab company buses to Ramallah and Jericho, and a few taxicabs as well, as throngs of Arabs in long robes and keffiyehs and tarbooshes milled and jostled between them. Fragments of Arab tunes floated up to my window on Arab-smelling breezes. The first wireless sets had just started appearing here and there in Jerusalem and the first sounds from them to reach my ears were these tunes, endlessly spiraling in the long-winded cycle, quacking with longings, of Arab love songs. The circle of Arab life which was revealed to me through the telescope in whose tube I lay—the tumultuous life swarming against the background of the Mount of Olives and the tower of Tur Malka, with its haggling and shouting and singing and smells, and its whole being which was dipped in a dream despite all its uproar—was like direct continuation of everything I had learned in the Bible about the lives of our forefathers in Eretz Israel; it was in some sense a materialization of those lives, awakening ancient chords like those of a long forgotten melody in my heart. (*Summer,* 24–25; 20–21)

This passage describes the narrator's youthful perception of Arab life through sight, sound, and smell. Though the life in question is clearly labeled "Arab" (Arab smell, Arab music, Arab clothes), there is nothing in this description to suggest that the presence of the ethnic other is experienced as strange or hostile. The Arab world appears natural to the boy-narrator, not only because he has always seen and heard and smelled it in his own life, but also because it seems to accord with what he imagines the national past to have been. His notion of what the past must have been is mediated by his experience in the Sephardic school, where he is the only Ashkenazi boy. Announcing the visit of a "famous" singer, the teacher in that school informs the boys that he will sing for them "as the Levites used to sing in the Temple" and will form them into a chorus that will "revive original Hebrew singing/poetry [*shira*]." Upon hearing the singer's performance, the boy-narrator concludes that the "original Hebrew singing/poetry [*shira*] that had once risen from the throats of the Levites in the Temple bore a remarkable resemblance to the Arab melodies issuing forth from the radio sets and record players in the Arab cafés in Mussrara and the Damascus Gate" (*Countess*, 83). This realization does not disconcert him at all, even though he is fully aware of the antagonism between this music and the music appreciated in his own cultural milieu.[18] Through its similarities to the world of oriental Jews in which he feels comfortable (though he does not entirely belong there), the Arab world appears to the boy as both familiar and different—the world of the past subsisting in the present.

As we have shown in chapter 1, the adult narrator is intent on finding material vestiges of his own personal past in the world of the here and now. It would seem that his youthful version was just as interested in seeing the historical past reappear in the present. Thus looking at the mosque of Nebi Samwil, he muses: "If only I could find the strength to look with total concentration, I would see the prophet Samuel coming home after making his circuit of Beit El and Gilgal and Mizpeh, just as it said in the Book of Samuel in the Bible" (*Summer*, 17; 16). The contemplation of the Arab present as a materialization of the biblical past is, therefore, a source of tremendous pleasure to him. The persistence of the Arabs in the old ways is never interpreted by the narrator as primitive, underdeveloped, backward, or the like. In this his attitude is ironically contrasted, for instance, with that of the supposedly progressive Lea Himmelsach, who pretends to go "on the barricades" to "enlighten" the Arabs. The material culture of the local Arabs, then, is seen by Shahar primarily as a valued living legacy of his own national past. The Arabs have been on the scene to carry on the material culture of biblical times and are thus both metaphorically and metonymically related to the ancient Israelites.

But if the Arabs "continue" the biblical past, the question must arise of the narrator's, and other Jews', status in the land. And so, in a direct sequel to the long passage quoted above, the narrator goes on as follows:

> But this materialization, despite its being a direct continuation, was not a natural continuation, for it was I who was the scion of the stock

> of Abraham, Isaac and Jacob, the natural and lawful heir of King David's dynasty here in David's city. Sometime, somewhere, something has gone wrong, as if a prince and a wanderer [*noded*] had changed clothes in a masquerade; the wanderer in the prince's clothes had settled in the king's palace, while the prince had taken up the staff of wandering [*makel hanedudim*] and set out on a long journey whose vicissitudes had transformed him beyond recognition. (*Summer*, 25; 21)

This passage, then, recognizes a direct continuity (and to that extent, a powerful historical link) between the Palestinian present and the biblical past, but it does so only to deny this continuity any grounding in "nature." The Arabs, then, are seen as, at best, the useful, temporary detainers of the local ancient material culture; at worst, as alien usurpers of a natural right not their own.[19] As the issue becomes more overtly that of the legitimate possession of the land, Shahar resorts to the motif of an exchange of clothes as a switching of identities in a clear allusion to Mark Twain's "The Prince and the Pauper" (and to that extent, Bilu was right to translate "*noded*" as "beggar" rather than "wanderer"). He uses the motif of the exchange of clothes to set up a little allegory according to which the present-day Arab is ultimately but the accidental look-alike of the ancient Israelite. Whereas in the passage from *Nin-Gal* the analogy between house, clothes, and body suggested that clothes may not be merely external, that what one wears may determine who one is, here the narrator insists that what the Jew and Arab wear is a matter of external paraphernalia and thus cannot affect the essential legitimacy of the one and the illegitimacy of the other. If in Twain's story the exchange of clothes was undertaken by mutual consent, here its allegorical counterpart is a historical mishap, a catastrophe that befell the Jewish people, for which no causal explanation is offered. Explicitly, Shahar's comparison does not go beyond the initial exchange, but it is possible to see it as having further implications: since the exchange that sent the Jews into exile and put the Arabs in possession was without reason, then there should be no problem in reversing it. In addition, the underlying symmetry that makes the exchange and its reversal possible is tendentiously enhanced by depicting the Arabs as an originally nomadic people, so that when the original owners of the land return from the aberrant nomadic phase of their history to reclaim it, it would only be natural for the Arabs to resume their former nomadic mode of life. The Jew literally would take the place of the Arab—become a settler in the land—and would thus assume his imaginary view of himself as "the natural and lawful heir of King David."

The narrator's claim to be the rightful heir is complemented by a quasi "nativist" stance: an articulation of his feeling of being at home in the local environment. This becomes clear when we compare his easy acceptance of the Arab way of life to the reaction of a newly arrived immigrant. Here is the description of Louidor's first encounter with the Arabs:

> When he arrived in Jaffa he was hit by a shock. . . . Jaffa was full of Arabs and Arab voices and Arab bustle and Arab smells. . . . In his first night in the land, in the small dirty hotel in Jaffa, he could not sleep not because of the fleas or the oppressive heat but because of the Arab language that rang all night in his ears as continuous calls of ya-la, ya-la, ya-la, ya-la, ya-la. (*Countess*, 99–100)

Offended and oppressed by Arab music, language, and smells, which are all strange and foreign to him, Louidor thinks with pity (which is, to a large extent, self-pity) what his hero, the Hebrew poet Konstantin Shapiro, would have felt had he been able to fulfill his dream and come to Eretz Israel:

> Here he is standing between the giant columns of the King's palace ready to sing to his people from the Songs of Zion just as the Levites used to sing the songs of King David in the Temple, when a sound comes to his ears. In a moment the crowd will welcome him with applause and the daughters of Jerusalem will crown his head with wreaths of flowers. He looks around and sees a growing crowd of Arabs in gowns and keffiyehs and tarbooshes waving their arms and calling at him in a threatening rhythm "ya-la ya-la ya-la ya-la." "I took the wrong way," says Konstantin Shapiro to the small, shriveled old man, with piercing eyes who stands by him. "Instead of arriving in Jerusalem I arrived in Baghdad." "You did not take the wrong way," says to him old Tolstoy, "Here is Jerusalem but you have nothing to do here. You can see that nobody understands you and nobody wants you in this place."[20] (*Countess*, 100–101)

Precisely those aspects of Arab culture that were so congenial for the boy-narrator, are experienced by the new arrival as utterly foreign and hostile. It is not clear what exactly a new immigrant like Louidor expected to find upon his arrival in Palestine, but one thing is certain: he did not expect to find the country populated by people of a culture entirely different from his own, in fact, people who appear to him to be little better than savages. Ironically, this attitude stems from the unquestioning acceptance of cultural norms prevailing in Eastern Europe. Louidor's dilemma is of one who has left a country whose way of life appears to him naturally normative (so much so that he did his best to assimilate), but where he was told that he does not belong, for a country that is supposed to be his true home but whose way of life appears to him alien and barbarous. The move to Palestine then does not solve the problem of homelessness for the likes of Louidor. Different as the narrator and Louidor are in their attitude toward local customs, their basic conception is quite the same: both feel that reclaiming the ancient homeland requires a displacement of the other people living in it now. In both cases, the idea is posited in terms of an exchange of clothes and a restoration of a former state. Just as in the narrator's metaphor at some point the historical mishap is to be corrected, and the Jewish prince is to resume his proper attire temporarily worn by the Arab wanderer, so Louidor will dress as a Bedouin and preach to the Arabs "to return to Medina the blessed and Mecca the sacred and to the land of Arabia, praiseworthy and spacious" (*Countess*, 93). It is Shahar's literary conceit that precisely the one who finds the Arab lifestyle so obnoxious should dress as an Arab and even convert to Islam (because otherwise he could not, in "good faith," urge them to decamp). Whereas the narrator does not seem to mind if the Arab way of life continues as long as the Arabs themselves make way for the true owners of the land, Louidor's primary wish is to make the Arab way of life disappear, and it is in order to accomplish this that he wants the Arabs to leave. In both cases, the proposed restoration will endow the Arabs with national traits defining the Jewish people: the narrator thinks they should revert to their "original" nomadic way of life and thus become like the wandering Jews of 2,000 years of exile; Louidor exhorts them to their own version of the return to Zion, which in their case would be Arabia and *their* holy places, Mecca and Medina.

Canaanite, Hebrew, Jew

Louidor's far-fetched adventure dramatizes some of the conceptual difficulties of renewed Jewish life and Jewish sovereignty in the land of Israel. Another figure in the novel who draws attention to these problems is Berl Raban, alias the poet Eshbaal Ashtarot, who, in *Day of the Ghosts* explains to the boy-narrator that a "Jewish state" ["*medinat hayehudim*," Herzl's expression] is an impossibility, just as "flying cats" are: if they fly there are not cats, and if they are cats they do not fly (*Ghosts*, 28–29).

Berl's status in the economy and composition of the novel is somewhat ambiguous. On the one hand, he is someone the narrator has known since his early childhood, a friend of the very central character, Gabriel Luria, a full-fledged resident of the Street of the Prophets community, discussed in chapter 3; he makes frequent appearances in several volumes of the novel, and one of the two episodes constituting the posthumous volume *To the Mount of Olives* is devoted to his fate after death. On the other hand, Berl's own discourse is only sparsely represented in the text. Much of what we know of his opinions (e.g., his admiration for the biblical figure of Joshua, conqueror of

Canaan) is due to reports by other characters. We are allowed into his consciousness only in one extended episode, that of his trip to Persia and its aftermath, and we are given to actually read only two lines of his poetry. These two lines make quite explicit what would be easily inferred by any reader familiar with Hebrew culture in the mid twentieth century, namely, that this character is based on the historical figure of Uriel Halpern, also known as the poet Yonatan Ratosh.[21] Ratosh was, of course, one of the founders and the undisputed leader of the group that came to be known as the Canaanites. It is possible that Shahar does not dwell on Berl's opinions, since he assumes the reader knows Ratosh's.

The Canaanites argued that the Jewish people do not comprise a real nation, defined by territory and a language, but a "faith community," and as such could not have a homeland other than the Diaspora.[22] In their view, the problem with Zionism was its attachment to the Jewish past and to the very definition of a Jewish people. They valorized the term *Hebrew* as denoting a pre-Jewish, and even a pre-Israelite, era in which various Semitic tribes formed a loosely allied political entity throughout the Fertile Crescent.[23] They sought to bring about a Hebrew revolution, whereby the Hebrew youth born in Palestine would break all ties with Judaism (and even with Zionism, insofar as it continues the Jewish past). In the words of the Israeli critic Hanan Hever, "Against the Jewish identity of Zionist culture, Canaanism proposed the Hebrew alternative of a native national culture deriving its authority from the local territory rather than from Jewish historical continuity. To this end the history of Jewish Diaspora was given up in favor of nostalgia for a distant past of Hebrew life in the ancient East."[24] This description by Hever encapsulates both the imaginative boldness and the fundamental ambiguity of the Canaanite stance. In deriving the definition of a Hebrew national identity from a territory rather than from a historical continuity, the Canaanites opened up and enlarged this definition to include, in principle, all of the peoples residing in the Middle East, regardless of their contemporary ethnic, religious, cultural, or political divisions. The new Hebrew nation would restore the glory of the alleged ancient Hebrew nation that was said to include (besides the Israelites) the Phoenicians, Ammonites, Moabites, Edomites, and other populations of the ancient East. The Canaanites thus depart from the purely spatial basis of their conception to recognize a historical dimension, but one that is not separable from the common territory. From the Canaanite point of view, the Arabs of today are in fact Hebrews, even though they may not acknowledge it, having undergone forcible Islamization and Arabization in intervening historical periods. Just as the Canaanites wished to skip over the hiatus of Jewish history, they hoped to bring the Arabs to renounce the imposed pan-Arab and pan-Moslem phases of their history and to come to the realization that they too are none other than the heirs of the ancient Hebrews.

As a serious cultural-political offer to the other, the obvious trouble with this theory is that the definitional term *Hebrew* is not valorized by any cultural or national tradition, either territorially or temporally based, other than the Jewish one. In inviting other ethnicities to identify themselves with the Hebrew nation, the Canaanites are in fact asking them to accept the hegemony of a national definition that, however self-declaredly inclusive, is still clearly Jewishly derived.[25]

Just as the impact of the Canaanites in Israeli culture may be felt far beyond the actual pronouncements of the spokesman of this group, so the implications of Canaanite thinking reverberate in Shahar's novel, even in the absence of any explicit mention of this group. The complex dialectic of territory, history, and national identity that characterizes Canaanite ideology is clearly related not only to Berl's pronouncements about the impossibility of a Jewish state but also to the attitudes embodied by the boy-narrator viewing Arab Jerusalem from his window and by Louidor landing in Jaffa harbor and later preaching at the Jaffa Gate. Louidor's solution to the Zionist problem with the Arabs, in its far-fetched naivete (or underhanded duplicity), can be seen as a parodic exaggeration of the Canaanites' belief that the Arabs may be talked into considering themselves members of the Hebrew nation. The fact that Louidor's premise is a loathing of the Arab is just another element of this parodic pattern. The basic ambiguity of the Canaanite ideology is even more tellingly reflected by the boy-narrator's musings on his windowsill. The narrator, like the Canaanites, is receptive to the sights, smells, and sounds of the local other, that is, the Arab, and outdoing their implicit move toward hegemony, showing equally little awareness of the inherent contradiction, he is quite explicit in asserting a sovereign birthright as legitimate heir to King David.

Both self-negating and imperial, the Canaanite idea, let us not forget, is the brainchild of Jewish poets and intellectuals born in the East European Diaspora. Such is the case of Shahar's fictional character of Berl Raban. Berl adopts the pen name Eshbaal Ashtarot, combining the names of two ancient pagan deities that have always been anathema to Jewish monotheism (as well as naming his children, Tammuz and Nin-Gal, after other ancient Semitic deities), but he never formally gives up his Jewish/Diasporic name (*Nin-Gal*, 109–10). In his portrait of Eshbaal/Ratosh, Shahar seems to be intent on highlighting not so much the contradiction in the Canaanites' relation to the other as the discrepancy between a Jewish, Ashkenazi, European, exilic type and the utopian dream of reinventing oneself as some sort of hyper-native. This incongruity does not escape the crabby, histrionic Mrs. Luria:

> Serenely pretending high seriousness, in a low, husky voice astonishingly echoing Berl's own, she would start uttering sententious phrases

> in energetic staccato, in a heavy, exaggerated oriental accent that so resembled Berl's contrived oriental way of speaking, that even Dr. Landau would burst into laughter. She would say about him, that "the face is the face of Red Ear and the voice is the voice of Rosa, senior Moise's sister." (*Countess*, 17)

Her witty parodic reference is, of course, to the biblical verse "The voice is Jacob's voice, but the hands are the hands of Esau" (Genesis, 27:22), as well as to the physical resemblance of Berl to his Ashkenazi ultra-orthodox relatives.

When the boy-narrator first encounters Berl's/ Eshbaal's/Ratosh's poetry, represented within the novel by a collection of poems bearing the pagan title "The Songs of Tammuz to Ashera," he jumps to the conclusion that its author must be Gabriel, since he heard stories about Gabriel's "idolatry" and "star worship" [*'Avoda zara, 'Avodat kokhavim umazalot]* (*Countess,* 77–78; see also *Summer*, 49–51, 62–68; 40–41, 48–55). Gabriel shares with Berl and the Canaanites more than just an interest in the pagan religions of the ancient East. In *A Tammuz-Night's Dream*, while walking around by the Valley of Kidron, Gabriel starts thinking, through some associative link, of "a question of language, of the meaning of a word that changes as time and place and luck [*mazal*] change":

> She took my place. The place: as long as our forefathers the ancient Hebrews lived in their land and ruled it, place was place, literally—this place, that place, my place, your place. But from the moment they lost control over a place, from the moment they turned into Jews ruled by others, dispersed and separated, from the moment all places, including Eretz Israel, became for them exile, place changed its meaning and became for them God—this God who has no body and no shape of a body and whom those who appreciate the body don't appreciate. The place [*Hamakom*], He will have mercy upon us. *Hamakom*, He will break the yoke off our necks and will lead us triumphant [*komemiut*] to our land. And until then, they lost the appreciation of place and the feeling of this or that place and the significance of this or that place, and the atmosphere of a place and its colors and smells and tastes and winds and sounds and the echoes of its hidden waves.[26] (*Tammuz*, 153–54)

Perhaps the first thing to note about this passage is that in speaking of the ancient Hebrews becoming Jews upon losing control of their land, Gabriel is using a terminology that clearly echoes the Canaanite valorization of "Hebrew" over "Jew." Gabriel's reasoning concerning the use of the word *makom* (place) to refer to God equally accords with the Canaanite insistence on the primacy of territory. The argument may be paraphrased as follows: in losing political control over the specific place which is their homeland, the Jews-to-be incurred a generalized loss of affinity for place as such, for any place, for immanence, thus ultimately physical existence and, by extension, the entirety of the empirical domain.[27] To the exilic Jewish mind, so Gabriel argues, "place" acquires precisely the opposite of its original, normal meaning: it comes to mean that which is not in existence, that which does not and cannot take place, at least not within this world and historical time, and having been pushed out of the realm of the actual, it becomes one of the names of this absence, which now merges with the idea of the transcendental God. The objective actuality of the concrete place has been displaced by a ritualized subjective longing for a nonplace doomed to nonexistence. This is particularly emphasized through one of the phrases Gabriel quotes with bitter irony as an example of this peculiar use of the term *makom* ("*Hamakom*, He will break the yoke off our neck and He will lead us triumphant [*komemiut*] to our land").[28] In a certain sense, it is possible to interpret the whole Zionist revolution as a replacement of the transcendental God perversely called "The Place," by the revived national subject who undertakes to bring about the return to Zion as a concrete, historical enterprise. It is therefore not irrelevant that Gabriel's meditation on place takes place in the vicinity of Mishkenot Sha-ananim, the first building venture by Jews outside the Old City walls and thus a symbol of their renewed contact with the land.[29] The tenor of Gabriel's meditation seems to suggest that this move should entail a detranscendentalization of the national god in view of regaining the long-lost immanence. It is as though, for him, for a people to have an affinity for its place, its divinity must reside in nature—a tenet that is just one step away from pantheism (a penchant for which Gabriel shows, especially during his stay in Brittany).

Another important aspect of the recovery of immanence—the renewed investment in the body—provides a motivating context for Shahar's incursions into the erotic, in which the character of Gabriel plays a major part. Strolling along and vaguely looking for Bella (whom he has just recently met), Gabriel temporarily mistakes a figure coming out of a house for that of Berl. This is only appropriate, since as the Canaanite poet Eshbaal Ashtarot, Berl probably shares in one way or another many of the thoughts now going through Gabriel's mind. The figure though turns out to be Bella (so close phonetically to Berl, and in Hebrew alphabet, just one little mark away, the short line distinguishing the letter "*reish*" from "*heih*"), with whom Gabriel is about to enter into a most carnal relationship. As the scene unfolds and the two strike up a conversation, it turns out that Bella herself is given to poetical daydreaming and mystical make-believe in imagery reminiscent of The Song of Songs and of Ratosh's erotic pagan poetry. She refuses to be called "Bella" (a name alluding to beauty, but not a Hebrew one) and "reminds" Gabriel that she is none other than *ayellet hashahar* (the doe of dawn, i.e., the Morning Star or Aurora). Pointing out the full moon that "has just reached the tip of Tur Malka" (*Tammuz*, 156), she enigmatically tells Gabriel that they are being beckoned by some presence. What she has in mind is not the Tower of David (the Turkish-built turret in the Old City ramparts that became a Zionist icon), as he surmises, but the "Gabriel Oak," an expression Gabriel is unable to relate to his botanical or literary knowledge. Upon arriving at the secluded place (under "a tall, proud, self-centered pine tree") where she has been leading him, Gabriel finds out the oak in question is none other than his own phallus. As she kneels before this object to administer to it, she "murmurs a silent prayer" and, refusing to let Gabriel lean her body against the tree, she insists on performing "the holy service" (*'avodat hakodesh*) herself (*Tammuz*, 157).

Clearly, then, the two lovers imagine themselves and are imagined by Shahar as enacting a pagan fertility rite, as was the practice, presumably, in biblical times, "atop every hill and under each evergreen tree." What is entirely absent here are the old prophets' bitter remonstrations against such doings. To sum up our reading of this sequence, we might say that in moving from his theologico-metaphysical meditation to outdoor sexual intercourse, Gabriel is just practicing what he preached. The project of restoring the national divinity to the concrete place of the homeland is symbolically enacted by reinvesting the body with positive meaning.[30]

The same set of issues with which Gabriel and Berl grapple appears also in the meditations of Srulik, the "little librarian from the Bnei Brit library," but lands him at a pole diametrically opposed to Berl's (as well as Gabriel's). Like the Canaanite poet, Srulik is fascinated with origins and the ancient East, most particularly with the patriarch Abraham, to whose birthplace, Ur of the Chaldees, he yearns to travel. But rather than being the father of a nation attached to and deriving its value from a specific place (the large Hebrew nation postulated by the Canaanites and extending over the entire Fertile Crescent or the smaller Hebrew nation living separate from other people in the Promised Land), for Srulik, Abraham is first and foremost the man who was commanded by God to leave his homeland.[31] This command serves Srulik as the foundation for an entire metaphysics of severance, "the metaphysics of get thee out [*lech lecha*]," which, as might be expected, is dualistic and transcendental:

> The soul accomplishes its journey on this earth in the body allotted it, and the journey always begins in severance and separation. Severance is the starting point, the birth of human individuality and independence. This severing begins on the loftiest and most abstract plane and continues on the lowest and most basic. In the beginning, the soul is severed from its root, from the universal soul, and sent to

> the body allotted it, to its vehicle. It is true that already at this initial stage all kinds of errors and confusions occur in the bill of consignment, such as a tiny dwarfish soul sent to drive a giant truck, and on the other hand a great soul obliged to squeeze itself into a shaky little car. But setting these initial confusions aside for the moment, we can clearly see how the driver's heavenly departure is immediately reflected on earth in the parting of his vehicle from its workshop—the body parted from its mother's navel, and later the man departing his father's house at the command: "Get thee out of thy country, and from thy kindred, and from thy father's house." And he was waiting and yearning for nothing else but the starting sign: "Get thee out!" (*Voyage*, 44; 259–60)

These reflections occur to Srulik at a phase of his Jerusalem existence to which he refers as "the dead end of my life": he experiences his situation as stagnant and confining, and the demands of the collective (in this case, primarily his family) as restrictive and oppressive: time and again his departure for Ur is thwarted by the needs of his family (his father's disappearance, his mother's illness, his aunt Elka's death). Psychologically speaking, then, the literary topos of life as a journey, as well as the doctrine of the transmigration of souls, are mobilized here in the service of a need for individuation and a desire for self-realization.

The chosen destination of this personal journey and the biblical expression "Get thee out" clearly suggest the figure of Abraham as its source of inspiration, but what exactly does it mean for Srulik to follow in the footsteps of Abraham? Though one traditional interpretation of the verse "*Lech lecha*" does indeed construe it as self-realization,[32] Abraham's severance from his homeland and his father's house also may be directly linked to his founding of monotheism. This is the thesis advanced by Leonard Woolley in his popular book on Abraham (a work, that, as we have shown in chapter 1, Srulik could hardly have read but that Shahar clearly has, since his text incorporates literal translations of several passages from it[33]). According to Woolley, Abraham did not simply leave his father's home but opted to exchange the life of a city dweller for the life of a nomad. To a large extent, it was this nomadic way of life that enabled or forced him to gradually detach himself from the belief in local gods (as practiced in his native city, Ur) and develop a notion of a God whose power is not limited to one specific place and whose "covenant" is with a family, a clan, a tribe, or a nation rather than with a city. Christians argue (and this is clearly the main purpose of Woolley's book) that the next and final stage in this detachment of God from "place" is the New Testament, whereby Christianity presumably abolished and rendered obsolete Abraham's old covenant, replacing Jewish particularism based on genetic filiation with a universal religion based on faith alone. Srulik's eventual conversion to Christianity, and his specific choice of Calvinism with its insistence on individual calling and unmediated relation to God, will then be the logical conclusion (and therefore a suitable substitute) for his search for Abraham.[34]

However, Srulik's desire to leave the land and wander in the footsteps of Abraham can also be interpreted as an adherence to and a valorization of a "Diasporic" view, according to which the Jews cannot and should not be rooted in a particular territory. From this perspective, being attached to a place means becoming *'am ha-aretz*: meaning literally "people of the land," this expression is used to designate the simple folk and/as "ignorant" (e.g., in the expression "*bur ve'am ha-aretz*"), and, by implication at least, the Gentiles. Unlike the Gentiles, the Jews are and should remain the "people of the book," with only a textual-spiritual homeland. From this perspective obeying the call "*Lech lecha*" means not only self-realization as a unique individual, not only belief in a transcendental disembodied divinity, but more specifically a particular view of the Jews as those who refuse to accept "settling down," identifying with one place as one's "home," the end of the road, fulfillment. It is important to emphasize that Srulik is not a Diaspora Jew waiting for a divine voice to tell him to go to the Holy/Promised Land; rather, he is a native of the land who wants to leave the land in order, one may say, to keep the promise alive (as a promise).[35]

We can see, then, that if Shahar/Srulik considers departure and voyage as symbolizing the condition for individuality, freedom, and self-fulfillment, then Shahar/Gabriel deplores the lack of investment in and appreciation for place and body that such departure entails. Together these two characters give voice to a tension within Judaism between, on the one hand, a desire to belong to the land, to "go native," to become (re-become) a people like all others, and, on the other hand, the rejection of such attachment to the land as "slavery" or "torpor," as an attitude which, by accepting the world as "given," restricts freedom and prevents self-reflection and critical distance. The narrator keeps these two positions in tension, since he neither chooses between the two poles nor uses one character to critique the position of the other.[36]

A Cautionary Tale

Perhaps an even more explicit discussion of the relation between identity and place in the concrete, political terms of the present-day Arab-Israeli conflict over the land is the parable of the rooftop in *A Tammuz-Night's Dream* (18–34). This rather long episode stands out from the rest of the *Palace* sequence in seeming to call for an allegorical reading as a rather transparent, didactic fable. This fable is embedded in the narrative in such a way as to make it appear, at first, rather difficult to assign the opinions and positions stated or implied in it to any particular character. Formally speaking, the narrator assumes no responsibility for the content of this text, whose composition he attributes to the character of Tammuz. Although Tammuz is nominally the author of the fable, we get no direct access to that text as written by him; what we do have is the narrator's paraphrase of the contents of a short play or scenario that Tammuz wrote and showed him soon after their graduation from high school many years before. But to the narrator, Tammuz is not simply another person; he often is presented in the *Palace* as the narrator's admired hero (who replaces, to a certain extent, Gabriel in the later volumes), a double who is the source of secret, forbidden knowledge (he is the one who tells the narrator the "rumors" about Gabriel and Orita, as well as the secret story of Heinrich Reinhold), who possesses the woman the adult narrator desires (Lutetia, in *The Nights of Lutetia*, and maybe Yaeli Landau in *A Tammuz-Night's Dream*) and, most importantly perhaps, a double who fails to recognize the narrator (and thus, symbolically, annihilates him).[37]

Abstract as it is, Tammuz's scenario is said to be grounded in personal experience. In his childhood, Tammuz was a quiet and nonbelligerent boy who took special pleasure in solitary games of building with wooden blocks (and in that he doubles the narrator of the short story "First Lesson," arguably the most autobiographical of all of Shahar's stories). The one exception to his peaceful demeanor occurs on a particular day when the nursery school that both he and the narrator attended took the children on an outing. As the children disperse around a field to play, Tammuz finds a platform, which later turns out to be the rooftop of an abandoned building, where he can do his building happily by himself, until he is rudely interrupted by two bullies; uncharacteristically standing up for himself, he routs them only to have the whole matter twisted around by the defeated aggressors, who succeed in getting him into trouble with the teacher, who never bothers to find out what really happened or to mete out proper justice. This personal childhood experience, whose meaning Tammuz could not explain even to his friend, the narrator, until years later (but still many years before the narrator's encounter with Thomas/Tammuz), serves Tammuz as the basis for the main development in his play or scenario.

In this scenario, of which Tammuz casts himself as the protagonist, following some nightmarish episodes taking place during some public celebration, Tammuz finds peace and quiet under a table. In this private and secluded space (which gradually merges with the rooftop of his childhood experience), he starts building, only to be set upon by two bullies,[38] aided and abetted by a third, slighter boy. Having defeated the two bullies, the hero tries to befriend the little boy, Hemmed, even though he tends to get in his way and is not much use to him in his building efforts. When the bullies reappear and the ungrateful little boy once again sides with them, the hero is pushed over the brink, and a kick from Hemmed at his grasping hand sends him falling into the abyss.

This schematic tale is used as a skeleton onto which are hung various small incidents and bits of discourse reflecting on the relationship between the protagonist and his fickle fellow-resident. Thus after the first act of aggression and before the disastrous second one, the protagonist falls into a protracted self-debate concerning the moral propriety of expelling the dangerous little nuisance from the rooftop:

> How can I drive him out of here—that is, what right do I have? True, I had been here a long time before him, and had already built and demolished here before it occurred to him to show up, but when I came back I did find him in this place, and after all he is not to blame for my going off. . . .When he got here he did not find me here so that from his point of view he preceded me, and has the right to drive me away. On the other hand, the fact still is that this had been my construction site before he ever came, so that I have right of precedence over this place, all the more since I came to build whereas he built nothing, had no aptitude for it . . . etc. (*Tammuz*, 26–27)

Quite clearly, this is a rather crude and tendentious conceptualization of Arab/Israeli relations and constitutes a particularly self-righteous version of the Zionist narrative of the conflict. Tammuz, with his building blocks, peaceful intentions, and moral sensibilities, clearly stands for the Yishuv (later, the State of Israel), that is, for Jews who came to Eretz Israel "to build and be built" ["*Anu banu artzah livnot ulehibanot bah*"]. The two bullies are the (seven, or twenty-two) Arab states, and the troublesome little brat on the rooftop represents the Palestinians. The Palestinian presence in the disputed territory seems to materialize only at the moment of the inexplicable attack from outside, very much in line with the characteristic hedging of Zionist discourse on this question. Childish and vulnerable, the Palestinians are not without some charm (*hemmed*) and are apt to arouse sympathy, but they remain backward and incapable of making a useful contribution to the construction of the country. Worst of all, they will always support any aggression by their Arab brethren against the Israelis and will treacherously and ungratefully gang up on them, regardless of the circumstances. The prospect of Tammuz, the protagonist, being literally kicked off his rooftop obviously echoes the Arab threats "to drive the Jews into the sea." Ending as it does, with Tammuz free-falling into the abyss, this scenario clearly reflects the belief that this is no idle threat but a real danger to the very survival of Israel. Given this turn of events at the literal level of the parable, the protagonist's moral deliberations over the possible expulsion of his sneaky nemesis appear as soft-headed naivete or misplaced bleeding-heart humanism. To put it quite bluntly: if the Israelis had not been so squeamish about expelling the Palestinians (in 1948, 1967, 1973, or some other opportune juncture), they would not "now," in the future projected by the parable, be faced with the nightmare of being, in turn, the victims of expulsion, nay, utter destruction. This, then, is a cautionary tale in the strictest sense of the word, a stern warning, whose polemical thrust is not really at the Arab side to the conflict but rather at those elements within the Jewish, Zionist, Israeli side who show a willingness to accommodate the Palestinians, to empathize with their plight, and to apply universalistic moral standards to their case. In authoring the scenario and attributing such tendencies to his namesake protagonist, Tammuz assumes the satirical mask of the ingénue to ironically criticize this stance.

Having concluded his paraphrase of Tammuz's fable, the narrator does not pause to draw an explicit moral. His indirect commentary, however, amounts to a tacit endorsement of the gist of our preceding paragraph. When he first read the scenario in Tammuz's presence, he suggested that its title should be changed from "The Vision" (which he found too vague and out of touch with the times) to "On the Roof," since it reminded him of the Yiddish popular saying, "Madman—get off the roof!"[39] The madness in question, by a double irony, does not refer to being on the roof in the first place or building there, but to the high-minded, self-endangering deliberations about the right of the Palestinians to inhabit the land. An additional spectacle of assent to this view of the fable is offered by the young Yaeli Landau, to whom the narrator tells the contents of the scenario. Her response is: "But this is terrible, terrible! This is exactly what is going to happen to us all if we keep on like this." To his faux naïf question, "What do you mean if we keep on like this?" she replies: "If we keep on letting them" (*Tammuz*, 33). Finally, after quoting Pascal's dictum that "Men are so necessarily mad that it would be mad by another turn of madness to not be mad," he concludes by urging ourselves "not to let them, those sane people, hurl us with a kick into the abyss" (34). By this point, perhaps in the interval between the fictional composition of Tammuz's scenario in the mid-1940s and Shahar's composition of this volume of his novel in the mid-1980s, the Jewish supporters of a compromise with the Palestinians seem to have progressed from being just overly squeamish to actually being the ones who are about to administer the lethal kick.

Two comments on the mechanism of representation in the parable of the roof are in order. The first concerns the very nature of this embedded narrative as a parable or an allegory—a representational mode not otherwise favored by Shahar. Thus, for instance, much of the opening of *Nin-Gal* revolves around a play authored by a character named Aharon Dan, who asks the narrator to deliver his manuscript to Thomas Astor at the *Paris Review*. Mistaking the narrator for the author of this play, Thomas/Tammuz criticizes it bluntly: "It is not a play. It does not have one single character who lives and breathes, one single sentence that expresses the life-truth of a particular person" (*Nin-Gal*, 114). The narrator agrees wholeheartedly with this harsh critique. If Thomas Astor is indeed Tammuz Ashtarot, then he must have come a long way since the composition of the scenario he first wished to entitle "The Vision" [*hazon, hizaion*], a title nearly identical to that of Dan's play, *Man's Vision* [*Hazon ha-adam*]. It may be, therefore, that on purely literary grounds, the narrator agrees with Tammuz, the critic, against Tammuz, the writer, that neither good drama nor good novels come out of such didactic parables.[40] This literary or aesthetic preference is grounded in Shahar's profound commitment to the open-ended richness of concrete individuals.

This leads us to our second point. We opened this chapter by showing the recurrent linkage suggested by Shahar between collective identity and violence. Time and time again he presents groups acting violently to suppress or punish nonconforming individuals. He further suggests that when individuals act as members of a unified group, their individuality is abrogated by this affiliation, and they are reduced to little more than part of a raging mob. In the allegorizing movement of the parable of the roof, the representation of the Arabs easily conforms to this view: they are many, and their inclination to violence is related to this fact. But the other side to the conflict—the Jews or the Israelis or the Zionist settlers—which in concrete historical reality is equally collective—is allegorized consistently and exclusively as an individual: the peace-loving, considerate, and creative Tammuz. In a further complication, the same technique is used in the fable's representation of a polemic within the Jewish side. In the opening section of the parable, Tammuz frustratingly finds himself the odd man out in a variety of situations arising from some kind of public celebration he attends. These eventually boil down to the fact that he is not in possession of "a red belt," apparently a sine qua non for any full-fledged member of the group. The color of this object leaves no doubt that the polemical target of the allegory at this point is the Zionist Labor movement. And so, while Tammuz remains an individual and is not hypostasized into any collective entity, such as the Revisionist movement, his implicit opponents are cast as an anonymous, tyrannical, collective body. Paradoxically, Shahar seems to be trapped here by the very tendency he ordinarily descries. The closer he comes to endorsing a nationalist position, that is, to demand a more zealous adherence to the national interest, the more he insists on allegorizing this stance as an individual, rather than as the conformity-demanding collective that it is.

Chapter 5

Remembering Proust

In 1978, in a review article devoted to Shahar's *Summer in the Street of the Prophets,* which had just come out in French translation, the journalist Jacqueline Piatier (who was then the editor of the book section of *Le Monde*) wrote: "David Shahar is a Hebrew author whose name the French should know since it is that of a master. . . . A few volumes of his *Jerusalem Scrolls* have already appeared in Israel where they received important recognition. . . . The Israelis are not mistaken; in Shahar they have an author of the stature of a Proust or a Faulkner."[1] The myth of the "Israeli Proust"—or the "Oriental Proust," as the article was entitled—has been launched.

Piatier, however, was not the first to draw the analogy. If our bibliographical records are accurate, then this honor should go to Israeli critic Ada Zemach who, in an article entitled "*Kirva yetera*" ["Too Close"], published in 1970, drew attention to Proust's influence on Shahar, indeed, to Shahar's "imitation" of the French master.[2] Haim Ganz in 1971 and Yosef Even in 1976[3] also mentioned thematic and stylistic similarities between the two authors. However, it was the warm French reception, beginning in 1971 (the date in which the first French translation of Shahar—a collection of short stories—appeared[4]) and culminating in the award of the Prix Médicis Etranger in 1981, which turned the analogy between Shahar and Proust from a simple critical observation into a sign of recognition. Indeed, the mention of Proust's name in Piatier's article was clearly meant as a great compliment; the name "Proust" functions there almost as an epithet, connoting a mixture of greatness, difficulty, and length. The laudatory implication persists, even when the validity of the comparison is denied, as in a review of the posthumous volume, *To the*

Mount of Olives, entitled "David Shahar Was Not Proust After All."[5] Thus the analogy between Proust and Shahar, once it was adopted by the French, facilitated the dichotomization between the French and Israeli reception of Shahar (now a commonplace of Shahar criticism); the myth of the "French Shahar" explains why other rapprochements that were proposed—such as between Shahar and Faulkner, or between *The Palace of Shattered Vessels* and Lawrence Durrell's *Alexandria Quartet*—did not catch, though they are, *prima facie*, no less plausible.[6]

The "propping" of an author from a relatively marginal culture on an older author who has achieved the status of a classic in a hegemonic culture must be a fairly common device used by reviewers to facilitate the reception of the new author. What interests us here is not only that in Shahar's case it seems to have misfired. We also note that as a promotional tactic, this device does not attempt to present an author as "new"—different, if not original and unique—since it is designed to render his newness acceptable by claiming him for an established and a reputable literary practice. This explains why reviewers (and many, though not all, of the critics who adopted the analogy) showed little interest in pointing out *differences* between Shahar and Proust, as the long established practice of "compare and contrast" instructs us to do.[7] Moreover, in looking over the similarities pointed out by reviewers and critics (often without supporting their claims with a close—or any—analysis of Proust's text), we note that the Proust to whom Shahar is compared has himself lost much of his specificity and originality, indeed, his radical edge. Many of the "Proustian" features critics found in Shahar's text are not particular to Proust (at least not in the way they were formulated by the critics in question) but rather are more or less common features or preoccupations of the European novel, of Romanticism and modernism, or even of Western culture in general.[8] We do not intend to deny that Shahar's and Proust's works belong to these traditions, but what makes them worth reading, in our minds, is that they intervened in these traditions and confronted the issues and problems they raise *in particular ways*, which it is, precisely, the task of the critic to specify.

It therefore seems to us that though the comparison between Shahar and Proust has by now become something of a cliché, the encounter between these two authors has not yet quite taken place. What we propose in the following pages is the beginning of such an encounter: we would like, on the basis of a close reading of selected passages in Proust and Shahar, to isolate a certain number of topoi they seem to share and, against the background of similarities, to point out important differences which, we hope, would allow us to better describe their respective literary projects (presuppositions, procedures, and goals). We should note at the outset that in comparing Shahar and Proust, our prime goal is to contribute to a better understanding of the former; our discussion of Proust draws on many of Proust's critics to give as nuanced an account as possible of his treatment of the topoi under discussion.

Similes of Memory

Shahar himself attracts our attention to Proust in the opening paragraph of his novel. There the narrator describes how Gabriel Luria, the hero of his childhood, first appeared to him while he was drawing water, so that "his figure was fixed in my memory as rising from [the cistern's] mouth together with the pail of water . . . rising and opening like the Japanese paper flower in its glass of water, which he himself was later to buy me from Hananiah's toy shop" (*Summer*, 9; 7). Notwithstanding the narrator's claim that this Japanese paper flower came from a Jerusalem toy store, its actual provenance is surely Proust's *Du côté de chez Swann* where, at the conclusion of the famous episode of the madeleine, the narrator evokes the image of Japanese pieces of paper which, dipped in water, receive different shapes and become flowers, houses, and people.[9]

What seems to us important in this case of "borrowing" is not so much the question of influence as the way in which the allusion to Proust in Shahar's text modifies the status of memory: while at one level the narrator is saying that now, as a grown man, he recalls an object given to him by another person when he was a child, on another level the author is showing us that while writing this text, he is remembering Proust (or, more accurately, the opening of Proust's novel). The Japanese paper flower is transplanted into Shahar's novel not from the world of physical objects but from the world of texts; moreover, it is borrowed from a text where it "originally" appeared not as an object in the world but as a figure—a simile for memory. While the transformation of the figure of the Japanese paper toy into a concrete physical object, well located in time and space, already suggests Shahar's need to anchor all remembrance in concrete material objects, the allusion to Proust invites us to direct our attention away from remembered reality and toward the process of remembering itself in its relation to textual production. A comparison between the passage in Proust from which the allusion to the Japanese paper flower is drawn and the opening passage of Shahar's novel where this Japanese paper flower reappears can shed light on this process and this relation.

In what is undoubtedly the most famous passage in Proust's entire work, the narrator tells how a certain vague feeling of something in the past, triggered by the taste in his mouth of a madeleine dipped in tea, gradually brings back to him the memory of dipping a madeleine in tea when, as a boy, he would visit his aunt. From this particular memory, a whole world comes out:

> And as soon as I had recognized the taste of the piece of madeleine soaked in her decoction of lime-blossom which my aunt used to give me . . . immediately the old grey house upon the street, where her room was, rose up like a stage set to attach itself to the little pavilion opening on to the garden . . . and with the house the town, from

> morning to night and in all weathers, the Square where I used to be sent before lunch, the streets along which I used to run errands, the country roads we took when it was fine. And as in the game wherein the Japanese amuse themselves by filling a porcelain bowl with water and steeping in it little pieces of paper which until then are without character or form [*indistincts*], but, the moment they become wet, stretch and twist and take on color and distinctive shape [*se différencient*], become flowers or houses or people, solid and recognizable, so in that moment all the flowers in our garden and in M. Swann's park, and the water-lilies on the Vivonne and the good folk of the village and their little dwellings and the parish church and the whole of Combray and its surroundings, taking shape [*forme*] and solidity, sprang into being, town and gardens alike, from my cup of tea.[10]

Proust's use of the image of the Japanese paper toy emphasizes the way an elusive past receives, through the process of remembrance, "form and solidity." As it emerges from the cup of tea, Combray ceases to be a dormant mental image, a private representation within the mind. It is no longer vague and shapeless but rather becomes distinct and differentiated—made of church, river, square, flowers—and gains "consistency" and "solidity." It thus acquires the attributes of an object in the physical world without, however, being an actual replica of the world, another object, a simulacrum: after all, the Combray that comes out of the cup of tea is only *likened* to a stage set or to the replicas of the real produced by dipping the Japanese pieces of paper in water. Thus Proust's text makes clear that the space where a memory trace acquires the form and solidity of physical reality and lived experience is neither the mind nor the world but the written page. What comes out of the cup of tea is a section of *La Recherche* entitled "Combray," from which the entire *Côté de chez Swann*, and all subsequent places/volumes of the novel, will be generated. The materiality we are dealing with here is a textual one, and what the passage describes is the originary scene of writing, the birth of the book.

The same can be said about Shahar's novel: what rises from the Jerusalem cistern in Shahar's opening paragraph is the figure of Gabriel Jonathan Luria and with it *Summer in the Street of the Prophets* and the entire *Palace of Shattered Vessels* with its manifold characters and tales:

> Four are the fathers of the feelings of memory: Light and cistern water, the mouth of the cave and the rock at its side—these four have been connected in my memory with the figure of Gabriel Jonathan Luria ever since the time he came to stay in our house when I was a child. From Paris he came straight to our house, and since he entered the yard just before the King of Abyssinia entered the Ethiopian

> Consulate across the road—which is to say, just as I was drawing water from the cistern—his figure was fixed in my memory as rising from its mouth together with the pail of water splashing radiant, dancing light in all directions, which I was drawing up with a peculiar kind of pleasure from its bottom: rising and opening like the Japanese paper flower in its glass of water, which he himself was later to buy me from Hananiah's toy shop. (*Summer*, 9; 7)

At first sight, "cistern water" seems to function as a trigger, much like the taste of the madeleine dipped in tea in the passage from Proust: as one of the "fathers of the feelings of memory," the sight or smell of the cistern water would generate or induce a "feeling of memory" that subsequently would result in a particular memory—that of drawing water from the well. But what is curious about this "originary" experience of memory (and sets it apart from subsequent ones) is that the memory of drawing water from the well is not triggered by any *actual* drawing of water—or even any actual sighting of a cistern or the smell of its water—in the present (close to the time of writing); the only "drawing" that occurs in the present is a *metaphorical* one—the drawing out of the well of memory—while the cistern itself and the act of drawing water are part of a past long gone and are now but a memory. Thus, on the one hand, Shahar turns the Japanese paper toy, which in Proust was only a figure for the process of remembering, into a real object bought "from Hananiah's toy shop"; but, on the other hand, he does not anchor or motivate the "feeling of memory" that inaugurates the novel—and hence the act of remembering and writing—in any actual sensuous experience. It should be noted that the experiential status of the episode of the madeleine in Proust is, too, far from simple, since it is difficult to locate it precisely in the chronology of the *Recherche*.[11] Yet Proust grounds his remembrance and writing in the fortuitous resemblance between two sensuous experiences, a resemblance that triggers "involuntary memory." Shahar, on the other hand, represents remembrance as voluntary: a deliberate act, initiated by the subject (the drawing of water), which does not depend on chance occurrences to trigger it.[12] The circular relation between the origin of memory and the originary event that is remembered (the memory of the well is at the origin of the memory of the well of memory) serves to assure the author of his independence of the vagaries of the real world, his control over his remembrance and writing.[13] Once the process of memory and writing is launched through this willed, self-generating act of "drawing," the narrator can represent characters (including himself) as subjected to "involuntary memory," à la Proust; this will be the case of Srulik's memory of his father (to be discussed below) or the case of Gabriel's memory of his grandfather, triggered by the smell of glue, as well as many other instances.

The memory of drawing water from the well is linked by association (by metonymy) to another memory—that of the first encounter with Gabriel Luria. However, the narrator goes on to say that not only Gabriel's memory but Gabriel himself somehow emerged out of the well: when seen for the first time, Gabriel appears to be rising out of the cistern just like—and at the same time as—the pail of water. Gabriel's appearance and the emergence of the memory of his appearance are here telescoped together to become indistinguishable. The shift in the text from past to present tense following the simile of the Japanese paper flower maintains the impression that the difference between remembered time and time of remembering has collapsed (especially since the use of the present tense in this case can be construed as indicating customary or routine events—the iterative—a use of the present peculiar to narrative). By collapsing Gabriel's first "actual" appearance with his reappearance in and through memory, placing them both in a "now" that is the now of narrating (and, by extension, of writing), Shahar's narrator, just like Proust's, is endowing memory with the concreteness, solidity, and presence ordinarily reserved to what we call "reality." This is achieved through an emergence of the remembered past—out of the well of memory, out of the cave of the mind—onto a material and potentially public space—that of writing. But in doing this, Shahar's narrator is also, and simultaneously, creating the opposite effect: the event of Gabriel's first appearance is ontologically "demoted" to the status of mere memory as writing. The "materialization" of memory has as its counterpart and corollary the "textualization" of experience.

In the Proustian scene of the madeleine, on the other hand, the "reality" of Combray does not seem to have diminished by its recollection and transposition onto the written page. This may account for the "popularity" of the madeleine episode and for the fact that readers who are familiar with only the beginning of Proust's novel would think of him as an author who celebrates the possibility of recovering past experience in and through art. As we shall see later on, however, Proust constantly undermines the distinction between experience and memory, between writing and reality, while continuing to practice an art that *appears* mimetic.

Metaphor and Metonymy

Early Proust critics, taking their cue from Proust himself, have emphasized the centrality of the figure of metaphor—and of its experiential equivalent, involuntary memory—for the *Recherche*. More recently, critics such as Gérard Genette or Paul de Man, arguing that Proust's novelistic practice is more complex, interesting, and "modern" than his theory, have somewhat downplayed the importance of metaphor and the epiphanic moments of involuntary memory in order to emphasize instead that of metonymy and the production of narrative. As Genette put it:

> The true Proustian miracle is not that one madeleine steeped in a cup of tea would taste the same as another madeleine steeped in tea, and would awaken its memory; it is rather that this second madeleine should resuscitate along with it a bedroom, a house, an entire town. . . . Whereas Proust says (or almost says) that without metaphor there are no true memories, we add for him (and for all): without metonymy there is no linking of memories, no story, no novel.[14]

Thus in Proust's text, metonymy operates in conjunction with metaphor. This produces, on the level of figures, hybrid forms (such as metaphors where the term of analogy is motivated by spatial proximity) and, on the level of narrative, a movement of expansion (or "irradiation," to use Proust's own term), a "chain reaction" that, beginning with an analogical relation, extends through contiguity.[15] This movement of metonymical expansion does not involve, strictly speaking, substitution: in the experience of the madeleine, for example, "the old grey house" does not take the place of "the little pavilion opening on to the garden" but rather, "attach[es] itself to [it]"; the town is seen simultaneously "in all weathers"; and the emergence of the whole town and its "good people" does not eclipse the centrality of the "I" who, in remembering the whole of Combray, sees "the Square where I used to be sent before lunch, the streets along which I used to run errands."[16]

The generation of Shahar's text depends just as much as that of Proust on the introduction of metonymical movement into metaphorical relations. The following scene, in which the boy-narrator watches Gabriel Luria as he shaves, sitting on the verandah of his home, can be read as an emblem (or a "mise en abyme") of metonymical narrative as practiced by Shahar:

> Since he [Gabriel] sat with his back to the balustrade, the top of the street, in the place where it joined Abyssinian Road, was reflected in the upper corner of his shaving mirror, enabling him to see what was going on in the triangle of the world behind his back as he shaved and to make his comments. The slightest movement, the most imperceptible stir, would create havoc in the landscape reflected behind his back, although it made no difference at all to his own lathered face in the mirror. One minute Gabriel's head would be floating by itself in a clear, empty sky, and the next people would be going in and out of the doors of the Café Gat. One after the other, the judge's car stopped on the corner and the chauffeur Daoud Ibn Mahmoud jumped out to have something to drink in his spare time, before his boss required his

> services again at the end of the court session; a flock of Ethiopian monks sailed past like black candles against the gray stone walls; and Dr. Landau peeped from his window before setting out for the eye clinic. (*Voyage*, 171; 405)

Following this passage, the text moves away from Gabriel looking at his face in the mirror, and from the boy-narrator, admiringly watching his hero—an idealized mirror image—to Dr. Landau talking to Daoud, then to Dr. Landau in his clinic, treating the Bedouin girl, then into the past, to Dr. Landau in his youth, and so on and so forth. The text, then, functions as a mirror of sorts whose "slight movements" disrupt both Gabriel's and the narrator's specular self-fascination. The mirror reflecting what happens "behind" the beholder may be interpreted as a spatial figure for the temporal dimension of memory, but then what is recalled through the action of this mirror is not only the beholder's own past experience, nor even the experience of the boy who beheld the beholder[17] but extends to the subjective experiences of others, in different places, on other occasions. In Shahar, in contrast to Proust, this extension entails substitution: when the mirror of narrative shifts to show us other characters, in other times and other places, the boy-narrator and Gabriel "go out of focus" and vanish.

This metonymical substitution is fundamental to Shahar's text and accounts for its particular character: a fictional autobiography that repeatedly digresses from its ostensible experiential domain—the hero-narrator's childhood—into the experiences of the adult characters who inhabited his world, and from them to those of yet other characters. In contrast to Proust's text, which remains centered on a self whose development through time (from protagonist to narrator) the novel tells, Shahar's text often takes leave of this self. We would have said that the narrator is not (or not only) the hero of his own story but (primarily) the witness of the stories of others, were it not for the fact that the stories the narrator tells are often not the product of any actual "witnessing."[18] Through an act of identification that abolishes the clear distinction between self and other, between what is inside the self and outside it, the narrator, more a medium than a witness, becomes the vehicle through which the stories of others (often remote in time and place) are told.[19] The story the narrator tells remains, then, "autobiographical," even when it tells of the experience of others, since those others are in some sense versions of the self. Thus, paradoxically, Shahar's narrator can so easily let go of his own self because he refinds himself in others; in contrast, if Proust's narrator remains "self-centered" it is, in part, due to the absolute impossibility he experiences of knowing others who remain, precisely, irreducibly other. (The impossibility of knowing the other is conveyed primarily through the experience of jealousy, so central to Proust's *Recherche*.) The exception that proves the rule is "Un amour de Swann," the story of Swann's love for Odette, which took place well before the narrator's birth and which the narrator tells near the beginning of his novel as though it were (part of) his own. It is this unique and anomalous part of the *Recherche* that many extended passages in Shahar's novel resemble most.

If metonymy is linked to narrative, then metaphor, as we have said, is linked to the return of the past in and through memory. Here, too, the differences between Proust and Shahar are revealing. The repetition of the same, which Genette presented as somewhat banal and trivial (one madeleine steeped in tea repeating another madeleine steeped in tea), would be represented by Shahar as an impossible miracle, and this impossibility marks for him an important limit of memory and writing. This becomes clear in a passage, from the second volume of the *Palace* (*Voyage*, 78–80; 300–302), whose protagonist is Srulik, Gabriel's best friend, whom the boy-narrator knew in his childhood as the little librarian from the Bnei Brit Library.

As in Proust, here, too, memory is triggered by a fortuitous resemblance between two moments in time. Coming home one day, Srulik spots through the window a hat hanging on a chair inside. He concludes that his father—who disappeared a few months earlier—is back home, since the view of the hat hanging on a chair reminds him of a day in his childhood when, returning home from the first day at school, he saw the same thing—a hat hanging on a chair—and, on that occasion, his father was home. The happiness caused by the father's apparent return now merges with another happy memory from that particular day—his happiness at a new suit of clothes in whose pocket he put a blue cellophane candy wrapper after having looked through it and seen the world in blue. The memory and the feeling of happiness are so intense that Srulik actually feels his arm flexing to move the fingers of the little hand that is no longer there, in order to straighten the wrinkles of the wrapper that is no longer there, for a blue-purple vision of a world that is no longer there. This lack of "material support" is enough to turn the momentary happiness of reliving the happy past into torture and misery. As the passage progresses, Srulik's feeling of being in paradise, of soaring into the seventh heaven (the happiness both of the past experience—of being lifted high up to the ceiling by his beloved father—and of reliving the past in the present through the superimposition of past on present), turns into the frustration of being in hell where, in Dantesque manner, one is placed within reach of the object of desire without having the bodily organs necessary to satisfy it.

The repetition of the past in the present would have been in Shahar a miraculous or an uncanny occurrence—that of the body and other material objects being exempted from the destructiveness of time. In contrast, what Srulik experiences is the "brittleness [*prichut*] of this world founded on the nothingness of the senses" (*Summer*, 147, 149; 132, 135). The senses, which are, according to Shahar, our only means of experiencing the empirical world, can also play tricks on us (especially when coupled with our wishful thinking) and even lead us to imagine that we have transcended temporality and the material world. At the same time, Srulik's tantalizing experience indicates, once more, to what extent Shahar is reluctant to divorce the process of remembering from its material support, refuses to consider the material support as immaterial. It is this commitment to the physical world that makes Srulik (as well as Shahar) wish for the exact recurrence of the very same (rather than a new edition of it, repetition with difference), thus pushing metaphor toward tautology. Paradoxically, this commitment also renders the desire for exact repetition impossible to realize, since in a world governed by irreversible time and irreducible space, resemblance (or even replication) can never be perfect identity.

In contrast, what Proust valorizes in metaphor is precisely the element of difference. In his text, metaphor verging on tautology stands for unproductive memory, memory fixated on one experience, and returning to it, obsessively.[20] Thus the narrating I in the opening pages of the novel (a narrating I who is not quite yet the narrator[21]), suffering from insomnia, waking up and not knowing exactly where he is, lighting a match to see what time it is, hoping it would soon be day—compares himself to a sick person who finds himself in an unknown hotel, wakes up and, misled by a ray of light, thinks it is soon going to be day, only to discover a minute later that it is only midnight, and that he has the whole night to suffer through without relief (I, 4; I, 4). This is memory as fixation and compulsion to repeat. For this narrating I the entire world of Combray is reduced to one single experience—the "going to bed drama"; and though he can, if asked, recall other aspects of his childhood in Combray, his interest in them is blocked by his obsession (I, 43–44; I, 46–47).

In contrast to the repetitive obsession that is entirely motivated from within the subject, "involuntary memory," as in the episode of the madeleine, is triggered by a fortuitous encounter with an object that turns out to be meaningful for the subject. Such encounters generate two kinds of movement that may in a sense appear contradictory: one is the movement of metonymization, described by Genette, and the other is a movement of abstracting from the two moments involved in the epiphanic experience a common essence. The latter is what allows Proust to speak of involuntary memory as the experiential analogue of the literary device of metaphor, yet metaphor understood as a figure that brings together two terms without erasing their difference.

In *Le temps retrouvé*, for example, dismissing the claim of "realism" to attain truth through detailed description of objects, the narrator states that

> truth will be attained by [the writer] only when he takes two different objects, states the connection between them . . . and encloses them in the necessary links of a well-wrought style; . . . when, by

> comparing a quality common to two sensations [*en rapprochant une qualité commune à deux sensations*], he extracts their common essence in joining them to each other, liberated from the contingencies of time, within a metaphor. (III, 889; III, 924–25)

The sameness that emerges through metaphor and involuntary memory is not literal or physical identity but a "common essence," and this common essence cannot become legible except against the background of difference.[22] In another passage, the narrator explains why the "miracle of an analogy," which allows one to apprehend "something that, common both to the past and to the present, is much more essential than either of them" (III, 871, 872; III, 904, 905), is so satisfying for him:

> So often, in the course of my life, reality had disappointed me because at the instant when my senses perceived it my imagination, which was the only organ that I possessed for the enjoyment of beauty, could not apply itself to it, in virtue of that ineluctable law which ordains that we can only imagine what is absent. And now, suddenly, the effect of this harsh law had been neutralized, temporarily annulled, by a marvelous expedient of nature which has caused a sensation—the noise made by the spoon and by the hammer, the same title of a book and so on—to flash [*miroiter*] at one and the same time in the past, so that my imagination was permitted to savor it, and in the present, where the actual shock to my senses of the noise, the touch of the linen napkin, or whatever it might be, had added to the dreams of the imagination the idea of "existence" which they usually lack, and through this subterfuge had made it possible for my being [*avait permis à mon être*] to secure, to isolate, to immobilize—for a moment brief as the flash of lightning—what normally it never apprehends: a fragment of time in pure state [*un peu de temps à l'état pur*]. (III, 872; III, 905)

This passage allows us to mark some important differences between Proust and Shahar. The "organ" through which the Proustian narrator enjoys beauty is not the eye but the imagination.[23] For Shahar, on the other hand, "the spiritual pleasure of light in all its colors and hues," and "the light of the whole world," "the pleasures of light and colors and melodies"—which stand for aesthetic experience but also for perception and cognition—always depend on the "ball of flesh" that is the eye (*Countess*, 33). This is not to suggest that Shahar is a more naive "realist" than Proust but to note the primacy granted by Shahar to sensory experience and his wariness about the possibility of nonsensory experience:

> I had, however, the flickering sensation that there may be feelings and emotions and visions and melodies that are not of this world, and exist without the mediation of the body; but the possibility of such bodiless, indefinite being fluttering in the empty void between nothing and nothing frightened me so much that I repressed it before it grew.[24] (*Countess,* 33–34)

Shahar's entire artistic project is played out between this fear of withdrawal into a disembodied, solipsistic spiritual sphere and the impossible desire to recapture the presence and plenitude attributed to the direct experience of the senses. As we have shown in chapter 1, the momentary fulfillment of this desire occurs in certain uncanny moments when a fragment of the past irrupts into the world of the here and now. In Proust, on the other hand, the encounter with reality experienced through the senses is devalued, since the presence of any "real" object *rules out* the working of the imagination; and yet imagination alone is not entirely satisfactory either. What happens in the brief moments of involuntary memory is an experience, as Beckett put it in his early essay on Proust, "at once imaginative and empirical, at once an evocation and a direct perception, real without being merely actual, ideal without being merely abstract, the ideal real, the essential, the extratemporal."[25] It seems as though it is Shahar who is more literally "in search of lost time," trying to retrieve the past and haul it back into the present. Proust's *recherche*, on the other hand, is not (as is commonly stated), for the past but for "a fragment of time in pure state," an apprehension of temporality per se, to be gained through the "subterfuge"of juxtaposing two separate moments in time.[26]

Autobiographical Narration

It is commonly agreed that autobiographical narration, by its retrospective nature, involves both a loss and a gain. In contrast to more immediate forms of recounting one's experience (such as letters or diaries), the greater temporal distance of autobiographical narration hampers its capacity to capture the full contingent richness of the original experience; but, on the other hand, this greater temporal distance allows the autobiographical narrator to gain an understanding of the story of his or her past, an understanding that often hinges on the ability to say when and how a certain process began. Of this point, Proust takes a particularly radical view. In the following discussion of "beginnings," in *La Prisonnière*, apropos of a sentence by Albertine, he says:

> I would have liked to recall exactly how the sentence had begun, in order to decide for myself, since she had broken off in the middle,

> what the conclusion [*la fin*] would have been. But since I had been awaiting that conclusion [*fin*], I found it hard to remember the beginning, from which perhaps my air of interest had made her deviate, and was left still anxious to know her real thoughts, the actual truth of her recollection [*son souvenir véridique*]. The beginnings of a lie on the part of one's mistress are, unfortunately, like the beginnings of one's own love, or of a vocation. They take shape, accumulate, pass unnoticed by oneself. When one wants to remember in what manner one began to love a woman, one is already in love with her; day-dreaming about her beforehand, one did not say to oneself: "This is the prelude to love; be careful [*faisons attention*]!"—and one's day-dreams advanced unobtrusively [*par surprise*], scarcely noticed by oneself. In the same way, save in a few comparatively rare cases, it is only for narrative convenience that I have frequently in these pages confronted [*opposé*] one of Albertine's false statements with her previous assertion [*assertion première*] on the same subject. This previous assertion [*assertion première*], as often as not, since I could not read the future and did not at the time guess what contradictory affirmation was to form a pendant to it, had slipped by unperceived, heard it is true by my ears, but without my isolating it from the continuous flow of Albertine's speech. Later on, faced with the self-evident lie, or seized by an anxious doubt, I would endeavor to recall it; but in vain; my memory has not been warned in time; it had thought it unnecessary to keep a copy. (III, 153; III, 149–50)

The narrator here not only admits that the account he has frequently opposed to Albertine's "lies," and hence presented as "true," is actually fictive, generated for "narrative convenience," but, more tellingly, he makes the epistemological point that it *could not* have been otherwise, since events, when they *begin*, "take shape, accumulate, pass *unnoticed* by oneself." What would subsequently turn out to have been a beginning—of a sentence and, by extension, of narrative, of love, of a vocation—can never be fully present to the self, whether in past lived experience or in present remembering and writing. It is not that retrospective understanding is gained at the expense of some loss to the richness of immediate experience; rather, since understanding of the future significance of the moment could not be had at the moment of experience, it was not *lived* in all of its fullness, hence, there is no "record" of it for future understanding. Accordingly, the retrospective structuring of a life into a totalized narrative with origin and end that we call "understanding," and autobiographical narration in the precise sense of a retrospective tracing of intelligible patterns can only be fictitious, acts of invention and representation.

A similar view is suggested in a crucial passage in Marguerite Duras's novel *L'Amant* (*The Lover*). We make this brief digression into the world of a third author for heuristic purposes: the Duras passage is concerned with an event having the outward form of a beginning, thus making the point more clearly. Referring to the event that will turn out to have fundamentally structured her experience and informed her vocation as a writer—the crossing of the river when, as a young girl of sixteen, she first saw the Chinese lover—she writes:

> I think it was during this journey that the image became detached, removed from all the rest. It might have existed, a photograph might have been taken, just like any other, somewhere else, in other circumstances. But it wasn't. The subject was too slight. Who would have thought of such a thing? The photograph could only have been taken if someone could have known in advance how important it was to be in my life, that event, that crossing of the river. But while it was happening, no one even knew of its existence. Except God. And that's why—it couldn't have been otherwise—the image doesn't exist. It was omitted. Forgotten. It never was detached or removed from all the rest. And it's to this, this failure to have been created, that the image owes its virtue: the virtue of representing, of being the creator [*auteur]* of, an absolute."[27]

The full apprehension of an originary event, demarcated and defined ("detached, removed from all the rest"), present to consciousness both in all of its minute detail and in its subsequent meaning, would be possible only to a subject possessing the attributes of God. This god-like position often appears in fiction in the guise of an omniscient narrator. Within the "normal" conventions of realism, however, the cognitive position we call "omniscient narration" is clearly incompatible with the position of a human first-person narrator. Duras's passage suggests that to the extent that any novelist (and that would include Shahar) wants to insist on the referential veracity or experiential nature of his or her tale (what one did, saw, thought, and felt when one was ten years old) he or she must relinquish the claim to recapture the reality he or she aims to represent; or, conversely, he or she may recount this reality in all of its detail and significance but only on the condition of renouncing the literal referentiality of the autobiographical project in the traditional sense. In either case, the text cannot be understood as the recapturing by the subject of his or her lived past experience as it really was, and the "reality" or "solidity" of what is remembered or represented cannot be judged by its adequation or approximation to such a past.

In comparison to Proust's and Duras's self-referential reflections, Shahar's representation of an originary event as both fully experienced and fully recaptured (or, at least, fully experienced at the moment of writing when it is fully recaptured) may seem naive. In a passage from *Summer in the Street of the Prophets*, the narrator describes a moment when he first saw, still without recognition, a figure from/of his past. The passage thus describes both a particular past event retained by memory, and the "event" of remembering, the return of the past:

> As was only expected, and as usual on all previous call-ups, time dragged on interminably in the uniform grayness of the world of external activities. However, as not to be expected, one moment—the moment when the man came out of the gate in the wall—suddenly detached itself from the course of time: this moment appeared before me like the vision of an orange sunset in which everything—the stone wall and the treetops beyond it and the dusty path and the black figure of the man—was immersed in a strange, wonderful, ample calm, as fixed and unchanging and outside the course of time as a picture hanging in a museum that you can go back to look at whenever you like and find exactly as it was when the artist finished painting it, without having to worry about the changes that may have taken place in the landscape during the passage of time—whether the sun has set and the sky darkened, or the wall collapsed and its stones scattered, or the man reached the end of the dusty path and turned off into the main road and disappeared. The strange and wonderful calming and uplifting flavor of this certainty that it was possible to return to this orange-colored moment of spacious sunset detached from the race of time, just as it was possible to return to a picture hanging in a museum, or to a place where you had already been before, remained with me even after I had returned to the course of time and the little black figure had turned the corner and disappeared. (*Summer*, 121; 104–105)

In contrast to Proust's and Duras's insistence on the impossibility of "isolating" or "detaching" a moment from the "continuous flow," here a moment in time does get detached; this both indicates that it is experienced as a privileged moment and explains why it can and will be recovered at will. Though the passage deals with the appearance of a figure, the emphasis is not, as in Duras or Proust, on the moment inaugurating a significant sequence. Rather, detached from the flow of time and thus remembered in all of its fullness, the "vision" of the moment signifies the power of memory to triumph over time, loss, and death: in memory, the sun never sets, the wall does not collapse, the man does not disappear (and since the man in question is Srulik, of whose death the narrator is about to hear, we can take this to mean that in his memory he remains alive). The narrator does not explain how and why the particular moment became detached; he merely says that this was unexpected, a small miracle. Rather than explain, he asserts the outcome: he both fully experienced this unique, out-standing moment and can fully recapture it. Curiously, however, the analogies proposed by the narrator in advancing his claim also may work to undermine it: the permanence of material objects is not more absolute, only of a different kind, than that of a memory trace, and so pictures in a museum may burn or deteriorate; the past is not an unchanging geography, as the narrator knows all too well. Much of the pathos of autobiographical writing is predicated on this latter realization—a realization that constitutes the "essence" of experience and provides the *raison d'être* of writing. Shahar's analogies, while designed to buttress his confidence in the adequacy and indestructibility of memory (and therefore the truth of his autobiographical narration), raise as many doubts as they dispel.

While Shahar does not offer an explicit theoretical discussion of the cognitive problems raised by Proust and Duras, his narrative practice (sometimes in spite of his narrator's efforts) exhibits the same difficulties in pinning down the original and originary event. If Proust narrates certain beginnings as though naturally, and only at some later point turns around and explains that this was done only for "narrative convenience," in Shahar, a certain incoherence in the representation of the event betrays its problematic mimetic status. Thus in describing Gabriel's first appearance, Shahar enhances this scene with all of the rhetorical hallmarks of an inaugural event. Yet, as we have already shown, it is not quite clear what essentially new pattern this "great and strange day," or even the entire brief period culminating in the "enchanted day," will turn out to have ushered. Likewise, the very punctuality of this event is both asserted and undermined in the text as it is inserted in contradictory descriptions of the surrounding circumstances. It is possible to infer from these textual contradictions that in his narrative practice Shahar experiences the impossibility of capturing such necessarily slippery events. It is perhaps because this impossibility is ever present in his mind that he so easily and frequently departs from a strictly personal, retrospective mode of narration and avails himself of the privileges of omniscient narration, most notably free access to other minds, entering the experiential domain of characters presented as other people existing in his world. One can even argue that it is through this alternation that Shahar attempts to overcome the double impossibility of the autobiographical project—an impossibility that, if we follow Duras, is the source of writing.

Apprenticeship

In Proust, the recovery of memory is intimately linked to the discovery of his vocation as an artist—a writer. Though, as we have seen, in both Shahar and

Proust the return of the past as a well-defined memory occurs at/as a moment of textual production, it is still the case that Shahar, unlike Proust, does not organize the story of the past as that of discovering his vocation as a writer. In spite of fairly frequent allusions to the act of writing, and in spite of fairly explicit hints that the narrator is identical to the author, David Shahar, there is no attempt in the novels of the *Palace* to trace the story of the young boy he was as leading to his having become the writer that he is.

This is related to another major difference between Shahar and Proust: in Proust, the discovery of artistic vocation is presented as the culmination of a process of demystification—a process whereby the errors of childhood and youth are recognized as such and replaced with some kind of truth. Commenting on the literary career of Bergotte after his death, Proust's narrator points out the role of disillusion and failed dreams for the artist:

> Desire is therefore not without its value to the writer in detaching him first of all from his fellow men and from conforming to their standards, and afterwards in restoring some degree of movement to a spiritual machine which, after a certain age, tends to come to a standstill. We do not achieve happiness, but we gain some insights into the reasons which prevent us from being happy and which would have remained invisible to us but for these sudden revelations of disappointment. Dreams, we know, are not realizable; we might not form any, perhaps, were it not for desire, and it is useful to us to form them in order to see them fail and to learn from their failure. (III, 183; III, 181)

Life is an error ("*cette erreur perpetuelle qui est la vie*," III, 585), and the narrator is someone who has recognized his errors and turned them into the material for a novel displaying this process of retrospective recognition.

Shahar's narrative, on the other hand, does not have the overall shape of a story of error discovered and corrected. This does not mean that the boy-hero knows and understands everything the moment it occurs. There are many instances in the text of the *Palace* where the narrator attracts our attention to a (momentary) gap in his knowledge or understanding of a particular event. Thus, for example, he mistakenly believes that the poems he has discovered under the peacock ashtray, *Songs of Tammuz to Ashera* [*Shirei Tammuz le-Ashera*] by Eshbaal Ashtarot, are "the very songs sung by the priestesses of Baal and the prophets of Ashtoret" (*Countess*, 12), only to discover, before the end of that very same day, that the poems were written six months earlier and not thousands of years ago (*Countess*, 32). When he discovers in the margin of the book its date of publication, he concludes that its author must be Gabriel, partially because of the stories he has heard about the latter's "pagan" tendencies (*Countess*, 77–78), but no sooner has he reached this conclusion than his error is dispelled by Gabriel himself who tells him that the poet is actually Berl (*Countess*, 78). For a while, the boy-narrator thinks that the young woman he keeps seeing coming out of Dr. Landau's house is his daughter, and again it is Gabriel who enlightens him and tells him that it is, in fact, "the famous Orita," Dr. Landau's wife (*Voyage*, 37–38; 252–53), and so on. But, as we can see, these errors, rather than structuring large movements of the plot, are corrected almost immediately and thus remain local.[28] Major attitudes or relationships, on the other hand, never fall into patterns of error and demystification.[29] The narrator is never led to a realization, say, that Gabriel is not the man he took him to be, or that Nin-Gal was not worthy of his love. Even when Srulik reappears as a Calvinist missionary, the narrator does not greet this astonishing transformation with any revision of his basic attitude toward him. Errors in Shahar's text, then, do not acquire a momentous weight that will make their dispelling a landmark in the development of the boy-hero, as is the case in Proust's text. There, for example, the hero's childhood belief that the two "sides"—that of Swann, or of Méseglise, and that of the Guermantes—are opposed to each other both literally (they lead in opposite directions) and symbolically (they represent two incompatible worlds) is dispelled only toward the end of the novel, when Gilberte proposes to him to go to Méseglise "by way of Guermantes," and this astonishing proposal causes him to revise his entire understanding of the relation between the two "sides" (III, 693; III, 711). In contrast, Shahar's novel as a whole does not show the boy-hero growing up and maturing, understanding his past errors, and attaining wisdom. This is most obvious in the later volumes of the novel (from *Nin-Gal* on), where the adult narrator, rather than effacing himself before his youthful self, whose experiences he represents, speaks to us directly without necessarily striking us as being wiser.

Indeed, the difference the narrator often remarks between his childhood self and his adult self does not amount to a gain in understanding but rather to a loss—loss of a certain intense experience possible only in childhood and which the first volume of the novel calls "the joy of awakening." Thus *The Palace of Shattered Vessels* is a fictive autobiography that differs in important ways from the tradition of the spiritual autobiography (from Saint Augustine on) as well as the tradition of the Bildungsroman and the Künstlerroman that reached one of its high points in Proust's *A la recherche du temps perdu*. In order to better understand these differences, we should take a closer look at what the process of apprenticeship in Proust entails.

The importance of apprenticeship in Proust's text was particularly emphasized by Deleuze. In *Proust and Signs*, he argued that however important the role of memory is in the *Recherche*, it "intervenes only as the means of an apprenticeship which transcends recollection both by its goals and by its principles." "Proust's work," says Deleuze, "is not oriented to the past and the discoveries of memory, but to the future and the progress of an apprenticeship. What is important is that the hero did not know certain things at the start, gradually learns them, and finally receives an ultimate revelation."[30] In other words, the practice of memory is a means for recovering the "lost" past as error, a recovery without which there could be no access to mature knowledge.

The hero of the *Recherche* (commonly called Marcel by critics) commits many errors. He creates in his mind an image of places—Balbec, Florence, Parma—based on their names, only to be disappointed when the real place proves to be totally different from the mental image of it he created in his mind. After several encounters with Charlus, he still does not understand that Charlus is a homosexual or that he is trying to seduce him. Jealous of his lover, Albertine, he tries to discover whether she tells him the truth and often fails. Walking as a child along the Méseglise way and meeting for the first time Gilberte Swann, he misinterprets a gesture she makes at him; walking in Paris during the war, he mistakes a brothel for a luxury hotel, and so on and so forth. All of these errors are errors of interpretation: faced with signs of different sorts, Marcel has to learn how to decipher them, and once he does, he understands certain truths (about the world, about love, about art). Marcel's errors of interpretation are not simply failures to read particular signs; they are also errors about the very nature and *modus operandi* of signs. His error about names, for example, stems from his assumption that there is a natural relation between signifier and signified and that the signified is the same as the referent.[31] Once he discovers this assumption to be false, Marcel develops an understanding of linguistic signs as symptoms: "Words themselves did not enlighten me unless they were interpreted in the same way as a rush of blood to the cheeks of a person who is embarrassed, or as a sudden silence" (III, 88; III 83).

Thus in Proust's world, all knowledge and understanding is mediated by signs, and signs tend to be opaque: their meaning is not immediately available to the interpreter who, on the contrary, has to learn the art of deciphering. Moreover, signs receive their meaning through time, hence, they cannot be understood on their first occurrence; understanding is retrospective, it depends on memory, which is not, as we have seen, quite dependable. Though Marcel is intelligent, sensitive, and precocious, he is not endowed with an intuitive, immediate understanding of these signs, and at the end of his long apprenticeship, he is all the more aware of the obliquity of signs and the impossibility of complete knowledge.

In Shahar, on the other hand, we begin with an experience of revelation. Far from being disappointed at the encounter with reality because of some previous misguided ideas about it, the child discovers on his own the sublime beauty of the night.

> The first meeting with the night sky shocked me and filled me with muffled dread. I saw the sky and suddenly it was black with tiny points of life in it. "Those are the stars," said Gabriel, and added, "the hosts of heaven." The Old City walls and the mountains around them, the Mount of Olives and Mount Scopus, were present in the darkness and heavy with the weight of an ancient-breathed quality, terrible in its dimensions which were beyond the dimensions of man, and its eternities which were beyond the eternity of man, and its indifference to the little men stirring on its back. (*Summer*, 13; 11–12)

The experience of the sublime—the immensity of the universe and the insignificance of man in it—is an immediate experience of the child, the result of his direct encounter with the night; the "naming" by Gabriel ("Those are the stars . . . the hosts of heaven") is secondary and follows the direct, immediate experience of beauty and dread.

The passage describing the first encounter with the world of the night appears also in the late short story "First Lesson" (where the figure of the father takes the place of that of Gabriel).[32] There it is followed by an important scene at school:

> When my teacher read aloud during the Bible lesson the words, "In the beginning God created the heavens and the earth and the earth was without form and void, and darkness was upon the face of the deep," the quality [*mahut*—essence] of the elements made tangible [*mitmameshet*—comes into being, realized] in the darkness suddenly welled up in me unendurably. "And God said, let there be light," and in the wall of darkness a crack was revealed and the imprisoned light burst through it to wrap the rocks and clods of earth in a mantle of day. I had sensed the things as they were [*devarim le-ashuram*], from inside myself, and the written and spoken words garbed them in phrases like currency which could be passed from hand to hand, from one man to another. On hearing these words from the mouth of my teacher, Mr. Avisar, for the first time, I waited with a pounding heart for a miracle like the miracle of the first night to happen. A great silence would fall on the classroom and in another little while the voice of God would be heard calling beyond it and I was already trembling with a terror that grew stronger with every moment that passed. (*Pope*, 248; *News*, 217)

Through the reading of the Bible by the teacher, the child experiences the moment of creation, the coming into existence [*hitmamshut*] of essence [*mahut*]. Though this takes place through the written and read word, the child can make a distinction between his unmediated experience of "things as they were" [*devarim le-ashuram*], which he senses "from inside [him]self," and the words, which communicate the experience of creation to others. Certainly the adult narrator, reporting this scene in the past tense, presents the boy as being somewhat naive, when following the logic of his visceral experience he awaits in awe to hear the voice of God; but this naivete is not considered a shortcoming. The narrator does not show any shame or embarrassment in telling this episode (even though he can no longer share the child's confidence) nor does he consider it an "error"; the other children and the teacher are seen as being deficient, since they cannot share the child's experience and take his silent waiting as a sign of his ignorance.[33]

The story "First Lesson" starts with the assertion of continuity between child and adult: "In the beginning was the miracle, and the miracle was, and is, and will be to be marveled at always. As for me, I have never stopped marveling to this day. . . . And not only have I not stopped marveling, but the marveling increases from day to day" (242; 209). Yet in the description of the child marveling at creation and expecting to hear the voice of God, the difference between the child and the adult narrator is clear. For the narrator, the fullness of immediate experience is no longer possible; indeed, as he tells us a bit later, he is full of yearnings and longings to an "essence beyond" [*ha'ikar*] (245; 213), which he cannot reach.

The child once possessed the immediate vision for which the adult can only long: Shahar is here closer to Wordsworth than to Proust without, however, subscribing in any obvious way to a conception based on anamnesis. Unlike Wordsworth, Shahar does not see the child's privilege as proceeding from prenatal knowledge, but unlike Proust, Shahar is full of nostalgia for his childhood. Something in the childhood of Shahar's protagonist-surrogates makes them susceptible to quasimystical experiences of unmediated revelation. What the adult narrator is nostalgic for in these experiences is not just their content but their intensity, so rarely, if at all, attainable in later life.

Though the capacity for "marveling" is what marks Shahar's protagonist for an artistic vocation, artistic production—or at least the art of writing—is seen as just a poor substitute for the experience of unmediated revelation. Unlike the child who fully experiences divine creation, lives the moment in which absence becomes presence, in which essence becomes manifest, the adult narrator can reach only the "veil" and the "limit," is ever on a voyage toward a goal he knows to be unattainable. Writing emerges out of this experience of loss: it is, the narrator of "First Lesson" tells us, the "tax" [*mas*] he has to pay in order to get the most out of the impossible voyage of longing and yearning (245; 213).

In the *Palace* novels, Shahar does not include elaborate discussions of his own art nor does he speak of the function of writing, but the allusion to the

Kabbalist theory of the "breaking of the vessels," most prominent in the novel-sequence's general title, provides us with a conceptual framework within which the particular kind of novel Shahar writes becomes comprehensible. According to the Kabbala, creation involved a catastrophe—the breaking of the vessels unable to contain the divine light. Human beings can help mend the "broken" world by working for "*Tikun*" (literally, mending)—picking up the sparks of light lying among the broken vessels. What would be the equivalent in the novel of the breaking of the vessels that requires *Tikun*? The happy world of childhood, the world of "summer in Street of the Prophets" with its "joy of awakening," is a world where there is no difference between "consciousness of sleep" and "consciousness of waking": "There was no abyss gaping between these two states of the soul—the abyss of birth and death—and I would run back and forth between sleeping and waking, and waking and sleeping, as if I were passing from one room to another in an enchanted palace [*armon*]" (*Summer*, 56; 46). It is also, as we have seen in the previous chapter, a world in which personal identities are fluid and porous, and where temporal distinctions are blurred. In other words, the world of childhood is presented as a world with neither beginning nor end, neither divisions nor gaps, an undifferentiated—unarticulated—wholeness. The equivalent of the "breaking of the vessels" would then be articulation—the introduction of spaces and difference, of absence, into an undifferentiated totality and unbroken continuity. The narrative procedures typical of Shahar's writing—entering the consciousness of other characters, collapsing different points in time, and creating an associative narrative flow where the boundaries between discreet "stories" are abolished—can be seen then as a means for an impossible task: creating through writing (which is articulation) an equivalent for the unbroken, unarticulated wholeness of the world of childhood.

Proust's trajectory toward writing is quite different. Starting with error and suffering rather than with revelation and joy, the narrator goes through a process of demystification at the end of which the superiority of art over life and his own vocation as a writer are revealed to him. The superiority of art is precisely in that it affords us knowledge. Unlike the elusive beloved who escapes the grasp and knowledge of the lover (even when imprisoned), the artist makes himself known in his work of art (known, that is, as an artist, not as a person[34]), and thus enables us to know otherness by lending us his eyes:

> . . . the art of a Vinteuil like that of an Elstir . . . exteriorizes in the colors of the spectrum the intimate composition of those worlds which we call individuals and which, without the aid of art, we would never know. A pair of wings, a different respiratory system, which enabled us to travel through space, would in no way help us, for if we visited Mars or Venus while keeping the same senses, they would

> clothe everything that we saw in the same aspect of the things of Earth. The only true voyage of discovery . . . would be not to visit strange lands but to possess other eyes, to see the universe through the eyes of another, of a hundred others, to see the hundred universes that each of them sees, that each of them is; and this we can do with an Elstir, with a Vinteuil. . . . Through art alone are we able to emerge from ourselves, to know what another person sees of a universe which is not the same as our own and of which, without art, the landscapes would have remained as unknown to us as those that might exist on the moon. Thanks to art, instead of seeing one world only, our own, we see that world multiply itself, and we have at our disposal as many worlds as there are original artists, worlds more different from each other than those which revolve in infinite space.[35] (III, 258, 895–96; III, 259–60, 932)

The discovery of his own vocation comes to the narrator when he realizes that self-knowledge also is possible only through art. Life itself, Proust tells us, is error and estrangement; art is not an imitation of this life of/as error and estrangement (as the practitioners of "realist" art ["*la littérature de notations*"] seem to think). Art is "true to life" not when it duplicates "what our eyes see and our intellect records" but when it reveals "the qualitative difference, the uniqueness of the fashion in which the world appears to each one of us." Hence, the narrator's conclusion: "Real life [*la vraie vie*], life at last laid bare and illuminated—the only life in consequence which can be said to be really lived—is literature" (III, 894–95; III, 931–32).

Artists

Artists play an important role in Marcel's education and apprenticeship. Though his first encounter with Bergotte's texts or with Berma's playing of Racine is rather disappointing (as the first encounter with most things is), Marcel subsequently learns to appreciate their art and, through this appreciation, he develops an understanding of what art is. The hearing of Vinteuil's music and the viewing of Elstir's paintings are important episodes in his life and landmarks in his development. They also are occasions for long discussions of and meditations on the nature of art.[36]

Artists do not have this kind of importance in Shahar's novel, and this is partially due to the fact we mentioned earlier: the *Palace* novels do not really tell the story of apprenticeship, the coming into being of an artist. Yet figures of artists abound in the *Palace*: the poet Eshbaal Ashtarot, the American poet Helen Morley, the playwright Aharon Dan, the filmscript writer Tammuz, the old English painter Holmes, the young painter Yaeli Landau (Orita's granddaughter), the photographer William Gordon, the violinist and composer Brunhilde, the pianist Paul Dornoy, also known as "the Polish owl," and the theater director Yehuda Shoshan; to this list we should add two craftspeople, the coppersmith Elka, Srulik's aunt, and the master carpenter Markel Cohen, Gabriel's maternal grandfather. Many of these figures remain rather marginal to the "plot" of the novel, and most are marginal figures in the society in which they live—misfits or, in Mrs. Luria's words, "broken vessels." Though the artistic excellence of some of them is never doubted, most do not achieve material success or public recognition. None is a "model" for the hero, though some (Helen Morely, Yaeli Landau, Aharon Dan) are used by the narrator as examples of what art should *not* be.

The most important artist in terms of the novel's plot is Eshbaal Ashtarot, otherwise known as Berl Raban. An intimate friend of Gabriel, he is also a constant presence in the boy's childhood world by virtue of working as Dr. Landau's assistant. The boy's discovery under the peacock ashtray of the book of poems *The Songs of Tammuz to Ashera* and his realization that their author, Eshbaal Ashtarot, is none other than Berl take place on the "enchanted day," which is also the day on which Berl quit his job in the eye clinic; Berl's move to the basement in Mrs. Luria's house occurs one week later, just before the beginning of the riots. Thus two important days in the life of Berl/Eshbaal are also important days in the life of the boy-narrator.

Berl's/Eshbaal's decision to quit his job in the clinic and leave his home in order to dedicate himself to writing his poetry in Mrs. Luria's basement is the novel's prime representation of the artist as someone with a "vocation." Artistic vocation is here understood as freedom from the usual obligations of middle-class life—earning a living and caring for a family. When Shoshi, whose life is transformed by her chance discovery of Eshbaal's poems, enters Berl's basement, "without ringing or knocking," this puts the last touch to the portrait of the artist as a rebel against the bourgeois way of life by adding to the freedom from daily cares the freedom of love.

But Berl's strike for freedom is not as rebellious as it may seem, since the social world in which he lives is not entirely committed to bourgeois values (work, riches, status). Berl's action, therefore, does not generate a dramatic conflict; it remains, in fact, without clear consequences. His ideological "transgression," symbolized by his name change, will be reversed only posthumously when the orthodox Jews, who symbolize the identity he rejected, claim him as their saint. During his life, Berl is censured only by one character—the new librarian, Devora Calmanson, who is elsewhere presented as intolerant and who, it is more than hinted at, is motivated by her own desires. Mrs. Luria, who first considers Berl's act sheer madness and condemns him for deserting his wife and three children to die of hunger (*Countess*, 120–21), ends up justifying his act in the following terms:

> This Berl, he has a dear soul. A person like him, who turns his back to all the pleasures of this world, who gives up a good job in order to realize the dream in his heart, is called in our days an idealist. And he is not like one of those rascals who call themselves idealists, who don't see anything but themselves, who are ready to return the world to a state of chaos only so that their heart's desires can be fulfilled, those spoiled brats who think that everything is owed to them, who claim that this world, since it does not give them all their pampering on a silver platter, deserves to be destroyed. (*Countess*, 123–24)

Shahar's novel represents several other "idealists" who, rather than looking for material and social success (or trying to change the world in order to better themselves), invest most of their energy in disinterested projects: the pharmacist Blum who thinks it is crucial to put the belief in the efficacy of sacrifice to a scientific test; Srulik, who dreams of going to Ur of Chaldees and ends up a Calvinist missionary; Gabriel himself, who occupies himself with a mysterious book of philosophical notations. Even Berl's brother, Haim Longlife, who dreams all his life of money-making inventions is, as Mrs. Luria shrewdly notes, an idealist, a dreamer, who never cares for the practical implementation of his inventions. Berl's devoting himself to writing poetry is thus but one manifestation of this "idealism" that the novel as a whole celebrates.[37] But Berl is a dreamer not only because he devotes himself to writing poetry and, hermit-like, turns his back on the world, "demand[ing] nothing from this world—neither riches nor honors nor yet pleasures" (*Countess*, 124). He also dreams of a world long gone and dead—"dreams of Malchitsedek, king of Shalem, and of Joshua Son of Nun, and of the prophets of the Baal" and, rather than seeking to turn these dreams into reality, retires from the world "to make poems out of his dreams" (*Countess*, 123). When Berl quits his job and moves into Mrs. Luria's basement, he does not simply free himself from certain obligations in order to make time to write his poetry; he rejects "the world" in at least three of its manifestations (the world of everyday obligations, the world of the present, and the world of political and social action). This rejection is reciprocated by the world: Eshbaal Ashtarot remains a rather obscure poet during his life and a misunderstood one after his death. The misinformation provided by his widow, Lea Himmelsach—that Eshbaal was influenced by Ezra Pound—causes critics to "find fault not necessarily with his opinions but rather with his poetry: from the poetic point of view, according to objective criteria and textual analysis, it became clear to them beyond any doubt that this was not poetry at all or, in the best case, bad poetry" (*Ghosts*, 13).

When Berl moves into Mrs. Luria's basement, he puts a sign on the door: "Please do not disturb. No ringing or knocking" (*Countess*, 116). At the end of *Time Regained*, Marcel also will shun the social world that may come knocking at his door: "I would not even permit people to come and see me at home during my hours of work, for the duty of writing my book took precedence now over that of being polite or even kind. . . . I should have the courage to reply to those who came to see me or tried to get me to visit them that I had, for necessary business which required my immediate attention, an urgent, a supremely important appointment with myself" (III, 986; III, 1034–35). And yet artistic vocation means something quite different in Proust than in the *Palace*.

We know that the *Recherche* is the story of a vocation, of how Marcel becomes a writer. But as Vincent Descombes notes in his discussion of vocation in Proust, Marcel's choice of artistic vocation is not played out against obstacles and restrictions in the world outside of him: rich and free, he does not have to quit his job or desert his wife in order to dedicate himself to his art, his parents do not interfere with his choices, and many of his friends and acquaintances encourage him.[38] If Marcel does not become a writer earlier on, it is not because the world puts obstacles in his way, but because he doubts his ability to write. And he doubts his ability to write because he cannot write on the kind of subjects he considers worthy of a great writer; he is blocked, because he doubts his inspiration. He will become a writer when he realizes that the subjects that interest him or make a strong impression on him do provide him with a worthy subject matter for a novel, since the worth of subjects for and in art has nothing to do with their worth "in life." Indeed, the true artist can make any subject a worthy material for art; therefore, choosing an artistic vocation does not entail a rejection of the contemporary, social world (which may be ugly or frivolous) for the sake of art, falsely understood as the representation of "beautiful" objects and the treatment of "serious" subjects.[39] On the contrary, the true artist shows his sovereignty by imposing his own scale of values. As the careers of Elstir and Vinteuil (not to mention Proust's own career) show, the reversal of values is something Proust's world not only accepts but even expects of the artist. Moreover, by making his impressions and sensations the subject matter of his book, Marcel succeeds in the project of self-realization (the realization of an inner self that is truly oneself by virtue of being one's own creation),[40] a project that other characters in the social world depicted by the novel attempt to achieve through action, but fail. In retiring to his room to write his novel, Marcel, the future great writer, dedicates himself to art; this, however, does not entail a rejection of/by the world.

Since, according to Proust, the artist re-forms the world and fashions himself through his work of art, and since what he reveals to us is a new world, never known before, it is not surprising that the metaphor of creation abounds in Proust's description of artists. The vocabulary of creation is most explicit in the case of Elstir:

> Elstir's studio appeared to me like the laboratory of a sort of new creation of the world in which, from the chaos that is everything we see,

> he had extracted, by painting them on various rectangles of canvas . . . here a sea wave . . . there a young man. . . . At the moment at which I entered, the creator was just finishing, with the brush which he had in his hand, the outline of the setting sun. . . . I was able to discern from [the canvases along the walls] that the charm of each of them lay in a sort of metamorphosis of the objects represented, analogous to what in poetry we call metaphor, and that, if God the Father had created things by naming them, it was by taking away their names or giving them other names that Elstir created them anew.[41] (I, 834–35; I, 892–93)

In Shahar's novel, it is the description of Elka, the coppersmith, working in her studio that evokes the metaphor of creation in the most explicit fashion. The studio is repeatedly called *beit hayotzer*—literally, the house of the creator, and the image that Elka has in her mind and that she then engraves is often called *tzelem*. The studio is full of vessels [*kelim*], and the light that comes pouring in through the small window (compared to an eye) is reflected in them. The "dance" of the light on the vessels is echoed by the tapping of Elka's fingers, "engraving a series of little lines . . . like sun rays [*kemin shemesh korenet*]" (*Voyage*, 32–34; 249–51). All of these small details suggest an analogy between Elka's artistic creation and the creation of the world (especially in its Kabbalist version, where creation involves the pouring of light into vessels). But Elka is no competition for God the creator. The "vessels" [*kelim*] she deals with are mere "copper utensils [*klei nehoshet*] of all shapes and sizes, plates, mugs, bowls, pots, coffeepots, casseroles, ashtrays, trays, and even . . . handles of soup ladles" (*Voyage,* 32; 249). Elka prefers to engrave them with her own original designs, and she reproduces the conventional scenes she was taught in the Betzalel art school "only when obliged to do so, as she said, 'to earn her bread,' in compliance with specific orders from souvenir merchants" (*Voyage,* 33; 250). Yet she does not sign her works and does not consider herself an artist or her products works of art, since they are, indeed, both objects of use and commodities. Elka's creation is modest and minor, and Elka herself, as a woman, as an artisan, and as someone who chooses not to reproduce dominant values (the conventional images reproduced by the Betzalel students—"the shepherd playing his pipe with three sheep bringing up the rear, the caravan of camels following a man riding a little donkey, Rachel's tomb in the shadow of a leafy tree, and David's Tower seen from various angles" [ibid.] played an important role in reproducing Zionist ideology), remains a marginal figure. It seems as though Shahar here is intent on downplaying the transgressive aspect of the artist who in his hubris dares to compete with God (though he retains the image of the artist as being ideologically "free"). The figure of the artisan represents a compromise between, on the one hand, the (transgressive) aesthetic impulse and, on the other hand, all that opposes this impulse, be it the injunction against creating images or the need to make a living.[42]

For Elka, creating a work of art means externalizing an inner vision. She does not copy reality, does not reproduce a conventional model, and does not even, as the narrator emphasizes, make her reliefs from previous drawings. At the moment of creation, she grabs the first vessel she can lay her hand on, and onto this preexisting material support, she transposes her inner vision and creates a work of art that has a material existence independent of her and can cause pleasure to others (*Voyage*, 32–34; 249–51; *Countess*, 10). The material support allows this vision to be realized and communicated to others.

Though the narrator insists that Elka's "choice" of an ashtray to receive the vision of the peacock was a blind one, the author's choice of an ashtray for Elka's masterpiece proves to be particularly appropriate for demonstrating the ability of the work of art to endure against all odds:

> I was sorry to see this beautiful ashtray serving the degrading function of a receptacle for cigarette ash: the entire inner surface of the ashtray was covered by a bas-relief of a peacock spreading its tail like a fan, and every cigarette placed on its rim would drop its ash onto the curves of the peacock's neck or the tufts of its crown or the tracery of its feathers until the peacock would disappear completely beneath the ashen avalanche, with only the tip of a feather peeping out here and there, like the limbs of a living soul buried alive. . . . And I always felt the same urge . . . to empty out the ashtray and wash the ash from the grooves of the peacock's tail. (*Voyage*, 194; 433–34)

The "ashen avalanche," the remnant and indicator of extinction and self-consumption, of death, covers the image of the peacock but does not destroy it: it is enough to wash the ashtray for this peacock to be born again, phoenix-like, out of the ashes. The work of art, an object in the real world and as such subject to destruction and extinction brought about by time, is seen here as repeatedly put to the test of time and repeatedly withstanding it. Its value resides not only in the aesthetic pleasure that it provides but also in its ability to endure and thus to preserve a momentary vision, unchanged.

It is instructive to compare the description of the peacock ashtray to the famous magic lantern scene in Proust. In the first pages of *Du Côte de chez Swann*, the narrator describes the transformation of his childhood room by the images projected on the wall by a magic lantern, telling the story of Golo, "filled with an infamous design," riding his horse toward the castle of Geneviève de Brabant:

> And nothing could arrest his slow progress. If the lantern were moved I could still distinguish Golo's horse advancing across the window

> curtains, swelling out with their curves and diving into their folds. The body of Golo himself, being of the same supernatural substance as his steed's, overcame every material obstacle—everything that seemed to bar his way—by taking it as an ossature and embodying it in himself [*se le rendant intérieur*]; even the door handle, for instance, over which, adapting himself at once, would float irresistibly his red cloak or his pale face, which never lost its nobility or melancholy, never betrayed the least concern of this transvertebration. (I, 10; I 10)

Here, too, an image is transposed onto a preexisting material surface. The comparison of the images projected by the magic lantern to stained glass windows (I, 9; I, 9) and, later on, to the paintings by Elstir ("The parts of the walls that were covered by paintings of his . . . were like the luminous images of a magic lantern, which in this instance was the brain of the artist," II, 419; II 435), allows us to think of this episode as describing, among other things, the creation of a work of art. As in the case of the peacock ashtray in Shahar, here, too, the material surface onto which the image is projected does not seem, *prima facie*, suitable, or "destined" to receive it: it belongs to the world of everyday life and serves other functions. This surface, this world, is completely transformed by the projected images. Golo's determination to ride on and bring about his "infamous design" is transferred to the images, which are seen as having the power to take over any element of the room and overcome all "material obstacles." The body of Golo "adapts itself" to the objects in the room (taking the shape of the doorknob), while at the same time it succeeds in "internalizing" [*rendant intérieur*] them. But this complete fusion or confusion between material support and image is only temporary. Whereas Elka's engraving changes the metal surface in an irreversible way, and, as we have seen, the engraved vision endures and withstands the ravages of time, in Proust, what is emphasized is the illusory and transitory nature of the projected image.

Obviously, medieval stained glass windows, Elstir's paintings, or the description of the magic lantern in Proust's novel are not transitory and ephemeral in the same way that the images projected by the magic lantern are. One can argue, indeed, that by transforming the "memory" of the magic lantern into a scene in a novel, Proust does something equivalent to Elka's transposing the vision of the peacock onto the ashtray: by passing from the private space of the mind (imagination or memory), symbolized in the scene itself by the child's bedroom, into the material and public space of the book, the images acquire a certain "solidity" and thus can endure (as well as be communicated to others). However, what endures and is communicated in this case is a representation of the ephemeral, transitory, illusory. It is in this sense that Elstir's paintings resemble the images projected by the magic lantern. Elstir's art (and, by analogy, Proust's) is not only "impressionist" rather than "realist," but the impressions it captures and fixes are fleeting ones: those first and passing impressions that may be called "optical illusions" (since they contradict what habit and intelligence tell us) or "poetic vision" (since they involve the metamorphosis of objects by a process analogous to the use of metaphor), as when we mistake the sea for the sky or the noise of a carriage for a street quarrel.[43] Elstir's goal, the narrator tells us, is "to reproduce things not as he knew them to be [*de ne pas exposer les choses telles qu'il savait qu'elles étaient*] but according to the optical illusions of which our first sight of them is composed [*est faite*]" or, positively put, to represent "the rare moments in which we see nature as she is, poetically" (I, 838, 835; I, 897, 894). The comparison between the different ways the two novelists conceive of art leads to conclusions similar to those we drew from the discussion of the different ways each one deals with temporality. Of the two, Shahar comes closer to considering art as a means of resisting time or recapturing the past; he sees the work of art as a material trace that endures and thus preserves, unchanged, an inner vision. Proust, too, is interested in the permanence of the work of art, but for him, art consists of capturing a fleeting, even an illusory vision, and "fixing" its very ephemerality.

Notes

Introduction

1. Thus, for example, in an article entitled precisely "Ein navi be-artzo" and published after Shahar's death, Ortziyon Bartana says of Shahar that he "reached the furthest point Hebrew literature of his generation could. . . . He eternalized life in Jerusalem of the Mandate period with force and breadth unequaled by any other author" (*Yedi'ot Aharonot*, April 11, 1997; The critic Amnon Navot considered Shahar's multivolume novel, *The Palace of Shattered Vessels*, "one of the important, if not the most important, work of new Hebrew literature in the generation after that of the founding-fathers" ("'Eynayim le-Eshbaal," *Davar*, September 19, 1986, part 1); Yosef Oren hailed him as an epic writer and described his narrative project in the *Palace* novels as unique ("Masekhet nashim shel David Shahar," *Ha-aretz*, December 23, 1983).
2. See, for example, Yonah Bahur, "Haherut lenapetz elilim," *Davar*, November 17, 1977; Lena Shiloni, "Tikun hakelim hashevurim," *Ha-aretz*, October 11, 1985; Yael Lotan, "David Shahar, Story-Teller," *Modern Hebrew Literature* (spring/summer 1982): 14–17; Yehoash Bieber, "Mi ata Gavriel Yonatan Luria?" *Davar*, February 22, 1985.
3. Yosef Oren, "The Sanctuary of the Broken Vessels," *Hebrew Book Review* (fall 1969): 15; Gilead Morahg, "Piercing the Shimmering Bubble: David Shahar's *The Palace of Shattered Vessels*," *AJS Review* (fall, 1985): 212.
4. See, for example, Sarah Katz's bitter review of *His Majesty's Agent*, "Diagnoza shel sofer shebagad bemasa hanefesh shelo," *Yerushalayim* (summer 1988): 92–98.
5. See, for example, Yael Lotan, op. cit.; Avi Garfinkel, "Ein sofer be'iro," *Yerushalayim*, April 11, 1997; Eli Shay, "Met be'emdat nivdal," *Kol Ha'ir*, April 11, 1997.

Chapter 1

1. For an account of the Freudian concept of *Nachträglichkeit*, see the entry "Deferred action" in *The Language of Psycho-Analysis*, ed. J. Laplanche and J-B Pontalis, trans. Donald Nicholson-Smith (New York : Norton, 1973), 111–14.

2. Thus, for example, Srulik, now the Calvinist missionary Dr. Shoshan, appears one day at the narrator's door, "like an apparition . . . like the materialization of a dim childhood memory" (*Summer*, 118; 101). Later on, three months after Srulik's death, the narrator hears his voice on the radio. He then tells a neighbor's son who Srulik was, and in the surprised look of the boy "as if he were seeing me for the first time in his life," the narrator recognizes his past self, as he was when he saw Gabriel for the first time (*Summer*, 149–50; 135–36).

3. For a discussion of the relation between Shahar's novel sequence and Lurianic Kabbala, see, among others, Morahg, "Piercing the Shimmering Bubble," 211–34; Malca Puni, "*Mekorot yehudiyim kiyesodot me'atzvim biyetzirat D. Shahar*," Ph.D. thesis, Bar Ilan University, 1980; Malca Puni, "'Itzuv hademuiot hasifrutiyot biyetzirat D. Shahar," *Zehut* (May 1981): 239–44; Nehama Rezler Bersohn, "David Shahar's Trilogy: *The Palace of Shattered Vessels*—A Combination of Literary Genres," *Modern Hebrew Literature* (summer 1980): 34–42.

4. See Gershom Scholem's discussion of Heikhalot mysticism in *Encyclopaedia Judaica*, vol. 10, pp. 500–506; Joseph Dan, *Gershom Scholem and the Mystical Dimension of Jewish History* (New York: New York University Press, 1987), 49–53.

5. "The Uncanny," in *The Standard Edition of the Complete Psychological Works of Sigmund Freud* (London: Hogarth Press, 1953–1974), vol. 17, pp. 219–52. The quotations are from p. 235.

6. A review of *Of Candles and Winds*, *Moznayim* 69:5 (February 1995): 47. The translation is ours.

7. The word *sha'ar* literally means "gate" but also "chapter," or part of a book; it is the term used by Shahar for each volume of the *Palace* sequence.

8. *The Autobiography of Emperor Haile Selassie I "My Life and Ethiopia's Progress" 1892–1937*, trans. Edward Ullendorff (Oxford: Oxford University Press, 1976), 263–66. The emperor embarked from Djibouti on May 4, 1936, and on the fifth day arrived in Haifa. From there, he proceeded to Jerusalem by train. Upon his arrival in Jerusalem, he visited Golgotha and then retired to the King David Hotel. The next day, he visited the Ethiopian monastery in Jerusalem. He left Jerusalem on May 23.

9. Sir Ronald Storrs, *Orientations* (London: Nicholson & Watson, 1943), 445. This is no doubt Shahar's source for this detail.

10. Sir Leonard Woolley, *Abraham: Recent Discoveries and Hebrew Origins* (New York: C. Scribner's Sons, 1936).

11. For example, as mentioned before, the narrator dates his meeting with Lutetia as taking place in 1988 (by reference to the fortieth birthday of the State of Israel). Through Lutetia the narrator meets again Tammuz-Thomas, who is Lutetia's lover. This second meeting with Tammuz, we are told, took place six months after the first meeting (*Lutetia*, 35), so the first meeting must have been some time in early 1988 or late 1987. That first meeting was described in *Nin-Gal* which, however, was published already in 1983.

12. This, however, would not quite explain why the narrator was worried "last year" about the flooding of this particular cistern when, according to these very pages, he moved into the Lurias' house only a few weeks prior to Gabriel's return, on a dry year.

13. In the revised edition, Shahar added the following: "I do not know how to explain the memory-image of that night, since I actually saw Gabriel for the first time only a few years later, when I was already a ten-year-old boy, on the day on which the Emperor of Abyssinia appeared in Jerusalem. Maybe before he returned to Jerusalem to settle, Gabriel had come for a short visit, since then forgotten, and whose memory came back to me only now, while writing; or maybe all this is the fruit of my imagination, which is deceiving me" (15). This attempt to reconcile textual contradiction reinforces our interpretation of this passage: the narrator both saw Gabriel for the first time on a particular, memorable day that can be objectively dated, and somehow in his memory or desire or imagination, Gabriel was already there prior to his return.

14. The listing of the emperor's attributes shows the rhetorical motivation for the coincidence between the private and public event: the emperor is "the conquering lion [*Ari*] of the Tribe of Judah [Yehuda]," and Gabriel Jonathan Luria, whose father's name is Yehuda, is a descendant of the famous Kabbalist Itzhak Luria Ashkenazi, best known as *Ha-ari* (the lion).

15. On the other hand, the description Shahar gives resembles remarkably historical accounts of the 1929 riots. Shahar describes the riots as erupting in Jerusalem with the mob coming out of the mosques of the Old City, where it was incited to violence by Islamic preachers and with the British police refraining from interference (see, e.g., *Countess,* 131–32). All of these features characterize the 1929 riots (see *Toldot hahagana,* ed. Ben-Tziyon Dinur et al. [Tel Aviv: Hasifria Hatzionit and Ma'arakhot Press, 1964], vol. 2, part 1, 312–20). *Toldot hahagana* even mentions that the mob turned back from Mea She'arim to Damascus Gate after two Arab rioters were killed (315); Shahar's account mentions the death of two rioters (Daoud and another, anonymous Arab) in this very neighborhood. The authors of *Toldot hahagana* draw attention to the difference in British attitude in 1936, when all police stations were ordered to open fire even at an early stage of disturbance as opposed to the delay of such an order "on the fatal Friday in summer 1929 in Jerusalem" (681). While the riots of 1929 fit better than those of 1936 the compositional needs of the novel, they have the disadvantage that the narrator, born, according to the novel, in 1926, cannot very easily represent himself as having witnessed them.

16. The revised edition adds that he was away from Jerusalem at the time of the funeral, having gone abroad again at that time. If anything, this "correction" only enhances a repetitive pattern in Gabriel's life, and thus suggests that his life after the riots was not much different than before.

17. In the entire novel, the narrator's parents are mentioned only once, and then as absent (*Summer,* 12; 11). The only figure who appears in anything similar to a

parental relation to the narrator is Gabriel's mother, Mrs. Luria. In the posthumous volume, *To the Mount of Olives,* many of Mrs. Luria's features (such as her talent for mimicry, her opinions of the grocer, the Red Ear) are attributed to the narrator's mother.

18. Could Srulik have reported the information he gained by eavesdropping to the narrator in some later, unmentioned conversation? This is not likely, given the intimate psychological details, which normally would not be a topic for conversation, and certainly not with a young child. Furthermore, this possibility is rendered irrelevant by the rehearsal of this scene also from Yaeli's point of view, this time without any shred of explanation as to how her experience could have become known (in contrast to the fact of Louidor's early-morning emergence from her room, noticed by Fat Pesach, who makes it common gossip).

19. Gershon Shaked, in his discussion of Shahar's work, reads, indeed, this passage as expressing the "main principle" of Shahar's "poetics of memory." See *Hasiporet ha'ivrit 1880–1980,* vol. 5 (Tel Aviv: Hakibbutz Hameuhad, 1998), 129–30.

CHAPTER 2

1. "The Myth of the Birth of the Hero" in *The Myth of the Birth of the Hero and Other Writings,* ed. Philip Freund (New York: Vintage, 1959).

2. The freedom she represents is seen as transgressive or otherwise reprehensible just as the freedom represented by the mother was. For example, she offers him some chewing gum—at the time of the narrated events and still at the time of writing a symbol of Western lax mores. At a deeper symbolic level, this chewing without ingestion or nutrition is a nonteleological activity, pleasure for pleasure's sake, suggesting mindless masturbatory self-absorption or a purely aesthetic pursuit.

3. On that particular night, the father did not wish the mother to go out (176); had she complied, she would not have been killed.

4. The story was translated under the title "Uncle Zemach."

5. Exceptions are Yehuda Shoshan's theater production in *Day of the Countess* and Daniel Koren's involvement with the puppet theater, especially with female puppets, in *His Majesty's Agent.*

6. A possibility that does not materialize in "First Lesson" but does in "Of Shadows and the Image," as well as in *Summer in the Street of the Prophets.*

7. Cf. Lukacs's famous utopian celebration of the lost immanence of the world of the epic in the opening sentences of chapter 1 of his *Theory of the Novel* (Cambridge: MIT Press, 1975), 29.

8. The grandmother's anti-Zionism is implicitly depicted as part and parcel of her ignorant disdain of concrete reality (discussed further on).

9. The biblical phrase used to dramatize Reuben's consternation at not finding Joseph in the pit where he and the other brothers threw him, since in his absence

they have sold him to slavery. An additional, and possibly relevant, irony is that Joseph was thus treated as punishment for the many-colored coat he was given by their father as a mark of preference.

10. Exactly what Ephraim's dream had his father do in "Of Shadows and the Image."

11. Thus in *His Majesty's Agent* the narrator says of his mother: "In her childhood her grandfather, who came from a small town in Eastern Europe, had told her that when he himself was a child, the rabbi had whipped him—bent him over the table and whipped him with a strap in front of all the other little boys in the *heder*—simply because he had a gift for drawing and liked making pictures of everything his saw. A Jewish child was not allowed to draw pictures, or even to look at the natural sights around him and enjoy the beauty of a tree. Whoever enjoyed the beauties of this world immediately lost his place in paradise, and like all the wicked, he would end up in hell" (214; 222).

12. Unlike the Christian European tradition from Prometheus to Frankenstein, which regards the human ambition to create as competing with or usurping divine prerogative, Jewish Kabbala seems to consider even the creation of anthropomorphic beings a worshipful emulation of God. See Moshe Idel, *Golem: Jewish Magical and Mystical Traditions on the Artificial Anthropoid* (Albany: State University of New York Press, 1990), passim.

13. An inner vision, but in typical Shaharian manner, dependent on the *sensory* sight of the stove fire shining in the darkness of the room.

14. Evidently we are thinking of Derrida's argument about *archi-écriture* as *différance* (*De la grammatologie* [Paris: Minuit, 1967], part I, passim, and "La différance" in *Marges de la philosophie* [Paris: Minuit, 1972], 3–29).

15. The published English version often tones down the original Hebrew text, leaving out some erotic excesses and other significant details. We restored omissions when necessary.

16. This text is roughly equivalent to the three brief paragraphs printed on the title page of the novel's part 1 in the guise of an epigraph. The Hebrew text, however, does not include the claim to authenticity and ends with a somewhat more slippery formulation: "Should a man be found bearing a like name, or who might say unto himself, 'why thus it has befallen me, too'—then the reality of this man's life must have been wilder than fiction" (7). Given the circumstances detailed below, the author could pretty much bank on it that the real Heinrich Reinhold would not step forward to protest.

17. See J. Bowyer Bell, *Terror Out of Zion: Irgun Zvai Leumi, LEHI, and the Palestine Underground, 1929–1949* (New York: St. Martin's Press, 1977); Thurston Clarke, *By Blood and Fire: The Attack on the King David Hotel* (New York: Putnam, 1981). Michal Ginsburg received an e-mail from a man named Bernie Baumohl, identifying himself as Heinrich Reinhold's nephew, who wanted to get in touch with David Shahar; he hoped that in doing research for his book, Shahar might have come upon some information about Reinhold's current whereabouts.

18. The English translation uses the Hebrew name "Yoël" in the dedication but refers to the character as "Joel," thus obscuring the fact that it is the same "person."

19. In his volume of memoirs, *Hadevarim gedolim hem me-itanu* (Tel Aviv: Hadar, 1994), Amrami himself devotes the whole of chapter 10 ("Mi lamavet umi lahayim: ma'aseh Yannai," 68–93) to an account of this affair along the same lines. In part 2 of the novel, the narrator, David Shahar, meets Reinhold again; he is now the Beverly Hills tycoon, Joseph Orwell, and he gives him an account of the events surrounding the King David sabotage. Cast as a personal story and not as a defense speech, this account addresses the incriminating details one by one, explaining them all away.

20. For a fuller discussion of these ambiguities, see Moshe Ron's review of *His Majesty's Agent,* "Heinrich Reinhold be-eretz hamar-ot," *Siman Kriah* 11 (May 1980): 147–56. In the sixth novel of the *Palace* sequence, *A Tammuz-Night's Dream*, published in 1988, the narrator mentions Reinhold as connected to a "secret" revealed to him by Tammuz. Shahar writes: "For a while I was angry with myself for having exposed in public the inscription of the traits of the secret—doing so, of course, with the positive intent of allowing anyone wishing for it the opportunity to hark to the arcane, vanishing music—but I soon found out I committed no crime, neither against Reinhold nor against Tammuz, by writing down and publishing the traits of the secret" (83).

21. In order to avoid overcomplication, we have left out several plot developments and strands of imagery that are quite pertinent to our theme.

22. See Ron, op. cit.

23. Soon after the beginning of part 2, prompted by Reinhold's spurious tale of being transformed into a eunuch Ethiopian priest as a punishment for overly admiring himself in the uncanny mirror (a cover-up for the disguises that he has been using at that stage in his underground activities), Jamilla tells another story of magic transformation, due to the evil eye of a spiteful stepmother, whose victim and finally victorious hero is one of Reinhold's several namesakes, a boy named Youssef (171–74; 176–80).

24. "*Yom hatzeva'im*" is also "day of the colors."

25. Soutine was a mother: reflecting on fate, Reinhold is reminded of a herd of gazelles he once saw in the desert while riding with Tamara in her car: "suddenly he saw that one of them had remained behind, rooted to the spot: she was in the process of giving birth. Like her, the hunted Soutine [who remained in France under Nazi occupation] was in the process of giving birth" (312; 324).

26. This scene echoes and prefigures other scenes in both *His Majesty's Agent* and the *Palace*. In the second telling of this episode, Reinhold, following the aborted attempt on the destroyer, is hiding in Haifa. Just before going back to Jerusalem he goes into a café and sees two policemen apparently about to arrest "a man of about fifty . . . nodding off in front of a foreign language newspaper lying open on the table." The man makes for the back door, bumps against a table, then a chair, loses his cap, and falls flat on his face to the floor. Reinhold attacks one of the policemen

and helps the man get away. In the "day of the crayons" episode, Reinhold's father sits in a café reading a newspaper when his son rushes in to show him his new crayons. When the father sees the court clerk, he attempts to escape through the kitchen door, bumps against a chair, and falls down, his hat rolling into the street; his son helplessly watches his humiliation (30–31; 27). In the fourth volume of the *Palace*, *Nin-Gal*, the narrator remembers how during the 1948 war he stood watch in an apartment in Jerusalem that belonged to a woman painter. The woman used to take off her clothes in order to paint herself naked without closing the door of her room, a behavior that was interpreted by the men standing watch as deliberate female provocation—"to show and not to give" (87–89).

27. Reinhold retreats from this sentiment by reminding himself of paternal responsibility, much as the narrator did in "First Lesson" in declaring world war on grandma, but adding the explicit vantage point of one who is an actual father: "If this world really and truly had a Father in Heaven, that father wouldn't let his child be blown up. . . . 'And in this universal explosion my son would be killed!'" (313; 326). Reinhold's suspicion-arousing behavior in the affair of the King David is all explained away by his concern for the safety of his child by Tamara. But *pater semper incertus est*: by the end of the novel, it is no longer certain that Emmanuel is really his biological son.

28. A rather curious variation on the figure of the mother is the narrator's elderly mother, who progressively loses her grip on reality—or so at least her son thinks. She dresses up in purple (Tamara's color, which she herself has previously identified as "the color of a prostitute," 208), dyes her hair red, and adorns herself with makeup and jewelry in a way the son thinks is somewhat scandalous; she wanders freely around the city, to distant parts, and on one particular occasion (later dubbed as "the day of the sovereigns"), she extravagantly throws gold coins out of the window; she turns Reinhold's old room into her "atelier," where she paints what her son considers "wild and primitive paintings" inspired by the Bible while humming to herself Reinhold's favorite song, "Liebe war es nicht." All of her paintings are, in fact, self-portraits, and she signs them "Joseph, Prince of Pithom." The son is scared by her behavior (including her painting) and tries to stop her (from roaming around the city, throwing the money out the window), but he cannot (222–33; 229–42). Clearly this mother is a composite of several figures: the mother as described, for example, in "Of Shadows"—free, extravagant, red-haired; Tamara—a woman dressed in purple, a "prostitute," who paints badly; and Reinhold—the would-be painter and lover. She is, in fact, a grotesque incarnation of the union/identification of mother and son so fondly described in "Of Shadows" but now seen from the point of view of a son who has adopted the point of view of the censoring (but weak) father.

29. It also brings up the uncontrollable anxieties associated with both repressed libido and the death drive analyzed by Freud in the essay on the uncanny. During the same sequence, Reinhold wishes Tamara's matrimonial photograph with Daniel to be turned to the wall and is then led to reflect, in quite a Freudian vein, on the covering of the mirrors in his childhood home following the death of a namesake cousin (87–88; 87–88).

30. The same is true of Gabriel: on his way to the King David Hotel to spend a week with Orita, he thinks about various slights he has suffered at the hands of Orita, and one of his grievances is her mistreatment of Srulik. Several other male characters in Shahar's fiction find themselves in some variation of this unenviable position.

31. The heart of Leonora, Miss Doris's cat, was buried in the yard of the Scottish Hospice on December 17, 1914 (32), and that was ten years before the King David encounter (31). However, as we have seen in the previous chapter, Gabriel's affair with Bella, which takes place around this time, is dated by reference to Brenner's death, that is, in 1921. But in both dates it would have been impossible for Gabriel to have his fling with Orita in the King David Hotel, which was built only in 1930 (when Gabriel was already presumably in France). This is another example of the collapse between the early 1920s and late 1930s, which occurs repeatedly in the novel sequence and on which we comment in the next chapter.

32. Thus Gabriel recalls an Indian legend about a righteous man who found himself after death in Paradise but next to an evil man he recognizes as his enemy on earth. "Above and beyond the metaphysical surprise rife with so many implications," Gabriel wonders how "the righteous man—or, more precisely, his soul" could have recognized his enemy who must, therefore, have kept some "shape," "some features from his earthly existence." Gabriel concludes: "So even in the soul-world the soul needs shapes and colors and traits and sounds and smells and whispers and even clothes—all those features of the world of matter that are perceptible to the senses" (33).

33. A quality of whose captivating charm Gabriel first became aware upon beginning his sexual liaison with his other, concurrent love, Bella.

34. An allusion to the biblical "turning" of the flaming sword [*haherev hamitahpekhet*], forbidding reentry into Eden.

CHAPTER 3

1. See, for example, Miriam Arad, "A Jerusalem Author's Doomed, Godlike Types," *Jerusalem Post*, November 20, 1970; Miriam Arad, "Jerusalem Novelist's Voyage," *Jerusalem Post*, December 31, 1971; Murray Baumgarten, "A Mythical City," *Jerusalem Post*, August 30, 1971; Yehoash Bieber, "Mi ata Gavriel Yonatan Luria?" *Davar*, February 22, 1985; Jean Blot, "L'Année dernière à Jérusalem," *L'Arche* 295 (January 1982); André Clavel, "David Shahar, conteur de Jérusalem," *Journal de Genève*, November 28, 1981; Jeffrey M. Green, "Jerusalem Daydreaming," *Modern Hebrew Literature* (spring/summer 1991), 24–27; Israel Harel, "Yerushalayim shel David Shahar," *Davar*, October 9, 1970; Tzvi Luz, *Metziut ve-adam basifrut ha-eretz yisre-elit* (Tel Aviv: Dvir, 1970), 122–43; Sarah Katz, *Marot biYerushalayim shel David Shahar* (Tel Aviv: 'Am 'Oved, 1985); Dan Miron, "Depictions [of Jerusalem] in Modern Hebrew Literature," in Nitza Rosovsky, ed., *City of the*

Great King: Jerusalem from David to the Present (Cambridge: Harvard University Press, 1996), 241–87; Jacqueline Piatier, "David Shahar, conteur de Jérusalem," *Le Monde des livres*, November 20, 1981; Malca Puni, "Yerushalayim ki-yetzirat omanut," *Ma'ariv*, May 21, 1982; Lena Shiloni, "Tikun hakelim hashevurim," *Ha-aretz*, October 11, 1985; Gideon Telpaz, "Remembrance of Things Past in Jerusalem: David Shahar," in *Israeli Childhood Stories of the Sixties* (Chico, Calif.: Scholars Press, 1983), 87–178.

2. To date, the only extended discussion of Jerusalem in Shahar's work is Sarah Katz, op. cit. Katz proceeds on the assumption that the Jerusalem represented in the short stories is the same as that represented in the *Palace* novels (of which she discusses only the first three volumes). She also takes at face value the autobiographical dimension of Shahar's novel. She thus reaches the conclusion—wrong, in our view—that the center of Shahar's Jerusalem—the narrator's "parental home"—is always "placed symbolically at the very heart of Mea She'arim," whether or not its location is indicated, whether it is placed on Street of the Prophets or on Mamilla Street (87). It is true that Shahar spent part of his childhood and adolescence at his grandmother's house in Mea She'arim and that the short story, "First Lesson," refers explicitly to this personal experience. However, it is highly important that in the *Palace* novels Shahar took a distance from his personal experience. Moreover, as we shall argue in this chapter, the Jerusalem of the *Palace* novels is very different from the Jerusalem of the short stories, and at least in the *Palace* novels, Street of the Prophets is a very different world than Mea She'arim.
3. For the most part, Shahar refers to his "real" places by their ordinary, familiar names; occasionally he uses a name of his own invention to refer to a place that exists or existed historically (by its location and phonetic similarity, Café Gat is clearly the historical Café Pat, just as among the characters of the novel, Judge Dan Gutkin is a transparent disguise for the historic Judge Gad Frumkin).
4. Roland Barthes, "L'Effet du réel," in *Communications* 11 (1968): 84–89.
5. This spatial qualification is unaccountably omitted from the English translation.
6. Bernard Keller, "La Jérusalem de David Shahar," *Foi et vie* 89 (1990): 42.
7. In an early story entitled "The Empty Packet of Cigarettes," and whose action begins at the intersection of Street of the Prophets and St. Paul Street, the narrator says of the latter: "The street was the border"—in that case, between Jews on one side and Arabs and British on the other side. See *The Death of the Little God*, 10; *News From Jerusalem*, 295.
8. The posthumous *To the Mount of Olives* shows the adult narrator going to different places in Rehavia.
9. Lea is the only character in the novel who mentions locations and institutions that embody Labor Zionism: the cooperative restaurant, the cooperative dairy, Tnuva, and the public meeting place Beit Ha'am.
10. Jeff Halper, *Between Redemption and Revival: The Jewish Yishuv of Jerusalem in the Nineteenth Century* (Boulder, San Francisco, and Oxford: Westview Press, 1991),

3. For other discussions of the Old and New Yishuv and the way they have been represented, see Ya'akov Barnay, "Hayishuv hayashan," in *Historyografia ule-umiyut* (Jerusalem: Magnes, 1975), 177–98; Israel Bartal, *Galut ba-aretz: yishuv Eretz Israel beterem tziyonut* (Jerusalem: Mossad Bialik, 1994), esp. 49–63, 74–89. Both Barnay and Bartal observe that not only was the category and name "Old Yishuv" created by the Zionist immigrants, but that their attitude toward it oscillated between two poles: on the one hand, they wanted to see the Old Yishuv as anticipating their own effort and goals and to that extent as being similar to them; on the other hand, they saw it as being continuous with Diasporic, "shtetle" Jewish life and therefore as representing the life they opposed and rebelled against. This specular relation, whereby the Old Yishuv is the same and opposite of the New Yishuv, prevented members of the New Yishuv and its historians from seeing the Old Yishuv as an independent phenomenon, a different response to the Jewish question. Our claim is that Shahar attempts to grasp precisely this difference.

11. Halper, *Between Redemption and Revival*, 194–229. In 1890, Jerusalem's Jews accounted for 60 percent of the total Yishuv; that figure dropped to 41 percent in 1922 and 12 percent in 1948 (ibid., 214).

12. *Nin-Gal*, *Day of the Ghosts*, and *The Nights of Lutetia*, which tell about the adult narrator's travel to and from France, mention the Ben Gurion airport.

13. For *Tmol Shilshom* see, among others, Yossi Katz, "Jerusalem in S. Y. Agnon's *Yesterday before Yesterday*," in *Writing the City, ed.* Peter Preston and Paul Simpson-Housely, 195–220 (London and New York: Routledge, 1994); Miron, op. cit., 263–70; for Ben-Zion's story see Nurit Govrin, *Ketivat ha-aretz: aratzot ve'arim 'al mapat hasifrut ha'ivrit* (Jerusalem: Karmel, 1998), 61–64.

14. For a discussion of the depiction of Jerusalem in Shahar's short stories, see Telpaz, op. cit., 90–93. Telpaz's main thesis is that stories, and part of stories, dealing with the narrator's childhood, depict the world of childhood and of the Old Yishuv, whereas "in stories lacking time gap between the actual period in which they were written and the period they depict . . . the scene is that of present day Jerusalem" (92). But his example of "present day Jerusalem" is the German Colony (in the story "The Woman with the Familiar Spirits") which, historically, is no more part of "present day Jerusalem" than Mea She'arim (the German Colony was founded in 1872 and Mea She'arim in 1875).

15. On the level of narration (rather than of story) the link between the *Palace* novels and *His Majesty's Agent* also takes place in the King David Hotel: it is there, the narrator tells us, that Tammuz told him the story of Heinrich Reinhold. The narrator has mixed feelings about having made this story public; one can say that he feels guilty for having betrayed what he calls, repeatedly, "the secret" (*Tammuz*, 82–83).

16. The information about the area around Street of the Prophets is gathered from the following: Yehoshua Ben-Arieh, *Jerusalem in the Nineteenth Century: Emergence of the New City* (Jerusalem: Yad Ben-Tzvi; New York: St. Martin's Press, 1986); Ruth Kark and Michal Oren-Nordheim, *Yerushalayim usevivoteiha: rova'im, shekhunot ukhefarim, 1800–1948* (Jerusalem: Akademon, 1995). Eyal Miron, ed. *Yerusha-*

layim vekhol netivoteiha: lesayer 'im Yad Ben-Tzvi (Jerusalem: Yad Ben-Tzvi, 1996); David Kroyanker, *Rehov Hanevi-im, Shekhunat Hahabashim veShekhunat Mussrara: sipuro shel makom—deyokana shel 'ir, Yerushalayim 1850–2000* (Jerusalem: Yad Ben-Tzvi & Keter, 2000); Natan Schur, *Toldot Yerushalayim*, vol. 3 (Tel Aviv: Dvir, 1987); Eliyahu Waguer, *Siyurim bi-Yerushalayim: madrikh lametayel* (Jerusalem: Keter, 1988).

17. Miron, op. cit., 198.

18. Frumkin, *Derekh shofet biYerushalyim* (Tel Aviv: Dvir, 1954), 126–27.

19. In a house at 5 Moshe Hagiz Street. Zikhron Moshe is on the northwest edge of our area and was the most modern Jewish neighborhood in Jerusalem until the First World War and a center for cultural life.

20. In the house of the Davidof family, 10 Rehovot Habukharim. The Bukharan neighborhood is to the north of Street of the Prophets. Founded in 1889 by rich Bukharan Jews, it was the most elegant and comfortable in Jerusalem; one of its houses, belonging to the Yehudaioff-Hafetz family, was considered the most luxurious house in all of Jerusalem, if not in the entire Eretz Israel, and this is where the official welcome reception for General Allenby was held in May 1918. In the 1920s when, as a result of the Russian Revolution and the First World War, the Bukharans in Jerusalem were cut off from their fellow countrymen in Bukhara and from their property there, they experienced economic hardship and started renting rooms to new immigrants of the "Second 'Aliya." Thus the Bukharan neighborhood became, for a short period, the center of the "New Yishuv" in Jerusalem, where workers, teachers, authors, government officials [*pkidim*], and Zionist leaders lived.

21. The Teachers' College was first under the direction of the Ezra society and was housed in the building of the Laemel School. Later on, when, following the "language wars," those who were committed to the teaching in Hebrew, headed by David Yellin, formed the Hebrew Teachers' College, it was housed on Yisha'ayahu Street in Zikhron Moshe. From there it moved to Beit Hakerem.

22. The Bnei Brit Library was a lending library for youth between 1930 and 1948; the Edison Cinema was built in 1932; the Rose Garden was created in the 1930s.

23. The narrator normally talks about the "gymnasia." In the case of Arik Wissotzky, however, he speaks of the "Gymnasia Sokolov," located on Chancellor Street (*Nin-Gal*, 78). Therefore, it may be that his other references are not to the Gymnasia Rehavia but to the Gymnasia Sokolov, though for Jerusalemites "the Gymnasia" *tout court* is normally the Gymnasia Rehavia.

24. See the account of the attempted murder in *Ha-aretz* of November 12, 1929 (reproduced in *Yerushalayim vekhol netivoteiha*, 245), where the location of the clinic is given in the same terms as those used by Shahar in describing Dr. Landau's clinic.

25. The rather marginal figure of the British painter Holmes may be seen as pushing the story even farther back into the past, since it is possible that he is, at least

partially, modeled after the pre-Raphaelite painter, William Holman-Hunt, who stayed in Palestine during the periods 1854–1856, 1869–1872, 1875–1878, and in 1892. Holman-Hunt's home in Jerusalem was on Street of the Prophets, and his preferred place for drawing views of Jerusalem and the Judean desert was on the way to Bethlehem, near the Monastery of Mar Elias. This is the exact place the novel designates as the home of Holmes, "who had spent fifty years painting landscapes of the country" (*Voyage*, 67; 286–87). One of Holman-Hunt's most famous paintings is that of the *Scapegoat*, a subject Shahar "describes" in Gabriel's dream in *Of Candles and Winds*. On Holman-Hunt, see Yehoshua Ben-Arieh. *Tzayareiha vetziyureiha shel Eretz Israel bameiah hatesha'esreh* (Jerusalem: Yad Ben-Tzvi & Tel Aviv: Yedi'ot Aharonot, 1992), 116–26; also see the entry Holman-Hunt in Ze-ev Vilnai, *Entzikolopediat Vilnai li-Yerushalayim* (Jerusalem: Ahi'ever, 1993), vol. 1, 376–77.

26. On the relation of Zionism to cities in general and Jerusalem in particular see, among others, Erik Cohen, "The City in Zionist Ideology," *The Jerusalem Quarterly* 4 (1977): 126–44; Arthur Hertzberg, "Jerusalem and Zionism" in Rosovsky, op. cit., 149–77; Hagit Lavsky, ed., *Yerushalayim batoda'ah uva'asiya hatziyonit* (Jerusalem: Merkaz Zalman Shazar, 1989).

27. "Of Other Spaces," trans. Jay Miskowiec, *Diacritics* (spring 1986): 22–27.

28. Amos Oz, *Mikha-el Sheli* (Tel Aviv: 'Am 'Oved, 1968). English translation by Nicholas de Lange, *My Michael* (New York: Knopf, 1972). All references to the novel are to these editions and will be given parenthetically within the text, Hebrew original followed by English translation. Translation has been silently modified when a more literal rendering was necessary.

29. A. B. Yehoshua, "Shlosha yamim veyeled" in *Mul haye'arot* (Tel Aviv: Hakibbutz hameuhad, 1968), 189. English translation by Miriam Arad, "Three Days and a Child" in *Three Days and a Child* (New York: Doubleday, 1970), 66.

30. See, for example, the interview with Hayim Be-er, *Ariel* (spring 1972), where Shahar says, among other things: "Jerusalem is a city of high density, full of tensions, of love and hate and jealousy, tensions between past and present" (15).

31. Mordekhai Naor, *'Ir va-em miDavid hamelekh 'ad yameinu* (Jerusalem: Yad Ben-Tzvi, 1995), 197.

32. Ibid., 197–98.

33. Though the official Jewish institutions had their seat in Jerusalem, the political parties and the powerful Histadrut kept their headquarters in Tel Aviv. This is where most of the newspapers were published and where the leading theaters as well as the opera and the philharmonic had their home. Though Jerusalem's population increased considerably during the Mandate period, it did not increase at the same rate as the Jewish population in the entire Eretz Israel (in 1917, the Jewish population of Jerusalem accounted for more than 50 percent of the entire Jewish population in Eretz Israel, whereas in 1947, the 100,000 Jews in Jerusalem were barely 16 percent of this population) or in Tel Aviv (between 1931 and 1936, the total population of Jerusalem increased from 90,000 to 120,00, but only

20,000 of these new residents were Jewish; in the same years, the population of Tel Aviv rose from 45,000 to 145,000, with the addition of 100,000 Jews).

34. M. M. Bakhtin, "Forms of Time and the Chronotope in the Novel," in *The Dialogic Imagination*, ed. Michael Holquist; trans. Caryle Emerson and Michael Holquist, 250 (Austin and London: University of Texas Press, 1981).
35. Ibid., 228–30. One may argue that in the Jewish tradition we find "provincial novels" in Bakhtin's sense in mid-twentieth century recreations of the "shtetle" and the "Jewish city" by some Jewish-American authors. See David Roskies, "Tzionut, makom vehadimayon hasifruti hayehudi," in *'Idan hatzionut,* ed. Anita Shapira, Yehuda Reinhartz, and Jacob Harris, 167–184 (Jerusalem: Merkaz Shazar, 2000). Roskies does not discuss these novels in Bakhtin's terms.
36. Walter Benjamin, "On Some Motifs in Baudelaire," in *Illuminations*, ed. Hannah Arendt, 155–201 (New York: Schocken, 1969); Franco Moretti, "Homo Palpitans," in *Signs Taken for Wonders* (London and New York: Verso, 1983), 109–29.
37. Bakhtin, op. cit., 230.
38. Hana Wirth-Nesher, *City Codes: Reading the Modern Urban Novel* (New York: Cambridge University Press, 1996), 20.
39. Ibid., passim.
40. Ibid., 20.
41. Sarah Katz already pointed out the importance in the novel of these two spaces. Katz, op. cit., 92.
42. This identification becomes explicit in the posthumous *To the Mount of Olives,* where the narrator's mother has many of the attributes and opinions of Mrs. Luria.

CHAPTER 4

1. In her book *The Arab in Israeli literature* (Bloomington and Indianapolis: Indiana University Press, 1989), Gila Ramras-Rauch mentions Shahar only once, as an influence on Anton Shammas (p. 199), and Warren Bargad, in his essay "The Image of the Arab in Israeli Literature" (in *From Agnon to Oz* [Atlanta: Scholars Press, 1996), does not mention Shahar at all. To the best of our knowledge there is to date only one study of the Arab issue in Shahar: Sarah Katz's article "Hakonflikt hayehudi—'arvi biyetzirato shel David Shahar," *Ha-uma* 136 (summer 1999), 454–70; English version, "The Arabe [*sic*]-Jewish Issue in the Works of David Shahar, *REEH* 1 (1999): 78–106. Some critics, however, discussed Shahar's representation of different ethnic groups. See Yael Feldman, "The 'Other Within' in Contemporary Israeli Fiction," *Middle East Review* 22:1 (fall 1989): 47–53; Madeleine Neige, "Jews, Muslims, and Christians in the Work of David Shahar," *The Jerusalem Quarterly* 6 (winter 1978): 41–46; Gideon Telpaz, "Remembrance of Things Past in Jerusalem: David Shahar," in *Israeli Childhood Stories,* esp. 93–100.

2. Baruch Link, in his review of the English translation of *The Palace of Shattered Vessels* (*Los Angeles Times*, January 1, 1989), says: "An important detail missing in the child's narrative is an awareness of the Jewish-Arab conflict."

3. As we pointed out in a previous chapter, the representation in the novel of the outbreak of violence between Arabs and Jews in Jerusalem in the summer of 1936 does not resemble any historical accounts of the 1936 riots but resembles remarkably historical accounts of the 1929 riots (which, however, the narrator, born in 1926, could not have very well witnessed).

4. Louidor is murdered two days after Berl and the narrator see him in the Jaffa Gate, on the evening of the "enchanted day," which took place one week before the riots.

5. Daoud was also concerned with Arab national honor at this point (see *Countess*, 45).

6. In the posthumous volume, *To the Mount of Olives*, the narrator makes explicit Gordon's pro-Jewish sentiments, describing him as one of the rare British who "can be called 'Zionist in their soul', those who believed in the need to renew the rule of the People of Israel in the land of Israel," and he compares him to Lawrence Oliphant and James Orde Wingate (*Mount of Olives*, 10–11).

7. It is also possible that Louidor's "conversion" was, at least in part, the result of being rejected by Yaeli Landau. The end result of this is that he is killed and castrated. Srulik, whose conversion to Christianity is never fully explained either, was in love with Orita. Though she did not literally reject him—since he never declared himself—we are told that after his sudden disappearance there were "rumors about something terrible that happened to him and forced him to flee the country in secret" (*Summer*, 80; 67). This enigmatic remark is inserted in between Srulik's explanation to the boy-narrator that the Ethiopian monks are castrated and Gabriel's telling him about the castration of pigs in Brittany. Gabriel himself left Jerusalem rather suddenly and, as we learn in *Of Candles and Winds*, as a result of being in some sense rejected or betrayed by Orita; the result of this is that he is a "broken vessel." Finally, as we shall see, Daoud's conversion to Arab nationalism—and subsequent death—is presented as possibly the result of his encounter with feminine sexuality. These four, partially similar cases suggest that inexplicable, sudden changes in the life of male characters in Shahar may be the result of their contact with women who are considered "castrating," since they seduce and betray.

8. The conflict between an individual and a group can be found already in the relation of various protagonists to their family. On this subject see Telpaz's discussion of Shahar's short stories in *Israeli Childhood Stories of the Sixties* esp. 100.

9. This same passage appears also in the short story "The Find" as the vision provided by the "magic stone" the boy and his Uncle Kalman find in the caves of the Sanhedrin (see *The Pope's Mustache*, 178–79).

10. In *Day of the Ghosts*, the narrator removes part of the ambiguity by asserting that Daoud Ibn Mahmoud, Gutkin's driver, is indeed Daoud, the son of Mahmoud

Effendi, who was murdered by Ali Ibn-Massrur when Daoud was a child. But this assertion is made when Daoud tells a story he heard in his childhood from Jamilla. This is the story of Rabah Effendi, the apricots, and the difference between human and divine justice—the story, in other words, which Jamilla tells Heinrich Reinhold in *His Majesty's Agent* (*Ghosts*, 154–55; *His Majesty's Agent*, 19, 14–15). At the very moment the narrator removes some of the ambiguity about Daoud's identity, he adds ambiguity by merging him with another character.

11. *Day of the Ghosts*, which ends with a return to the 1936 riots (188–91), begins with the description of a violent demonstration by orthodox Jews, which the adult narrator watches from the window of the basement in his childhood home (24); in *To the Mount of Olives*, the narrator is almost killed by Arabs when he walks by himself near the Mount of Olives cemetery after his mother's funeral, and Tammuz is attacked by a group of orthodox Jews near his apartment in the Nahlaot area (*Mount of Olives*, 10–18, 41).

12. Though polygamy is permitted according to biblical law and was practiced throughout the Talmudic period, it nevertheless was frowned upon by the sages and ultimately banned by Rabbenu Gershom b. Judah and his court. But whereas the ban [*herem*] was accepted as binding by Ashkenazi communities that lived, for the most part, in Christian countries where polygamy was forbidden by both religion and secular law, this was not the case in Oriental countries, since Islam permits polygamy. In practice, however, in Oriental communities, a provision was inserted in the *ketubbah* precluding the husband from taking an additional wife, unless his first wife consented and the court permitted (see "Bigamy and Polygamy," in the *Encyclopedia Judaica*, vol. 4, 985–90). Thus though the old Bey whispers in the young girl's ear, "You are sanctified to me through intercourse [*beviah*] according to the Law of Moses and Israel" (*Countess*, 122), he is probably acting in violation if not of the law at least of established customs. Through his bigamy he becomes so Oriental as to almost not be a Jew anymore. It is interesting to note that this transgression does not seem to have any effect on the old Bey's social status, and its only possible negative consequence is that it made it impossible for Mrs. Luria's sister, Pnina, to find a "God-fearing Jew" who would be ready to marry her (*Summer*, 48; 38). This confirms the characterization of his milieu, his world, as being tolerant of unorthodox individuals.

13. It is important to note that though the Bey's excessive sexuality codes him as "Oriental," the novel as a whole does not portray Oriental or Arab characters as being full of uncontrolled lust. In general, as we have seen in chapter 2, male lust is described by Shahar under the heading "*'Eynaim ro-ot vekhalot*," that is, as a male's legitimate response to female provocation. Daoud, and later on an anonymous prisoner of war whom the narrator meets after the Six Day War, are portrayed as examples of restraint in the face of provocation and are motivated by a sense of self-respect and honor rather than by lust. They are contrasted to two Arab prisoners who could not control their lust (*Countess*, 46–49) and are implicitly likened to Gabriel in his relation to Orita (*Candles*) and Rahamim in his relation to Anastasia (*Nin-Gal*, 87–96).

14. For another discussion of "Oriental fantasies" and the relation between imagination, on the one hand, and mimicry or mimetic representation, on the other hand, see Yael Sagiv-Feldman, "Hafantaziot hamizrahiyot shel David Shahar, *Bitzaron* (1982): 14–23.

15. In the posthumously published *To the Mount of Olives*, the narrator's mother merges with Mrs. Luria.

16. As most critics claim; see, for example, Dov Landau, "Heshbono shel David Shahar 'im yefei hanefesh lemineihem," *Hatzofeh,* October 3, 1986.

17. For a comparison between this scene and a scene from Gérard de Nerval's novella, "Sylvie," see Michal Peled Ginsburg, "Sketching Literary Influence: Gérard de Nerval and David Shahar," in *The Spirit of Poesy: Essays on Jewish and German Literature and Thought in Honor of Géza von Molnár,* ed. Peter Fenves and Richard Block, 167–75 (Evanston: Northwestern University Press, 2000).

18. At the very beginning of *A Voyage to Ur of the Chaldees,* the narrator talks of the "nocturnal battle for control of the air space over the Street of the Prophets (which raged between the Chopin waltzes emerging from the home of Dr. Landau, the eye specialist, and the love songs of Farid el-Atrash blaring from the newly installed radio sets in the Arab cafés)" and describes their intermingling as explosive: "Sometimes the notes dropping from the keyboard would splash into the Arab tunes streaming up from the Damascus Gate and the Mussrara Quarter into my round east-facing window, and the night air would vibrate with a growing tension. For the Western rhythms did not blend with the Oriental tunes to create a smoothly flowing harmony—as sometimes happens when music absorbs a melody from a foreign culture and succeeds in assimilating and digesting it—but instead produced an explosive compound which needed only a spark to ignite it" (*Voyage,* 9–10; 223). Western and Arab music clash rather than harmoniously blend, but the boy in his window seat occupies a median position and seems to hear both with pleasure.

19. This is not the only view represented in the text. Mrs. Luria, for example, gives a long speech where she argues that the Arabs are the descendants of the Israelites. Mrs. Luria is far from arguing, however, that the Arabs, therefore, are not only the inhabitants of the land but also its rightful owners. Her main point in the passage is, rather, to devalue the Bible (the study of which leads to the "Jerusalem idleness" she abhors). By saying that the old fellah she saw at Dr. Landau's clinic is probably "a descendant of the Prophet Jeremiah," "descended from the people of Anathot," she tries to argue that "the prophet Jeremiah . . . was no more, when all is said and done, than a fellah from el-djabel, from the distant mountains, from Anata or Nebi Samwil" (*Voyage,* 169; 403).

20. In his introduction to the poems of Konstantin Asher Shapiro (*Shirim Nivharim,* Warsaw: Tushiya, 1911), Ya'akov Fichman mentions one of Shapiro's poems "which remained in manuscript and in which the poet describes his terrible mood after the contempt shown him by the young people [i.e., *Hovevei Tzion*]. He tells how in his dream he stands in the streets of the newly rebuilt Jerusalem and sings

to his people from the songs of Zion. The people welcome him with applause [*betru'ah*], and the daughters of Jerusalem are about to crown his head with a wreath of flowers. Suddenly a horrible voice is heard: What are you to us? [*ma lecha velanu*?]—it is the voice of the youth of Zion [*tze'irei tzion*] who will throw the wreath off his head and will trample over it" (xv). Though Louidor tells Yaeli that he has never read Shapiro's poems, Shahar apparently read something, maybe Fichman's account. Fichman mentions many of the facts of Shapiro's life that "Louidor's father told him"; however, the episode where the successful photographer is rejected by Tolstoi because he is a Jew is not mentioned by Fichman. The *Encyclopedia Judaica* states that Shapiro did photograph Tolstoi.

21. In *Day of the Countess,* Shoshi discovers Berl/Eshbaal's poetry when in a store on Geula Street she receives her package wrapped in newspaper on which she reads "the first line of a poem "*Shefi heshek 'aravot*" that penetrated her like a column of flickering sunrays (*hadra kesilon meratzed karnei shemesh*]" (*Countess,* 163). "*Kotefet shefi heshek 'aravot*" is the last line of Ratosh's poem, "*Raveh ori*" (first published in May 1951). In *Day of the Ghosts,* we hear about Berl's frantic search for a poem he wrote late at night in Café Gat, "the poem that ended with the line '*Al mut laba'al be-eshun leil kaitz*" (*Ghosts,* 33). This is the first line of Ratosh's poem "'*Al mut laba'al*" (first published in January 1952). In the collection of Ratosh's poems, *Yohemed* (published in the summer of 1952), where both poems were reprinted, "'*Al mut laba'al*" follows "*Raveh ori.*"

22. For the Canaanite movement, see Yonatan Ratosh, ed. *Minitzahon lemapolet* (Tel Aviv: Hadar, 1976); James S. Diamond, *Homeland or Holy Land? The "Canaanite" Critique of Israel* (Bloomington and Indianapolis: Indiana University Press, 1986); Ya'akov Shavit, *The New Hebrew Nation: A Study in Israeli Heresy and Fantasy* (London: Frank Cass, 1987); Nurit Gertz et al., eds., *Hakevutza hakena'anit: sifrut ve-ideologia* (Tel Aviv: Ha-universita hapetuha, 1987); Hanan Hever, "Kehila yelidit medumyenet: sifrut kena'anit batarbut hayisre-elit," *Sotziologia yisre-elit,* 2 (1999): 147–66.

23. Berl's presumed interest in the Hebrews is mentioned when a journalist, writing a book about Eshbaal Ashtarot (who, after his death, has gained some fame as a poet), asks the narrator to comment on "the meaning in the poetry of Eshbaal of the root "'ever" and all that derives from it: '*Ivri* [Hebrew], the-land-beyond-the big-river [*me'ever lanahar*], the land of the Hebrews [*eretz ha'ivrim*], to cross the river [*l'avor*] and so on" (*Ghosts,* 17).

24. Hever, op. cit., 147.

25. Shavit sees the basic contradiction in Canaanite thought as one between "pluralistic, democratic, liberal aspect of their platform and the compulsory, totalitarian aspect" through which they sought to impose a common civil, cultural, and national consciousness. The latter also contradicts the Canaanites' geographical determinism (see Shavit, op. cit., esp. 122–30).

26. For a discussion of the use and meaning of the term *makom,* see Ephraim E. Urbach, *The Sages: Their Concepts and Beliefs,* trans. Israel Abrahams (Jerusalem:

Magnes Press, 1979), chapter 4. Urbach argues that the term was used when one wanted to emphasize the immanence of God, "whose place is the world" (63), and his proximity to man, as opposed to the term *shamayim* (Heaven), which was used to emphasize God's distance and the awe one feels toward him.

27. This clearly echoes the depiction of the grandmother in "First Lesson," discussed in chapter 2.

28. One should note that at least in the Hagadda of Passover, where this phrase appears, God is referred to as "the Merciful" (*Harahman*) rather than as *Hamakom.*

29. Though the building of Mishkenot Sha-ananim by Sir Moses Montefiori was motivated by philanthropic ideas rather than Zionist ideals, it has subsequently acquired the status of a milestone in the Zionist narrative of the revival of the Land of Israel.

30. In Zionist practice, on the other hand, the return to the land, to working it "with one's own hands," and the valorization of male physical beauty in the figure of the "Sabra" were strangely coupled with puritanical attitudes toward sexuality.

31. This, however, does not mean that Srulik is indifferent to the notion of a Hebrew nation. Back in Jerusalem and as a Calvinist missionary who insists he has remained a Jew, he holds maximalist views about the "natural" borders of Israel (*Countess*, 68).

32. See Malca Puni, "*Mekorot yehudiyim kiyesodot me'atzvim biyetzirat D. Dhahar.*" Ph.D. dissertation, Bar-Ilan University, 1980, 76.

33. Compare *Voyage*, 128, 129, and 130, to Sir Leonard Woolley, *Abraham: Recent Discoveries and Hebrew Origins* (New York: C. Scribner's Sons, 1936), 66–67, 118–19, 64–65.

34. The convergence of Abraham and Jesus occurs when the text tells us that Srulik "went down into Egypt" [*yarad mitzraima*] (*Summer*, 138; 122), an expression that connects him to both Abraham (who also "*yarad mitzraima*," Genesis, 12:10) and Jesus (of whom we are told "*vayelech mitzraima*," Matthew, 2:15).

35. See Zali Gurevitch, "The Double Site of Israel," in *Grasping the Land: Space and Place in Contemporary Israeli Discourse and Experience,* ed. Eyal Ben-Ari and Yoram Bilu, 203–16 (Albany: State University of New York Press, 1997). See also Zali Gurevitch and Gideon Aran, "Al hamakom (antropologia yisre-elit)," *Alpayim* 4 (1991): 9–44.

36. Gurevitch argues that the ultra-orthodox Jews in Israel and the Canaanites resolved this dialectic each in an opposite way: the ultra-orthodox by living a "book-cult," and the Canaanites by "hailing Hebrew identity and its primordial autochtonic relation to the land" (214). In his opinion, these solutions are reductive, and the ambiguity in which the rest of Israel lives is a productive one. See also Harry Berger Jr., "The Lie of the Land: The Text beyond Canaan" in *Representations* 25 (winter 1989): 119–38. Berger introduces a third term between "land" and "book": the divine voice that speaks, in the book, of the land, from a nonplace, such as the desert.

37. Tammuz was first introduced into the novel as Berl's son; his name is one of the elements in the characterization of Berl as a Canaanite poet, modeled on Ratosh. But Tammuz develops in the later volumes: as Thomas Astor, literary and political figure, he lives in Paris, his politics are far from Canaanite, and he is (or at least may be) the narrator's rival for the love of Lutetia, whom he meets regularly at the church of St. Sulpice, by Delacroix's painting of Jacob's struggle with the angel. It seems possible, then, that the adult Tammuz is to some extent modeled after the novelist Benjamin Tammuz, who started as a Canaanite but changed his politics, lived in Paris and London, and wrote allegorical novels, among them *Ya'akov,* whose skeleton is the story of Jacob's struggle with the angel. Tammuz's novel contains many autobiographical elements from the life of its author; it also includes long descriptions of Canaanite ideology as well as meditations on Jewish history and the Diaspora.

38. The text identifies the two bullies as "the same bullies he had driven away from his building area" (22), as though the nursery school experience was part and parcel of the play.

39. This expression reentered circulation in Israeli public discourse during the tenure of Yigael Hurwitz as finance minister when he used it to push through an unpopular economic plan.

40. Though, on the other hand, Shahar chose to publish this passage in 1985 as a separate piece under the title "On the Roof." See *Moznayim* 58 (March–April 1985): 4–7.

CHAPTER 5

1. Piater, "David Shahar, un Proust oriental," *Le monde des livres,* April 14, 1978.

2. Zemach, "Kirva yetera," *Molad* 3:13 (January/February, 1970): 108–13. Other critics who discussed textual echoes of Proust in Shahar's works are: Piatier, in her article of March 8, 1985 in *Le Monde des livres,* mentions the return of the past in *Nin-Gal,* occasioned by the uneven steps (*Nin-Gal,* 43), as an echo of the illumination caused by the uneven paving stones at the end of *La Recherche*; Lena Shiloni, in her essay "'Tikun hakelim hashevurim" (*Ha-aretz,* October 11, 1985), mentions the image of the Japanese paper toy used by Proust in the scene of the madeleine and by Shahar at the beginning of *Summer in the Street of the Prophets*; Yael Sagiv-Feldman finds textual echoes in a passage in Shahar about memory and claims that the "Proustian influence here is obvious" ("Hafantaziot hamizrachiot shel David Shahar," *Bitzaron* [1982]: 17).

3. Ganz, "*Hamas'a le-Ur Kasdim* leDavid Shahar," *Ha-Aretz,* December 10, 1971; Even, "Im hofa'at helek gimel shel *Heikhal hakelim hashevurim,*" *Moznayim* 43 (November 1976): 390–97.

4. *La Colombe et la lune,* trans. Madeleine Neige (Paris: Gallimard, 1971). All of Shahar's works to appear in French were translated by Madeleine Neige. They are:

Un été rue des Prophètes (1978); *Un voyage à Ur de Chaldée* (1980); *Le Jour de la Comtesse* (1981); *L'Agent de Sa Majesté* (1983), *Nin-Gal* (1985); *Riki, un enfant à Jérusalem* (1987); *Le Jour des Fantômes* (1988). All were published by Gallimard. *Les Marches du palais* (Paris: Payot, 1989); *Lune de miel et d'or* (Paris: François-Bourin, 1991); *Les Nuits de Lutèce* (Paris: François-Burin, 1992); *Les Petits péchés* (Paris: Julliard, 1994); *La Nuit des Idoles* (Paris: Laffont, 1997).

5. Yohanan Reshet, "David Shahar bekhol zot lo haya Proust," *Ha-Aretz*, October 11, 1998. The critic Amnon Navot, on the other hand, uses the analogy as a term of praise, saying that Shahar's work gives the Israeli reader something "of the same value [*shveh 'erekh*]" to Proust's work. "'Einayim le-Eshbaal," part 1, *Davar*, September 19, 1986.

6. Piatier herself suggests a comparison with Faulkner as did Ortziyon Bartana in his review "Shahar shavar et hakelim," *Ma'ariv*, August 22, 1986. Navot, op. cit. drew the analogy with both Faulkner and the *Alexandria Quartet*.

7. Exceptions are Ganz (op. cit.), who states (but does not substantiate this statement) that "the remembrances of Shahar's heroes are not as purely autobiographical as those of Proust"; Even (op. cit.) contrasts the concept of character in the two authors (a contrast that was challenged by Zemach, see *Moznayim* 44:3 [February 1977]: 217); Hilel Barzel, in "Lemahut hazikaron biyetzirat David Shahar" (*Moznayim* [December 1980]: 15–27), claims that memory in Proust is nocturnal, lunar, soft, delicate, and feminine, whereas memory in Shahar is solar, viril, and eruptive; Gilead Morahg, in "Piercing the Shimmering Bubble: David Shahar's *The Palace of Shattered Vessels*" (*AJS Review* [fall 1985]: 211–34), concludes part of his analysis by stating that "Whereas Proust explores memory in an attempt to discover the essential identity of the self, Shahar evokes memory as means of relating the self to a greater, transcendent essence that lies beyond it"(227); Yael Feldman, in an article entitled "Gender In/Difference in Contemporary Hebrew Fictional Autobiographies" (*Biography* 11 [summer 1988]), draws our attention to the fact that Shahar's use of autobiography differs from Proust's, in that his narrator is a witnessing narrator rather than a protagonist-narrator (195); Juliette Hassin contrasts the two authors by claiming that Proust created a "complete world" ['*olam shalem*], whereas Shahar, "a broken world" ["Marcel Proust veDavid Shahar: 'Olam shalem ve'olam shavur," *Moznayim* 66 (January/February 1992), 41–46]; finally, N. Bar-Tov, in his review "Peras beTzarfat lesefer al Yerushalayim" (*Hatzofeh*, November 27, 1987), reports that Shahar himself drew some oppositions between himself and Proust: Proust's writing, according to Shahar (according to Bar-Tov), is "passive—a kind of receptacle to impressions, voices, sights, and smells," whereas his own approach in describing reality is "active" and "dramatic."

8. Some of the thematic preoccupations or stylistic peculiarities that critics considered common to Shahar and Proust are: digressive or associative manner of narrating (Jacqueline Piatier, "David Shahar et les rêveurs de Jérusalem," *Le Monde*, June 27, 1980; Yael Feldman, "In Pursuit of Things Past: David Shahar and the Autobiography in Current Israeli Fiction," *Hebrew Studies* 24 [1983]: 99–105; Yael Feldman, "Mi*Nin-Gal* el *Kayitz bederech hanevi-im*," *Hado-ar* 34 [September 13,

1985]: 599, 609; Baruch Link, "The Israeli Proust," *Los Angeles Times*, January 1, 1989); similarity of "style" or "language" (Jérôme Garcin, "Et si David Shahar était le frère israélien de Proust . . . ," *Nouvelles Littéraires* [December 3–10, 1981]; Yosef Even, op. cit.); predilection for long, winding sentences (Madeleine Neige, "De l'hébreu au français,' *Le Monde des livres*, November 20, 1981; Feldman, op. cit., 1983); search for childhood (Jacqueline Piatier, "David Shahar, conteur de Jérusalem: Le roman de la déchirure," *Le Monde des livres*, November 20, 1981); a narrator who merges with the author and resembles, at least partially, the hero (Jacqueline Piatier, op. cit., April 14, 1978); importance given to memory and the awakening of memory through association and through the stimulus of the senses (Ganz, op. cit.; Even, op. cit.; Hilel Barzel, op. cit., Yael Feldman, op. cit., 1982, 1983; Haya Shaham, "Kefel hapanim shel hahavaya," *Yedi'ot Aharonot*, January 8, 1984; Gilead Morahg, op. cit.); search for lost time (Even, op. cit.); the large cast of characters, who are all left free to speak and narrate (Benny Ziffer, 'Misterei hakosmopolitiyut," *Ha-aretz*, November 27, 1981); serial composition ("roman-fleuve") (Shiloni, op. cit.); transcendence or synthesis of opposites (Feldman, op. cit., 1985); excess of detail in relation to paucity of action (Avi Garfinkel, "Ein sofer be'iro," *Yerushalayim*, April 11, 1997).

Other critics who mention the Shahar-Proust analogy and who are not mentioned elsewhere in this chapter are: Dan Omer, "Heikhal ha'etim hashevurim," *Kol Ha'ir*, July 30, 1982; Omer, "Hasheki'a shel David Shahar," *Ha'olam Hazeh*, January 18, 1984; Sarah Katz, "Hamehaber shemaha et shemo misefer hayav,' *Moznayim* 69 (February 1995); Gila Ramras-Rauch, "*Un Voyage à Ur de Chaldée*," *World Literature Today* (summer 1981); Jean-Yves Guérin, "*Le Voyage à Ur de Chaldée*," *Esprit*, (January 1981); Henri Raczymow, "Un Proust israélien," *L'Arche* 253 (April 1978); Ghislain Sartoris, "David Shahar," *Le Royaliste*, December 17–30, 1981; Clara Malraux, "L'Eternel espoir juif," *Le Figaro*, December 8, 1981; Yael Lotan, "David Shahar, Story Teller," *Modern Hebrew Literature* (spring-summer 1982): 14–17.

9. Both Zemach and Shiloni mention this textual echo in their articles, previously cited.

10. Marcel Proust, *A la recherche du temps perdu* (Paris: Gallimard, Pléïade ed., 1954), vol. 1, 47–48; *Remembrance of Things Past*, trans. C. K. Scott Moncrieff and Terence Kilmartin (New York: Vintage, 1982), vol. 1, 51. All references to Proust's work will be to these editions and will be given parenthetically in the text, by volume and page number, first the French original, then the English translation. When a more literal rendering seemed necessary, the translation was silently modified.

11. See Marcel Muller, *Les Voix narratives dans la* Recherche du temps perdu (Geneva: Droz, 1965), 43–44.

12. For another reading of the scene of drawing from the well, in its similarity and difference from Proust, see Morahg, "Piercing the Shimmering Bubble," 227–230.

13. This insistence on the voluntary character of the initial act of remembrance which launches the whole novel can be interpreted as the need of the subject to control

an experience of loss through symbolic representation as theorized by Freud in *Beyond the Pleasure Principle*, (trans. James Strachey [New York: Norton, 1961], especially in the discussion of the "fort/da" scene.

14. Gérard Genette, "Métonymie chez Proust," *Figures III* (Paris: Seuil, 1972), 57–58, 63. According to Leo Bersani, "The narrator's book cannot be written in the ecstatic trance induced by the taste of the *madeleine* or the sound of a spoon hitting a plate. The chance experience must be transformed into a deliberate investigation, a conscious *recherche*. The title of the work indicates how unimportant the experiences of involuntary memory are for the actual writing of the work: Marcel was certainly not in search of his past when he tasted the *madeleine* or stumbled on the flagstones. But now, in writing, he must use his intelligence to undo retrospectively the distorting of his intelligence in the past" (*Marcel Proust: The Fictions of Life and of Art* [New York: Oxford University Press, 1965], 215; emphasis in the text). For Paul de Man's treatment of metaphor and metonymy in Proust see "Reading (Proust)," in *Allegories of Reading* (New Haven and London: Yale University Press, 1979), 57–78.
15. Genette, op. cit., 56.
16. Similarly, Proust does not actually use metaphors but rather similes in which both terms of the comparison are co-present rather than one being substituted for the other (see Genette, op. cit., 58).
17. In the opening pages of the novel, it is the boy who is the beholder and Gabriel who beholds the beholder: having watched the Ethiopian Emperor enter the Consulate, the boy "turned to face the other way" and discovered "a man sitting on the wicker chair next to the verandah table, regarding me and the scene before me with smiling eyes" (*Summer*, 23; 19, see also *Summer,* 153; 137–38). This symmetrical reversal shows the specular relation between Gabriel and the boy-narrator, a specularity that needs to be refracted for the narrative to continue.
18. Yael Feldman, in op. cit., 1988, characterizes the narrator of the *Palace* novels as a witness, in contradistinction to the model autobiography, exemplified by Proust.
19. In the late short story, "First Lesson," to which we shall return later, the narrator describes himself as "nothing but a pipeline, a record playing the tune impressed upon it, a kind of medium" (*The Pope's Mustache*, 247; *News From Jerusalem*, 216).
20. In his reading of *Du côté de chez Swann*, Jeffrey Mehlman emphasizes the collapse of differences in Combray. He argues that the failure of Marcel's father (on that memorable night, when Marcel stayed up to receive his goodnight kiss) to function as a father (as Abraham, to whom he is likened), as the figure of the Law that prohibits incest, the law of difference, locks the child in a world of sameness. Mehlman links the lack of difference in the world of Combray to its closed matriarchy, created by the exclusion or weakening of all males. The emblem of this tendency to eliminate otherness is Aunt Léonie, whom Mehlman reads as a parody of the union between the child and his mother. See "Proust's Counterplot," in *A Structural Study of Autobiography* (Ithaca and London: Cornell University Press, 1974), 20–64.

21. This is, in Marcel Muller's helpful terminology, the "Intermediary subject"—the I who serves as an indispensable relay for the narrator, who, in turn, remembers the hero (Muller, op. cit., 8).

22. On the meaning of "essence" in Proust, see Gilles Deleuze, *Marcel Proust et les signes* (Paris: Presses Universitaires France, 1964); translated by Richard Howard under the title *Proust and Signs* (New York: George Braziller, 1972).

23. This, of course, does not mean that the eye and the gaze have no importance in Proust's world. On the contrary, the many scenes of voyeurism attest to the crucial role played in the novel by the "scopic drive." But as these scenes suggest, the gaze in Proust entails both less and more than perception of a real object. To take just one example: in the scene in which Marcel sees Gilberte for the first time (and where, in fact, he watches her watching him watching her), the narrator, on the one hand, deplores (as he will many times in the novel) his lack of talent for observation ("*esprit d'observation*"), which makes him misperceive the color of her eyes, and, on the other hand, characterizes his gaze as "a gaze eager to reach, touch, capture, bear off in triumph the body at which it is aimed [*qu'il regarde*], and the soul with the body" (I, 141; I, 154). For a psychoanalytic reading of the eye and the gaze in Proust, see Michel Erman, *L'Oeil de Proust* (Paris: Nizet, 1988).

24. Though Shahar grounds everything in the experience of the senses, hence, in the material body, he also claims that all pleasure is spiritual. In *Day of the Ghosts*, Haim Longlife tells the narrator: "Pleasure is always spiritual, even when its cause is something material, like chicken soup, or a cup of coffee, or intercourse with a beautiful woman. There is no pleasure without consciousness of pleasure, without spiritual wonder [*hitpa'alut nafshit*]. Without spiritual pleasure, what taste is there to wonderful sights and good smells and beautiful melodies?" (*Ghosts*, 145). Rather than striving to transcend the material, to reach a spiritual realm divorced from "reality" (as many critics of Shahar have claimed) Shahar is fully invested in the reality of matter and the body and looks for the spiritual within the material. This accounts, among other things, for his fascination with paganism.

25. Samuel Beckett, *Proust* (New York: Grove Press, 1957), 56.

26. "Le temps perdu n'est pas chez Proust, comme le veut un contresens fort répandu, le 'passé,' mais le temps à l'état pur, c'est-à-dire en fait, par fusion d'un instant passé et d'un instant présent, le contraire du temps qui passe: l'extra-temporel, l'éternité." See Gérard Genette, "Proust palimpseste," in *Figures* (Paris: Seuil, 1966), 40, note 4. "The search for lost time is in fact a search for truth. If it is called a search for lost time, it is only to the degree that truth has an essential relation to time" (Deleuze, op. cit., 15).

27. Marguerite Duras, *L'Amant* (Paris: Minuit, 1984), 16–17; translated by Barbara Bray under the title *The Lover* (New York: Harper and Row, 1986), 10.

28. In this respect, it is interesting to note that one "discovery" of the narrator—that *The Palace of Shattered Vessels* actually was written by Gabriel Luria—mentioned in the first pages of the novels (*Summer*, 19; omitted from both English and French translation) remains without sequence or consequence in spite of the narrator's

promise of future clarification. It is as though the novel's structure cannot accommodate a retrospective illumination that will cast a doubt on the boy-narrator's grasp of the reality around him.

29. This is an important difference between the *Palace* novels and *His Majesty's Agent,* which in many other respects resembles the novel sequence. In the latter novel, the hero, Heinrich Reinhold, repeatedly commits errors of judgment and later discovers them.

30. Deleuze, op. cit., 4; 25.

31. See Gérard Genette, "Proust et le langage indirect," *Figures II* (Paris: Seuil, 1969), 223–94. Genette's essay elaborates on and corrects in an important way Roland Barthes' essay "Proust et les noms," in *Le Degré zéro de l'écriture. Suivi de nouveaux essais critiques* (Paris: Seuil, coll. Points, 1972), 121–34.

32. Two other key passages from "First Lesson," discussed below, reappear in the *Palace*: the opening sentence, "In the beginning was the miracle, and the miracle was, and is, and will be to be marveled at always," appears as part of Gabriel's long interior monologue at the end of *A Tammuz-Night's Dream*, where the "miracle" is his sexual relations with Bella (169); the passage about the body being "the veil and the limit, and penetrating it does not lead to the essence beyond, and you can journey beyond it only in it and through it, and in order to get everything there is to get out of the journey itself, you must pay the price of yearning and longing in advance" appears toward the end of *Day of the Countess* as part of Shoshi's interior monologue where this thought is attributed by Shoshi to Herod, who despairs of being loved by Miriam (209).

33. For a different interpretation of this scene of reading, see Naomi Sokoloff, "Metaphysics and Metanarrative in the Stories of David Shahar," *Hebrew Annual Review* 6 (1982): 179–97; "Discoveries of Reading: Stories of Childhood by Bialik, Shahar, and Roth," *Hebrew Annual Review* 9 (1985): 321–42.

34. The confusion of the artist and the person was a main target in Proust's writing "Contre Saint Beuve."

35. For an interpretation of the concept of works of art as "worlds," see Deleuze, op. cit., especially the chapter "Essences and the Signs of Art."

36. For a general discussion of the importance of "fictive" artists in Proust's novel, see Michel Butor, *Les Oeuvres d'art imaginaires chez Proust* (London: Athlone Press, 1964).

37. The figures of dreamers can be found also in the short stories. See, for example, "The Pharmacist and the Salvation of the World," "Of Dreams" (in *The Death of the Little God*), and "The Fortune Teller" and "The Find" (in *The Pope's Mustache*).

38. Vincent Descombes, *Proust: Philosophy of the Novel*, trans. Catherine Macksey (Stanford: Stanford University Press, 1992), esp. chapter 16, " Self-Realization in the Institution of Literature."

39. In the *Palace,* it is Daoud who represents the false view of art as representation of "beautiful" objects, as opposed to the photographer Gordon who seeks to impose

a new, "modernist" aesthetic (see, e.g., *Countess*, 41). But unlike Elstir or Vinteuil, Gordon dies appreciated only by a few people (and those, marginal figures in a deserted corner of the British Empire); after his death, his pictures are misattributed to famous photographers (*Countess*, 70).

40. Descombes, op. cit., 283.

41. We find images of creation also in discussions of Vinteuil's music: "It was upon flat, unbroken surfaces like those of the sea on a morning that threatened storm, in the midst of a harsh silence [*aigre silence*], in an infinite void, that this new work [i.e., the septuor] began, and it was into rose-red daybreak that this unknown universe was drawn from the silence and the night to build up gradually before me" (III, 250; III, 251–51). It is interesting to compare this passage to the description of music in the opening pages of Shahar's *A Voyage to Ur of the Chaldees*. Though music is described in these pages as an almost physical force that invades space, produces, in its contact with other music, "an explosive compound," and has strong effects on the body (it causes Mrs. Luria severe headaches), it also is seen as ephemeral and immaterial. The narrator tries to give the music some shape that will endure, imagining the notes as stars that create constellations. But when the music is over, all traces of it are gone, and the narrator is left only with a void: "Only when the music died away did the dread come slowly back to take its place, the dread of the infinite spaces of the cold, dark void separating the stars which were meaninglessly suspended on nothing" (*Voyage*, 11; 224–25). Whereas Proust describes the moment in which music emerges from the dark void, revealing to the listener a new world, Shahar dwells on the moment in which music fades and disappears in the void. Since the traces left in the mind—the patterns or constellations that music leaves in our memory—are never enough for Shahar, who needs a material trace, outside the subject, when the music is over, there is nothing left.

42. It is interesting to note, however, that Elka's decline—which is never explained either psychologically or economically, and which is introduced abruptly—occurs right after the creation of her masterpiece, the peacock ashtray. Thus, her decline can appear as a punishment for having presumed to create an image.

43. On Elstir's impressionism, see Michel Erman, *L'Oeil de Proust.*

Bibliography

Amrami, Yoel. *Hadevarim gedolim hem me-itanu*. Tel Aviv: Hadar, 1994.

Arad, Miriam. "A Jerusalem Author's Doomed, Godlike Types." *Jerusalem Post*, November 20, 1970.

———. "Jerusalem Novelist's Voyage." *Jerusalem Post*, December 31, 1971.

Avishai, Mordekhai. "'Od perek biyetzira lo gemura." *Ma'ariv*, December 31, 1971.

Bahur, Yonah. "Haherut lenapetz elilim." *Davar*, November 11, 1977.

Bakhtin, M. M. *The Dialogic Imagination*. Edited by Michael Holquist and translated by Caryle Emerson and Michael Holquist. Austin and London: University of Texas Press, 1981.

Bargad, Warren. "The Image of the Arab in Israeli Literature." *From Agnon to Oz*. Atlanta: Scholars Press, 1996.

Barnay, Ya'akov. *Historyografia ule-umiyut*. Jerusalem: Magnes, 1975.

Bartal, Israel. *Galut ba-aretz: yishuv Eretz Israel beterem tziyonut*. Jerusalem: Mossad Bialik, 1994.

Bartana, Ortziyon. "Ein navi be-artzo." *Yedi'ot Aharonot*, April 11, 1997.

———. *Hafantasia besiporet dor hamedina*. Tel Aviv: Hakibbutz Hameuhad, 1989.

———. "Omanut—oman—emuna: he-arot le*Leilot Lutetia*." *Moznayim* 66 (1992): 47–50.

———. "Shahar shavar et hakelim." *Ma'ariv*, August 22, 1986.

Barthes, Roland. "L'Effet du réel." *Communications* 11 (1968): 84–89.

———. "Proust et les noms." *Le Degré zéro de l'écriture. Suivi de nouveaux essais critiques*. Paris: Seuil, coll. Points, 1972, 121–34.

Bar-Tov, N. "Peras beTzarfat lesefer al Yerushalayim." *Hatzofeh*, November 27, 1987.

Barzel, Hilel. "Lemahut hazikaron biyetzirat David Shahar." *Moznayim* 52 (December 1980): 15–25.

———. "*Nin-Gal* ve*Yom harefa-im*: tahanot beroman entziklopedisti." *Bitzaron* 9 (1988): 40–48.

Baumgarten, Murray. "Engaging Rascal." *Jerusalem Post*, March 17, 1978.

———. "A Mythical City." *Jerusalem Post*, August 30, 1971.

Baziz, Orna. "Demut ha-isha biyetzirat David Shahar al pi hare-i haluriani. *'Alei siah*, 42 (1999): 51–72.

———. *La Femme dans l'oeuvre de David Shahar*. Thèse de doctorat. Institut national des langues et civilisations orientales, 1995.

Beckett, Samuel. *Proust*. New York: Grove Press, 1957.

Be-er, Hayim. "Le-esof et shivrei hakelim, la'asot rekonstruktzia: siha 'im David Shahar." *Ha-aretz*, August 27, 1971.

———. "*Moto shel ha-elohim hakatan* leDavid Shahar." *Ha-aretz*, September 25, 1970.

———. "Shattered Vessels: An Interview with David Shahar." *Ariel* (spring 1972): 15–18.

Bell, J. Bowyer. *Terror Out of Zion: Irgun Zvai Leumi, LEHI, and the Palestine Underground, 1929–1949*. New York: St. Martin's Press, 1977.

Ben-Arieh, Yehoshua. *Jerusalem in the Nineteenth Century: Emergence of the New City*. Jerusalem: Yad Ben-Tzvi; New York: St. Martin's Press, 1986.

———. *Tzayareiha vetziyureiha shel Eretz Israel bameiah hatesha'esreh*. Jerusalem: Yad Ben-Tzvi & Tel Aviv: Yedi'ot Aharonot, 1992.

———. *Yerushalayim hahdasha bereshita*. Jerusalem: Yad Ben-Tzvi, 1979.

Ben-David, Sylvia. "Heikhal hakelim hashevurim." *Hayom*, August 29, 1969.

Benjamin, Walter. "On Some Motifs in Baudelaire." In *Illuminations*, edited by Hannah Arendt, 155–201. New York: Schocken, 1969.

Berger, Harry Jr. "The Lie of the Land: The Text beyond Canaan." *Representations* 25 (winter 1989): 119–38.

Bersani, Leo. *Marcel Proust: The Fictions of Life and Art*. New York: Oxford University Press, 1965.

Bersohn, Nehama Rezler. "David Shahar's Trilogy: *The Palace of Shattered Vessels*—A Combination of Literary Genres." *Modern Hebrew Literature* (summer 1980): 34–42.

Bieber, Yehoash. "Mi ata Gavriel Yonatan Luria?" *Davar*, February 22, 1985.

Blat, Avraham. "Mas'a el hehalal hapenimi." *Hatzofeh*, November 21, 1976.

Blot, Jean. "L'Année dernière à Jérusalem." *L'Arche* 298 (January 1982).

Butor, Michel. *Les Oeuvres d'art imaginaires chez Proust*. London: Athlone Press, 1964.

Clarke, Thurston. *By Blood and Fire: The Attack on the King David Hotel*. New York: Putnam, 1981.

Clavel, André. "David Shahar, conteur de Jérusalem." *Journal de Genève*, November 28, 1981.

Cohen, Erik. "The City in Zionist Ideology." *The Jerusalem Quarterly* 4 (1977): 126–44.

Dan, Joseph. *Gershom Scholem and the Mystical Dimension of Jewish History*. New York: New York University Press, 1987.

Deleuze, Gilles. *Marcel Proust et les signes*. Paris: Presses Universitaires de France, 1964. Translated by Richard Howard under the title *Proust and Signs* (New York: George Braziller, 1972).

de Man, Paul. "Reading (Proust)." *Allegories of Reading*. New Haven and London: Yale University Press, 1979, 57–78.

Derrida, Jacques. *De la grammatologie*. Paris: Minuit, 1967.

———. *Marges de la philosophie*. Paris: Minuit, 1972.

Descombes, Vincent. *Proust: philosophie du roman*. Paris: Minuit, 1987. Translated by Catherine Macksey under the title *Proust: Philosophy of the Novel* (Stanford: Stanford University Press, 1992).

Diamond, James S. *Homeland or Holy Land? The "Canaanite" Critique of Israel*. Bloomington and Indianapolis: Indiana University Press, 1986.

Dinur, Ben-Tziyon et al. eds. *Toldot hahagana*. Vol. 2, part 1. Tel Aviv: Hasifria Hatzionit and Ma'arakhot Press: 1964.

Duras, Marguerite. *L'Amant*. Paris: Minuit, 1984. Translated by Barbara Bray under the title *The Lover* (New York: Harper and Row, 1986).

El Khayatti, Reddouane. *La Notion du temps dans le cycle romanesque* Le Palais des vases brisés *de David Shahar*. Thèse de doctorat, Université de Paris VIII, 1998.

Erman, Michel. *L'Oeil de Proust*. Paris: Nizet, 1988.

Even, Yosef. "Ha-omnam Proust sheli bilvad?!" *Moznayim* 44 (1976): 217.

———. "'Im hofa'at helek gimel shel *Heikhal hakelim hashevurim*." *Moznayim* 43 (1977): 390–98.

Feldman, Yael. "Mi*Ningal* el *Kayitz bederekh hanevi-im*: ehad tirgum ushenayim mikra." *Hado-ar* 34 (August 13, 1985): 599, 609.

Feldman, Yael S. "Gender In/Difference in Contemporary Hebrew Fictional Autobiographies." *Biography* 11 (summer 1988): 189–209.

———. "The 'Other Within' in Contemporary Israeli Fiction." *Middle East Review* 22:1 (fall 1989): 47–53.

———. "In Pursuit of Things Past: David Shahar and the Autobiography in Current Israeli Fiction." *Hebrew Studies* 24 (1983): 99–105.

Foucault, Michel. "Of Other Spaces." Translated by Jay Miskowiec. *Diacritics* (spring 1986): 22–27.

Freud, Sigmund. *Beyond the Pleasure Principle*. Translated by James Strachey. New York: Norton, 1961.

———. "The Uncanny." *The Standard Edition of the Complete Psychological Works*. Vol. 17. London: Hogarth Press, 1953–1974, 219–52.

Frumkin, Gad. *Derekh shofet biYerushalayim.* Tel Aviv: Dvir, 1954.

Furstenberg, Rochelle. "History through a Cracked Mirror: On David Shahar's *His Majesty's Agent.*" *Modern Hebrew Literature* (winter 1980): 30–33.

Ganz, Hayim. "*Hamas'a le-Ur Kasdim* leDavid Shahar." *Ha-aretz,* December 10, 1971.

Garcin, Jérôme. "David Shahar: *Le Jour de la comtesse.*" *Nouvelles Littéraires* (March 22–28, 1984).

———. "Et si David Shahar était le frère israélien de Proust..." *Nouvelles Littéraires* (December 3–10, 1981): 41–42.

Garfinkel, Avi. "Ein sofer be'iro." *Yerushalayim,* April 11, 1997.

Genette, Gérard. "Métonymie chez Proust." *Figures III.* Paris: Seuil, 1972, 41–63.

———. "Proust et le langage indirect." *Figures II.* Paris: Seuil, 1969, 223–94.

———. "Proust palimpseste." *Figures.* Paris: Seuil, 1966, 39–68.

Gertz, Nurit et al., eds. *Hakevutza hakena'anit: sifrut ve-ideologia.* Tel Aviv: Ha-universita hapetuha, 1987.

Ginsburg, Michal Peled. "Sketching Literary Influence: Gérard de Nerval and David Shahar." In *The Spirit of Poesy: Essays on Jewish and German Literature and Thought in Honor of Géza von Molnár,* edited by Peter Fenves and Richard Block, 167–75. Evanston: Northwestern University Press, 2000.

Govrin, Nurit. *Ketivat ha-aretz: aratzot ve'arim 'al mapat hasifrut ha'ivrit.* Jerusalem: Karmel, 1998.

Green, Jeffrey M. "Broken Vessels." *Jerusalem Post,* January 27, 1980.

———. "Drawer of Water." *Jerusalem Post,* July 14, 1989.

———. "Jerusalem Daydreaming." *Modern Hebrew Literature* 6 (spring/summer 1991): 24–27.

———. "Misunderstandings." *Jerusalem Post,* September 19, 1986.

Gurevitch, Zali. "The Double Site of Israel." In *Grasping the Land: Space and Place in Contemporary Israeli Discourse and Experience,* edited by Eyal Ben-Ari and Yoram Bilu, 203–16. Albany: State University of New York Press, 1997.

Gurevitch, Zali and Gideon Aran . "Al hamakom (antropologia yisre-elit). *Alpayim* 4 (1991): 9–44.

Hagorni, Avraham. "Uma zot kol hasipurim?" *Davar,* November 18, 1983.

Haile Selassie I. *My life and Ethiopia's Progress, 1892–1937: The Autobiography of Emperor Haile Sellassie I.* Translated by Edward Ullendorf. Oxford: Oxford University Press, 1976.

Halper, Jeff. *Between Redemption and Revival: The Jewish Yishuv of Jerusalem in the Nineteenth Century.* Boulder, San Francisco, and Oxford: Westview Press, 1991.

Halperin, Sara. "Komiyut vehumor biyetzirat David Shahar." *Moznayim* 64 (1990): 62–65.

———. "Yesodot komiyim basipur hakatzar shel David Shahar." *Hakongres ha'olami lemada'ei hayahdut* 10 (1990): 267–73.

Harel, Israel. "Yerushalayim shel David Shahar." *Davar*, October, 9, 1970.

Hassin, Juliette. "Marcel Proust veDavid Shahar: 'olam shalem ve'olam shavur." *Moznayim* 66 (January/February 1992): 41–46.

Hever, Hanan. "Kehila yelidit medumyenet: sifrut kena'anit batarbut hayisre-elit." *Sotziologia Yisre-elit* 2 (1999): 147–66.

Idel, Moshe. *Golem: Jewish Magical and Mystical Traditions on the Artificial Anthropoid.* Albany: State University of New York Press, 1990.

Kadari, Sheraga. "Hahalomot shel *Heikhal hakelim hashevurim*." *Hayom*, October 18, 1969.

Kark, Ruth and Michal Oren-Nordheim. *Yerushalayim usevivoteiha: rova'im, shekhunot ukhefarim 1800–1948.* Jerusalem: Akademon, 1995.

Katz (Mark), Sarah. "Hakonflikt hayehudi-'arvi biyetzirato shel David Shahar." *Ha-uma* 136 (summer 1999): 454–70.

Katz, Sarah. "The Arabe (*sic*)-Jewish Issue in the Works of David Shahar." *Révue européenne d'études hébraïques* 1 (1999): 78–106.

———. "Bu'ot ubavu-ot be'olamenu." *Moznayim* 34 (1972): 74–77.

———"Diagnoza shel sofer shebagad bemasa hanefesh shelo." *Yerushalayim* (1979): 92–98.

———. *Ha-ani vegiborav besipurei David Shahar.* Tel Aviv: Eked, 1975.

———. "Hamehaber shemaha et shemo misefer hayav." *Moznayim* 69 (February 1995): 46–49.

———. "Heikhal hekelim hashevurim leDavid Shahar." *Moznayim* 29 (1969): 145–47.

———. *Marot biYerushalayim shel David Shahar.* Tel Aviv: 'Am 'Oved, 1985.

———. "Nishmat hadevarim vehazman: 'im hofa'at *Heikhal hakelim hashevurim* leDavid Shahar betirgum angli." *Yedi'ot Aharonot*, March 19, 1976.

———. "*Yom harozenet* leDavid Shahar: 'iyun minekudat re-ut ideologit veyitzugit." *'Alei Siah* (1976): 203–207.

Katz, Yossi. "Jerusalem in S. Y. Agnon's *Yesterday Before Yesterday*." In *Writing the City*, edited by Peter Preston and Paul Simpson-Housely, 195–220. London and New York: Routledge, 1994.

Keller, Bernard. "La Jérusalem de David Shahar." *Foi et vie* 89 (1990): 39–49.

Kroyanker, David. *Rehov Hanevi-im, Shekhunat Hahabashim veShekhunat Mussrara: sipuro shel makom—deyokana shel 'ir, Yerushalayim 1850–2000.* Jerusalem: Yad Ben-Tzvi & Keter, 2000.

Landau, Dov. "Heshbono shel David Shahar 'im yefei hanefesh lemineihem." *Hatzofeh*, October 3, 1986.

Laplanche, Jean, and J-B Pontalis. *Vocabulaire de la psychanalyse*. Paris: Presses Universitaires de France, 1971. Translated by Donald Nicholson-Smith under the title *The Language of Psycho-Analysis* (New York: Norton, 1973).

Levine, Etan. "Les petits pechés." *World Literature Today* 69 (winter 1995): 217.

Levski, Hagit, ed. *Yerushalayim batoda'a uva'asiya hatzionit*. Jerusalem: Merkaz Zalman Shazar Letoldot Israel & Hamerkaz Leheker Hatziyonut Vehayishuv, 1989.

Link, Baruch. "The Israeli Proust." *Los Angeles Times*, January 1, 1989.

Lotan, Yael. "David Shahar, Story-Teller." *Modern Hebrew Literature* (spring-summer 1982): 14–17.

———. "Might As Well Laugh." *Jerusalem Post*, November 23, 1979.

Loufer, Tzipora. *Tefisat hazeman be*Heikhal hakelim hashevurim *leDavid Shahar*. Master's thesis, Bar Ilan University, 1974.

Lukacs, Georg. *Theory of the Novel*. Cambridge: MIT Press, 1975.

Luz, Tzvi. "Hamemad ha-epi biyetzirat David Shahar." *Bitzaron* 9 (1988): 49–53.

———. *Metziut ve-adam basifrut ha-eretz yisre-elit*. Tel Aviv: Dvir, 1970.

Malraux, Clara. "L'Eternel espoir juif." *Le Figaro*, December 8, 1981.

Meged, Eyal. "David Shahar: beseter hamadrega (re-ayon)." *Yedi'ot Aharonot*, September 14, 1984.

Mehlman, Jeffrey. "Proust's Counterplot." *A Structural Study of Autobiography*. Ithaca and London: Cornell University Press, 1974, 20–64.

Meudal, Gérard. "Le Sens du poêle." *Libération*, April 28, 1994.

Miron, Dan. *Im lo tiheyeh Yerushalayim*. Tel Aviv: Hakibbutz Hameuhad, 1987.

Miron, Eyal. *Yerushalayim vekhol netivoteiha: lesayer 'im Yad Ben-Tzvi*. Jerusalem: Yad Ben-Tzvi, 1996.

Moretti, Franco. "Homo Palpitans." *Signs Taken for Wonders*. London and New York: Verso, 1983, 109–29.

Morahg, Gilead. "Piercing the Shimmering Bubble: David Shahar's *The Palace of Shattered Vessels*." *AJS Review* (fall 1985): 211–34.

Muller, Marcel. *Les Voix narratives dans la* Recherche du temps perdu. Geneva: Droz, 1965.

Naor, Mordekhai. *'Ir va-em miDavid hamelekh 'ad yameinu*. Jerusalem: Yad Ben-Tzvi, 1995.

Navot, Amnon. "'Einayim le-Eshbaal." *Davar*, September 19, 26, 1986; October 10, 1986.

———. "Harikat hakelim hashehukim." *Davar*, January 1, 1989.

———. "Havayot mitpatzlot: 'al sifro shel David Shahar *Nin-Gal*." *'Akhshav* 49 (1984): 309–13.

Neige, Madeleine. "De l'hébreu en français." *Le Monde des livres,* November 20, 1981.

———. "Jews, Muslims and Christians in the Work of David Shahar." *The Jerusalem Quarterly* 6 (winter 1978): 41–46.

Omer, Dan. "Hasheki'a shel David Shahar." *Ha'olam Hazeh,* January 18, 1984.

———. "Heikhal ha'etim hashevurim." *Kol Ha'ir,* July 30, 1982.

Oren, Yosef. "Haheikhal hashalem vekhol agapav. *Ma'ariv,* January 13, 1984.

———. "Masekhet nashim shel David Shahar." *Ha-aretz.* December 23, 1983.

———. "The Sanctuary of the Broken Vessels." *Hebrew Book Review* (fall 1969): 13–16.

———. "Shavuy baheikhal." *Yedi'ot Aharonot,* August, 8, 1986.

Oz, Amos. *Mikha-el sheli.* Tel Aviv: 'Am 'Oved, 1968. *My Michael.* Translated by Nicholas de Lange. New York: Knopf, 1972.

Piatier, Jacqueline. "David Shahar aux prises avec le Paradis." *Le Monde des livres,* February 25, 1990.

———. "David Shahar, conteur de Jérusalem: Le roman de la déchirure." *Le Monde des livres,* November 20, 1981.

———. "David Shahar davant l'éternel fanatisme." *Le Monde des livres,* March 11, 1988.

———. "David Shahar et l'histoire d'Israël." *Le Monde des livres,* June 24, 1983.

———. "David Shahar et les rêveurs de Jérusalem." *Le Monde des livres,* June 27, 1980.

———. "David Shahar, un Proust oriental." *Le Monde des livres,* April 14, 1978.

———. "Rêver de Jérusalem sur la place des Vosges." *Le Monde des livres,* March 8, 1985.

———. "Le Roman de Saint Sulpice." *Le Monde des livres,* December 9, 1992.

———. "Samuel Agnon, David Shahar, Amos Oz." *Le Monde des livres,* December 10, 1971.

Plantz, Richard. "A Voyage to Ur of the Chaldees." *Hebrew Book Review* (spring 1972): 16–20.

Proust, Marcel. *A la recherche du temps perdu.* Paris: Gallimard, Pléïade ed., 1954. *Remembrance of Things Past.* Translated by C. K. Scott Moncrieff and Terence Kilmartin. New York: Vintage, 1982.

Puni, Malca. "'Itzuv hademuyot hasifrutiyot biyetzirat D. Shahar 'al pi deyoknaot min hamasoret." *Zehut* (1981): 239–44.

———. "'Ma'aseh berokeah uge-ulat ha'olam' biyetzirat David Shahar." *Ma'alot* 13:5 (1982): 19–24.

———. "*Mekorot yehudiyim kiyesodot me'atzvim biyetzirat D. Shahar.*" Ph.D. dissertation, Bar-Ilan University, 1980.

———. "Yerushalayim ki-yetzirat omanut," *Ma'ariv*, May 21, 1982.

Raczymow, Henri. "Un Proust israélien." *L'Arche* 253 (April 1978).

Ramras-Rauch, Gila. *The Arab in Israeli Literature*. Bloomington and Indianapolis: Indiana University Press, 1989.

———. "*Un voyage à Ur de Chaldée*." *World Literature Today* (summer 1981): 523.

Rank, Otto. *The Myth of the Birth of the Hero and Other Writings*. Edited by Philip Freund. New York: Vintage, 1959.

Ratosh, Yonatan, ed. *Minitzahon lemapolet*. Tel Aviv: Hadar, 1976.

Raviv, Yair. "'Al haheikhal ve'al hakelim." *Davar*, September 12, 1969.

Reshet, Yohanan (Yoram Bronowski). "David Sharar bekhol zot lo haya Proust." *Ha-aretz*, October 11, 1998.

Rogani, Hagay. "*Hebetim mivniyim biyetzirat David Shahar uvetekst talmudi: 'iyun mashveh*." Master's thesis, Haifa University, 1990.

Ron, Moshe. "Heinrich Reinhold be-eretz hamar-ot." *Siman Kriah* 11 (May 1980): 147–56.

Roskies, David. "Tzionut, makom vehadimayon hasifruti hayehudi." In *'Idan hatzionut*, edited by Anita Shapira, Yehuda Reinhartz, and Jacob Harris, 167–84. Jerusalem: Merkaz Shazar, 2000.

Rosovsky, Nitza, ed. *City of the Great King: Jerusalem from David to the Present*. Cambridge: Harvard University Press, 1996.

Sagiv-Feldman Yael. "Hafantaziot hamizrahiyot shel David Shahar: kama he'arot 'al omanut hasipur shel *Heikhal hakelim hashevurim*." *Bitzaron* (1982): 14–22.

Sartoris, Ghislain. "David Shahar." *Le Royaliste*, December 17–30, 1981.

Schur, Natan. *Toldot Yerushalayim*. Vol. 3. Tel Aviv: Dvir, 1987.

Segal, Nili. "David Shahar 'al omanut ve-emuna (siha)." *Bitzaron* 9 (1988): 28–34.

Shaham, Haya. "Kefel hapanim shel hahavaya." *Yedi'ot Aharonot*, January 8, 1984.

Shaked, Gershon. *Hasiporet ha'ivrit 1880–1980*. Vol. 5. Tel Aviv: Hakibbutz Hameuhad, 1998.

Shalom, Gershom. *Pirkey yesod behavanat hakabbala usemaleiha*. Jerusalem: Mossad Bialik, 1977, 107.

Shapiro, Konstantin Asher. *Shirim nivharim* (preface: Ya'akov Fichman). Warsaw: Tushiya, 1911.

Shavit, Ya'acov. *The New Hebrew Nation: A Study in Israeli Heresy and Fantasy*. London: Frank Cass, 1987.

Shay, Eli. "Met be'emdat nivdal." *Kol Ha'ir*, April 11, 1997.

Shiloni, Lena. "Tikun hakelim hashevurim." *Ha-aretz*, October 11, 1985.

Sokoloff, Naomi. "Discoveries of Reading: Stories of Childhood by Bialik, Shahar, and Roth." *Hebrew Annual Review*, 9 (1985): 321–42.

———. "Metaphysics and Metanarrative in the Stories of David Shahar." *Hebrew Annual Review* 6 (1982): 179–97.

Storrs, Ronald, Sir. *Orientations*. London: Nicholson & Watson, 1943.

Tamar, David. "Ta'uyot sofrim vahakhamim." *Yedi'ot Aharonot*, July 2, 1982.

Telpaz, Gideon. *Israeli Childhood Stories of the Sixties: Yizhar, Aloni, Shahar, Kahana-Carmon*. Brown Judaic Studies, 40. Chico, Calif.: Scholars Press, 1983.

Urbach, Ephraim E. *The Sages: Their Concepts and Beliefs*. Translated by Israel Abrahams. Jerusalem: Magnes Press, 1979.

Vilnai, Ze-ev. *Entzikolopediat Vilnai liYerushalayim*. Jerusalem: Ahi'ever, 1993.

Waguer, Eliyahu. *Siyurim biYerushalayim: madrikh lametayel*. Jerusalem: Keter, 1988.

Wirth-Nesher, Hana. *City Codes: Reading the Modern Urban Novel*. New York: Cambridge University Press, 1996.

Woolley, Leonard, Sir. *Abraham: Recent Discoveries and Hebrew Origins*. New York: C. Scribner's Sons, 1936.

Yardeni, Galia. "David Shahar." *Moznayim* 15 (1962): 166–70.

Yehoshua, A. B. "Shlosha yamim veyeled." In *Mul haye'arot*, 173–257. Tel Aviv: Hakibbutz Hameuhad, 1968. "Three Days and a Child." in *Three Days and a Child*, translated by Miriam Arad, 53–129. New York: Doubleday, 1970.

Zemach, Ada. "Kirva yetera." *Molad* 3:13 (January/February 1970): 108–13.

———. "Marcel Proust shel Yosef Even." *Moznayim* 44:3 (February 1977): 217.

Ziffer, Benny. "Misterei hakosmopolitiyut." *Ha-aretz*, November 27, 1981.

Zoran, Gavriel. "Likrat teoria shel hamerhav basipur." *Hasifrut* 30–31 (1981): 20–34.

Index